Received on

D0211233

CONVERSATIONS
IN BLACK

NO LONGER PROPERTY OF
THE SEATTLE PUBLIC LIBRARY

CONVERSATIONS IN BLACK

ON POWER, POLITICS, AND LEADERSHIP

ED GORDON

hachette
BOOK GROUP

Copyright © 2020 by Ed Gordon
Cover design by Amanda Kain
Cover copyright © 2020 by Hachette Book Group, Inc.

Hachette Book Group supports the right to free expression and the value of copyright. The purpose of copyright is to encourage writers and artists to produce the creative works that enrich our culture.

The scanning, uploading, and distribution of this book without permission is a theft of the author's intellectual property. If you would like permission to use material from the book (other than for review purposes), please contact permissions@hbgusa.com. Thank you for your support of the author's rights.

Hachette Books
Hachette Book Group
1290 Avenue of the Americas
New York, NY 10104
hachettebookgroup.com
twitter.com/hachettebooks

First Edition: January 2020

Hachette Books is a division of Hachette Book Group, Inc.
The Hachette Books name and logo are trademarks of Hachette Book Group, Inc.

The publisher is not responsible for websites (or their content) that are not owned by the publisher.

The Hachette Speakers Bureau provides a wide range of authors for speaking events. To find out more, go to www.hachettespeakersbureau.com or call (866) 376-6591.

Library of Congress Control Number: 2019954809

ISBNs: 9780316532860 (hardcover); 9780316533058 (ebook); 9780316535656 (library ebook); 9781549123689 (audio)

Printed in the United States of America

LSC-C

10 9 8 7 6 5 4 3 2 1

To Black folks who, for generations, have fought and beat the odds at every turn.

To all the great people who gave me their time to participate in this conversation, thank you for your dedication to our community.

CONTENTS

INTRODUCTION

When I first started this project in 2012, seventeen-year-old Trayvon Martin had just been senselessly killed by a neighborhood watchman nearly twice his age. Though Michael Brown, Laquan McDonald, and Sandra Bland were still alive, they, too, would soon become synonymous with injustice. Bill Cosby was stirring up controversy in the Black community for chastising African American parents and educators, but even so, he was still America's beloved TV dad. Maya Angelou was alive and dispensing sage wisdom as only she could. Barack Obama was finishing up his first term in the White House. The only Black people Donald Trump was (publicly) antagonizing were the African American contestants on *The Apprentice*. We were still jammin' to R. Kelly's "Ignition (Remix)" despite whispers of involvement with underage girls. Maxine Waters was an outspoken congresswoman, but she hadn't quite reached "Auntie" status yet.

Oh, how times have changed.

From local activism and social justice to national leadership and politics, conversations—good and bad—are bubbling up all across Black America, and with passionate pundits, vocal social media influencers, and empowered activists, no one is short on opinions. All in all, we—as a community—are expressing our sentiments more than ever before. As a career journalist, I have conducted award-winning and personally rewarding interviews with countless leaders and celebrities, iconic figures who are leading our culture, setting trends, raising visibility, and blazing new trails. Though many of these televised interviews have garnered significant attention, I've often been most intrigued by the conversations that transpired just after the camera's red light was turned off. I've always wished that others might be privy to what is said behind closed doors. I started thinking about how powerful and transcendent it could be if a number of these voices were in the same room at the same time. So I decided to put together a series of virtual conversations between Black influencers, in the hope of moving our community forward.

With the glow of Barack Obama's victory still shining over much of Black America, in some respects, the change was coming, just as Sam Cooke had promised. A man of color was in the White House with a first family that was the ideal American family. In the years between then and now, much *has* changed—and not all for the better. Through it all, our discussions, questions, and concerns have ranged from the sublime to the ridiculous to the inspiring. We talked about the record number of candidates of color who entered political races on local, state, and federal levels; ABC's new series *Scandal*, in which fictional Black superwoman Olivia Pope cleaned up colossal messes and saved the nation time and time again; the night *Moonlight* first didn't win and then, seconds later, won the Oscar for Best Picture; Kanye's ridiculous statement that slavery was a choice; and even how good *Black Panther* was!

We talked about all kinds of things. Yet, more frequently—and rightfully so—the discussions drifted toward areas where people of color saw little or no change. We expressed concern about backsliding (or, as I call it, "*Black*-sliding") as many of the measures of civil rights progress and equality began to decline. We talked ad nauseam about the continued lack of higher education and job opportunities for Blacks, the growing wealth disparity between Blacks and Whites, the danger of simply being born Black that makes the mundane—from driving to shopping—dangerous, even deadly. Our conversations reveal that, in many cases, the playing field for most African Americans has not changed.

Today, amid a drastically changed political and social landscape, this book resurrects the best strategic moves, new narratives, and next steps the Black community needs to adopt to move the needle back toward progress. This book is intended to be a discussion starter, and I hope you will form your own groups to extend the conversation about the ideas and thoughts expressed here. Have these conversations in your home, dorm room, club meeting, barbershop, hair salon, church, workplace, and anywhere else you gather. Each chapter ends with questions to help you jump-start these discussions, and the goal is to prompt action. *Conversations in Black* should be used as a catalyst for furthering positive change in our communities, a tool to enable us to speak with a more collective voice and to find a way forward. With a united voice, we can develop new approaches to dismantle the systemic stumbling blocks to equality and, in some cases, outright racism that hinder our progress.

No monolithic thought can be—or should be—reached by all African Americans on any subject. Our beliefs on how best to achieve the goal of equality are shaped by, among other things, our experiences, backgrounds, education, and social status. However, we can and should work toward building consensus. More constructive debates within our community and individual introspection are equally necessary, especially by those of us who have attained some measure of success. We must ask ourselves if we've done enough for those who haven't found more secure footing.

We owe it to one another to live as our brother's keeper. It's time we have a talk with folks who live with the misguided notion that somehow their superior nature alone brought them to the C-suite or a suburban house or delivered six- or seven-figure incomes.

I am grateful to those who took the time to be a part of this book, and I am excited to see where it may lead. Now, let's get the conversation started!

WHAT'S GOING ON?

THE STATE OF BLACK AMERICA

STACEY ABRAMS	Politician & Author
HARRY BELAFONTE	Entertainer & Activist
TODD BOYD	Academic & Author
CHARLAMAGNE THA GOD	Radio Personality & Author
LAURA COATES	CNN Analyst & Radio Host
RICHELIEU DENNIS	Founder & Chair of Essence Ventures
MICHAEL ERIC DYSON	Academic & Author
ALICIA GARZA	Cofounder of Black Lives Matter
JEMELE HILL	Journalist & Broadcaster
ERICKA HUGGINS	Activist & Educator
D.L. HUGHLEY	Comedian & Author
DERRICK JOHNSON	President & CEO of the NAACP
KILLER MIKE	Rapper & Activist
DeRAY MCKESSON	Author & Social Activist
MARC MORIAL	President & CEO of the National Urban League
BRITTANY PACKNETT	Vice President of Teach for America
AL SHARPTON	President of the National Action Network
SUSAN TAYLOR	Former Publisher of *Essence* & Founder of the National Cares Mentoring Movement
T.I.	Rapper & Activist

Often, you'll find the music and rhythms of the iconic Marvin Gaye album *What's Going On* playing throughout my house. It's one of the greatest albums of all time. From the sounds of party banter and the sweet opening notes of Eli Fontaine's wailing saxophone on that first track, I am transfixed; when Eddie Brown's bongo backbeat drops in, it moves me. Every. Single. Time. Then, Marvin's smooth voice declares:

> Mother, Mother
> There's too many of you crying

Instantly, I'm transported back to 1971, and Marvin is talking about the state of the nation, pointing out the ills that have kept America from becoming the nation she claims to be. It's the era of the Vietnam War, and the country is in a state of unease. Gaye's own brother had returned from the war a different man. At the time, the nation was plagued by poverty, police brutality, and drug abuse. It's not hard to switch back and forth from the past to the present day; many of the issues that Gaye sings about are still with us today.

The truth is, ever since Africans were first brought to America in chains, we've asked ourselves, "What's going on?" We're frequently marginalized or left out of the American narrative because the narrative that America so often weaves is not entirely ours. Take policing. White America's story line about law enforcement is very different from that of people of color. America has portrayed policing over the years as a heroic, feel-good story line—for White America. But the reality is that the story about these supposed "heroes" in law enforcement looks a lot different for people of color. Rather than solely depending on mainstream media or Hollywood to tell us what's going on, we must rely on each other. Barbershops and beauty shops, dinner tables, cookouts, town hall meetings, Black Twitter—these are just some of the places we go to learn what's really going on. This is where we measure ourselves against White America. It is only among ourselves that we can learn about whether we're getting our fair share and strategize about what we need to do on our quest for equality.

Since the 1950s, progress on the racial equality front in America has been remarkable and dissatisfying all at once, sometimes moving at warp speed and other times at a glacier-like pace. We've seen monumental achievements: the passage of the 1965 Voting Rights Act, the landmark federal legislation that prohibits racial discrimination in voting; the launch of Black Entertainment Television in 1980 by businessman Bob Johnson; a peak of seven African Americans heading Fortune 500 companies in 2007 (today, there are three); the historic election of Barack Obama in 2008, arguably the biggest symbol of America's advancement in the area of racial equality. However, victory was not, as some suggested, a signal of a post-racial America. The notion of a color-blind nation is a myth, at best, and likely a foolish and even dangerous impression to consider. If this country wants to be great, we must continue the ongoing quest for fairness and respect for all our citizens. A realistic look at certain indicators shows the striking disparity that African Americans and other minorities still face.

The tremendous wealth gap between Blacks and Whites, for example, has not diminished in decades. In 1962, the average wealth of White households was seven times greater than that of Black households. After decades of "declining discrimination," that ratio remains essentially the same. Police brutality and law enforcement inequities continue to ravage people of color. Just being Black can still be seen as "criminal"—and can be as good as a death sentence. We cry out for America to say their names: Eric Garner, Tamir Rice, Sandra Bland, Michael Brown...and yet, tragically, there are many, many more.

The proof that race is still a polarizing force is seen in the growing number of hate crimes and the carelessly callous dog-whistling rhetoric of Donald Trump. In August 2017, this veil of collective ignorance was lifted when a viral video showed torch-carrying hate-mongers in Charlottesville, Virginia, spewing abhorrent rhetoric and creating chaos that would lead to the death of a counterprotester. Many ultraconservatives feigned surprise at this level of hate, and President Trump attempted to minimize the vitriol of August 12. Yet just three days later, Trump would say, "You also had very fine people on both sides." However Americans spin the national narrative, race is still a polarizing force, and the state of Black America, at least in some quarters, is precarious.

Over the years, I have debated the direction of Black America with friends and foes. Are we making progress? Do we have a plan to bring equality to all? Are we able to work together as a community? As a journalist, I have moderated or have been a member of panels that have earnestly convened to map out ways to better allow people of color to fully participate in the promise of America. Unfortunately, too often these gatherings produce too few answers. The lingering unanswered question is, what is the state of Black America? That seemed to be a fitting place to start our conversation.

WHAT'S THE STATE OF BLACK AMERICA TODAY?

MICHAEL ERIC DYSON: It's the best of times; it's the worst of times. It's the best of times because we've had an exponential increase in the Black middle class's upward social mobility, in comparison to the Jim Crow, postsegregation culture in America. There's been an extraordinary opening of educational opportunities to Black people. On the other hand, there are indications that [a large part of] Black America is suffering greatly. When you think about the deliberate attempts to control the housing of Black people, that reinforces persistent and troubling rates of Black poverty.

We've had an exponential increase in the Black middle class's upward social mobility.

TODD BOYD: It's hard to describe Black America as one thing. There are things going on with young Black people that may be different than for older Black people. There may be things going on with Black women that are exclusive to women. The Black community has never been one thing. It's never been monolithic, even though a lot of people like to think of it that way. So it's broad, and diverse, depending on what you're talking about.

T.I.: I think we've been distracted. I think people are kind of submerging themselves in entertainment and other things that are going on around them. We aren't necessarily speaking to the needs of the community. The things that need to be done to advance *us*, the things that deserve attention. The actions that need to be taken aren't being addressed. The sacrifices that need to be made aren't being made. I feel like Black America is distracted, and therefore we're stagnant to a certain degree.

DeRay Mckesson: In so many ways, we have changed the conversation about race and justice in this country in ways that are really powerful. People are talking about injustice, talking about disparity in ways we have never done in public. Unfortunately, the outcomes have not changed all that much. We're in this interesting moment where the conversation has changed and people think because the conversation has changed the outcomes must have changed, and they haven't. We're in a pivotal moment to see if we can change both. Otherwise, we will reflect on this and say, "Wow, we changed the conversation, but the things we really cared about didn't actually change that much."

Police have actually killed more people since 2014, not less, but that is not what people believe. People think because you've seen a million videos, it's better. The awareness is at an all-time high, but the outcomes are actually just sad. They are worse than they were when the protests began. This is actually true of education and incarceration; the conversation is really growing, but the outcome is not moving at that pace.

Alicia Garza: I would say it's getting more and more complex and could certainly use an update in terms of Black America's political orientation to make sure that all of the components of our communities are powerful. Black America is changing; unfortunately, our politics are not changing in tandem with our demographics. We've seen an increase in immigration from African countries over the last decade, but we still talk about Black communities as Black folks who are born in the US. We have seen an increased level of visibility of Black people who identify as lesbian or gay or bisexual or transgender.

Todd Boyd: When I was growing up, most Black people were descendants of slaves, and that was their experience. We've since had a lot of immigrants from Africa, from the Caribbean. Biracial people have grown in numbers and how they identify. The Black community now looks very different than how it was back in the '70s. It's necessary to think about what it means to be a Black person, now. You can't just assume that what it meant thirty or forty or fifty years ago is the same as [what it means] today, because then we're not accounting for all the change.

According to the Pew Research Center's analysis of the US Census, the number of Black immigrants living in the United States rose from 816,000 in 1980 to 4.2 million in 2016.

The Pew Center also suggests that the mixed-race population is growing three times faster than the US population as a whole. The US Census Bureau predicts that, by 2060, the number of multiracial Americans will be three times larger than it is now.

ERICKA HUGGINS: I agree. When we discuss Black America, we're thinking in a monolithic way. We're thinking that there's one Black America, and there's not. The state of people of color in the United States is in a similar place as it was in the '60s, in a similar place as it was in the '40s. It's structural; it's institutional. If these institutions and structures change, then the state of Black America would shift.

*   *   *

The diversity of the community adds another level of complication to the Black equation. Many of the subgroups that fall under the umbrella of "Black" don't always share the same issues; at times, they even conflict. That makes forging a harmonious ideology more difficult. The growing LGBTQ community of color, for instance, is at times demonized by those who adhere to the traditional religious leanings of many African American families. Immigrant people of color are often still ostracized by Blacks born in America. Conversely, some immigrants identify themselves not as Black but by their place of origin; for example, Jamaican or African. This presents a growing complication and complexity in defining what it means to be "Black" in America.

However, no matter what the class or the country of origin of Black Americans, or the status of their entry into the country (as slaves or as free people), the inequities still apply to all of us. Now that we have greater access to education, some believe that things will shift if we're able to also achieve financial success. But they haven't. One of the largest differences we have seen since the civil rights advancements of the 1960s is the great economic bifurcation of Black America. While these advancements have enabled some Blacks to improve their financial status, there is still a large economic underclass that has never escaped poverty. Perhaps the biggest hurdle for our community—the greatest obstacle to reaching equality—is closing this wealth gap, a division that has caused classism to grow within our race.

ARE BLACKS GAINING GROUND ECONOMICALLY?

D. L. HUGHLEY: We [do] have Black women, who are the most educated segment of our society, the most entrepreneurial, the most forward-leaning, but that has to be coupled with the notion that in 2000, the median income for Black households was $41,000, and now it's $39,000. It still tells a story of how we are looked at differently, because there's no other way to explain how everybody else's income rose except ours, even with the great strides that Black women are making. It's a mixed bag, but at the bottom of it is the sh*t we've always dealt with.

JEMELE HILL: I think there are some things that we can certainly be proud [of], like our legacy of civil rights advancements. There are just other things that you look at and wonder, *Will this ever change?* Especially when you look at the fact that the income gap, for example, between Black Americans and everybody else, is continuing to widen. It's almost as if we're still in Jim Crow.

SUSAN TAYLOR: The Census Bureau calculates poverty as a [family income of $12,195 or lower] for a family of four with two related children. It's insane.

KILLER MIKE: Since the late 1930s, land ownership has shrunk. If you look at cities that are predominantly Black, many of them, from an infrastructure perspective, are falling and are not where they could be. We're in danger. Even though unemployment is lower, you gotta say to yourself, what kind of jobs are we getting if we can't buy houses? The jobs we're getting are not [paying] enough to create homeowners in America, which is the cornerstone of wealth. I fear for us now.

The Economic Policy Institute, using the definition of poverty as whether a family has sufficient income to meet basic material needs, reports that in 1968 the median Black household earned 63 percent of the income the median White household earned in a year. In 2016, the median Black household earned 61 percent of the annual income the median White household earned.

The report also showed that, in 1968, with a poverty rate of 33.5 percent, African Americans were three times more likely to live in poverty than Whites. In 2016, the Black poverty rate was 22 percent, lower than it was almost fifty years ago but still 2.5 times higher than the White poverty rate.

ED GORDON: Aside from the wealth gap, what other factors hold us back from achieving racial equality? What should we focus on next?

JEMELE HILL: Basic civil freedoms have been addressed, [like] the right to vote, [and] we're not drinking out of separate water fountains anymore. There are signs of tremendous progress, but I also see areas where it seems nothing has changed. There are a lot of systemic issues that haven't been addressed in this country. So all the advances are either through policy— forced policy that finally had to be reckoned with—or basically because people have overcome in such a phenomenal manner that the progress couldn't help but tag along.

STACEY ABRAMS: We continue to suffer from judicial, electoral, and financial systems that were not only designed to disadvantage us but also isolated us from opportunity. We continue to have to work to fix what was broken, but we should not ignore the important progress that we have made.

MARC MORIAL: Our generation is tasked with trying to ensure that this post–civil rights progress that we sort of inherited, remains. There's been too much three steps forward, two steps backward, four steps forward, two steps backward, since the 1950s and '60s. We have to make sure not to turn into the second Reconstruction era.

AL SHARPTON: Throughout Black history, we've *always* had step-forward, push-back. From the abolitionist movement finally getting Lincoln to reluctantly bring the enslaved into the Union Army; [this] was the trade-off to get the Emancipation Proclamation. That was followed by Andrew Johnson, who took it all back, and then *Plessy v. Ferguson*. So that has been the pattern and the trend. I expected [that] what we're seeing now would happen after eight years of Obama.

*   *   *

The state of Black America has changed since the political rise of Donald Trump. Black America's status has become more tenuous, more dubious since June 16, 2015, when Trump officially announced he was a candidate for the presidency of the United States. Arguably, the single biggest tactic Trump used for his victory was divide and conquer. His greatest line of division is race. Trump's wink and a nod at bigotry has given license to those who harbored intolerant racial feelings secretly to freely display them with little concern. Their attitude seems to be, "Why keep your views latent when they are shared by the president of the United States?" The dogmatism Trump spouts is allowing figurative and literal attacks on people of color.

There is a growing environment of hate and intolerance in this country. White privilege runs from the annoyance of "Becky" calling the police because a Black person she's never seen is walking their dog on "her" block to White privilege run amok with the life-and-death mob mentality that rose in Charlottesville, Virginia. The election of Donald Trump and the ascending alt-right have emboldened much of the far right's detest for minorities, yet, in a strange way, these developments have awakened Black America to what surrounds us.

IS IT FAIR TO SAY THAT PART OF THE STATE OF BLACK AMERICA IS UNDER ATTACK?

MARC MORIAL: Black America is under assault by Trumpism, which is the philosophy of White nationalism wrapped in twenty-first-century political clothing. It's an assault on the gains of the last thirty years and an assault on the browning of America.

AL SHARPTON: I am disappointed that both White and Black America have not reacted. I saw more Blacks who called themselves activists raise questions in the streets under Obama than [under] Trump. It's like they're afraid to fight a guy [who'll] fight back. When I say we're in a precarious position, it's not only what they're doing to us, it's our reaction I'm disappointed in.

CHARLAMAGNE THA GOD: Donald Trump has made Black people realize we really don't have anything but ourselves at the end of the day. In a way, it's good because we're getting back to a lot of old-school values. Whether it was Dr. Martin Luther King Jr., Elijah Muhammad, or Malcolm X, they all talked about doing it as a people. I feel like we're getting back to that. We really did get lost in trying to assimilate into pop culture, mainstream culture, White culture, whatever that is. People are getting back to being proud of their Blackness, and they're taking pride in being Black again. That is very important.

ED GORDON: Mr. Belafonte, I am curious how you see all of this. Your history of fighting for equality gives you a unique purview of the state of Black America and what can only be seen as a rise in racist activity and intolerance.

HARRY BELAFONTE: I see promises denied. I see participation in the oppression of Black culture and Black life still very active in America. I see that we've come to a horrible normal, where the president of the United States is not only stirring up racist animosity but also adding fuel to his own comments on what he thinks of people of color.

ED GORDON: In spite of these setbacks, what progress have we made under Trump? And what will help us continue to move forward?

RICHELIEU DENNIS: Transformation. We are entering a new level, or we have entered a new level, of self-awareness, a new realization of our modern vulnerabilities, and a significant understanding of how we realize our potential.

LAURA COATES: This is a time of optimism, but one of a real sense of agency that we are no longer waiting [for] and being reactive [to] people [who] come to us as allies or for people to approach us with solutions. We are being far more proactive about knowing that we not only have a seat at the table, we can command every seat.

BRITTANY PACKNETT: We also seem to be in a place of imagination and creativity, another Renaissance—in art, fashion, music, politics, literature, journalism, and academia. Bright Black faces, Black voices, Black philosophy, Black public thinking. That is advancing the cause. And that is evolving in a very different way. The kind of movement-making that Black people have always been capable of is on display right now in really new and innovative ways.

DERRICK JOHNSON: We have people in positions that we could have never imagined, whether it's corporate boards or political office. We have a strong class of entrepreneurs. We have workers accessing positions that some of our foreparents would've never imagined.

SUSAN TAYLOR: You're right; some of us are living lives that our great-grands could have never imagined. However, so many of us are struggling, and that suffering is really heart-wrenching. It's what I'm trying to figure out with a whole host of other leaders of organizations; how we can create a Marshall Plan for our people and do it in a way that helps those who typically want to tread carefully. I don't believe that we can be oppositional when we're trying to get people to do what is more than just the right thing, but it's the morally right thing. I believe in the depth of their hearts everybody really wants to do that.

*   *   *

No matter what your station in life, no matter what heights you've reached, the reality of prejudice still hovers over our nation like an ominous cloud—not because of political discord but because of racism. There is not a singular state of Black America. There are groupings of economic status, age, gender, education, and a multitude of things that make up our rich and diverse culture as Blacks. But one commonality remains: racial inequality. Successful African American actors are overlooked for roles, not for lack of talent or box office draw but because of racism. Black hedge funds are often left out of the most lucrative deals on Wall Street, not because of underperformance but because of racism. The universal state of Black America is unequal and always has been.

Almost fifty years ago, Marvin Gaye implored us in "What's Going On" to ask questions about why America was suffused with racism. A half century later, rapper Childish Gambino recorded "This Is America," a smash hit that points out that these same issues still stand uncorrected.

The lack of understanding, empathy, or care for Black America has always been fluid, manic, and, at times, even schizophrenic. Four hundred years is a long time to be unsettled. America is our home, even though we are still fighting to be welcomed in through the front door. We, too, love this nation; we, too, pledge allegiance to it. So what's going on? The future of Black America is uncertain; the only certainty is that we will continue to love this country and fight for it until America delivers on her promise. Once that happens, our state will be at ease, because the chance to succeed and flourish will finally be in our hands—and that's all we've ever wanted. Until then, our posture and stance will be bold and defiant; we will be in fight mode. However you define that.

STARTING YOUR OWN CONVERSATION

- What are your thoughts on the current state of Black America? Where do we stand?

- Does the rise of Trump—and White nationalism—mean that our cause has taken a step back? Why do you think so or not?

- How does the past look different from the present? Have we made progress or not?

- What role might financial and economic progress play in advancing our status in other areas?

- In what areas do you feel that we have become stagnant, and what is most needed for us to move forward?

- In what areas does Black America today find itself on the verge of real change?

- What can you do in your community to inspire collective interest and activism?

- What kind of progress is most pressing for your community? And what resources do you need to help combat racism?

OBAMA

A REFLECTION

STACEY ABRAMS	Politician & Author
HARRY BELAFONTE	Entertainer & Activist
BRITTNEY COOPER	Academic & Author
MICHAEL ERIC DYSON	Academic & Author
ALICIA GARZA	Cofounder of Black Lives Matter
JEMELE HILL	Journalist & Broadcaster
ERIC HOLDER	Former US Attorney General
D. L. HUGHLEY	Comedian & Author
HAKEEM JEFFRIES	US Representative from New York
VAN JONES	Commentator & Author
VAN LATHAN	Television Producer
MALCOLM D. LEE	Film Director & Screenwriter
TAMIKA MALLORY	Social Activist
DᴇRAY MCKESSON	Social Activist
MARC MORIAL	President & CEO of the National Urban League
ANGELA RYE	Attorney & Political Analyst
BAKARI SELLERS	Attorney & Political Commentator
AL SHARPTON	President of the National Action Network
SHERMICHAEL SINGLETON	Republican Strategist
MICHAEL STEELE	Former Chair of the Republican National Committee
MAXINE WATERS	US Representative from California

When I was in elementary school, my teachers used to encourage us to excel by saying, "You can be anything you want to be when you grow up." Really? I am a cynical adult, and I was just as cynical as a child. My ten-year-old self would mumble back, "Yeah, anything but president!"

I truly believed I would never, in my lifetime, see a Black president of the United States, until a mixed-race, former community organizer, Democratic senator from Illinois proved me wrong. Others had tried. Shirley Chisholm's "Unbought and Unbossed" presidential campaign in 1972 was inspirational. Jesse Jackson energized us in presidential primaries in 1984 and 1988, telling us to "keep hope alive." In 2004, Al Sharpton tossed his hat in the ring, and others, like Lenora Fulani and Alan Keyes, brought color to the presidential race from time to time.

Then, in 2005, Barack Obama was elected the junior senator from Illinois, and by 2006, there were whispers that he was considering a run for the highest office in the land. He had delivered a rousing, attention-getting speech at the 2004 Democratic National Convention, but few, including me, woke the next morning thinking this man would be the one to make history. The word on the political landscape had always been that the presidency was an unbreakable glass ceiling, and I concurred.

By late 2006, these whispers grew louder, and rampant speculation followed. That speculation had reached a fever pitch in early 2007 when I interviewed the senator in question, who hadn't even served a full term yet. We were weeks away from what everyone believed was going to be his official announcement to launch his presidential campaign. A man who hadn't even served four years in the Senate, a man often described as a moderate, rank-and-file Democrat. He had yet to make his mark legislatively. Some believed his biggest accomplishment was being named to *Time* magazine's annual list of the "World's Most Influential People" or when the audio edition of his memoir, *Dreams from My Father*, earned him a Grammy for Best Spoken Word Album. Fine accolades, but was that White House–worthy? Not to mention that he was a Black man!

I arrived in Chicago not knowing what to expect. I knew him to be intelligent and charismatic. I knew he was a young Turk in the Democratic Party.

We'd spoken on the phone briefly. He walked in confident and affable, working the room and greeting everyone with a smile. We started the interview, and eventually, I asked if the rumors about his presidential run were correct. That cynical child from elementary school came out. As he spoke, all I could think was, *Yeah, yeah, whatever, man. Good luck, make us proud—or at least don't embarrass us—but you ain't winning.* He kept talking, and I just thought in awe, *Wow, he really seems convinced he has a fat chance.* Ha!

A few weeks later, on February 10, 2007, he made it official: he was running. By June 2008, the presumptive nominee Hillary Clinton had dropped out of the race, and in November of that year, Barack Obama accomplished what I thought was impossible.

I vividly recall waking up before dawn and heading to Washington, DC, on January 20, 2009. I was going to be stationed to anchor the soon-to-be-president Barack Obama's swearing-in ceremony. The day felt more than historic for the nation; it was euphoric for Black America. Thousands upon thousands of Blacks, many of them descendants of slaves, had come from all across the country to witness this momentous occasion; the sight was overwhelmingly moving. People brought their entire families and took photos, all to archive the moment and be able to say, "I was there." Nothing touched me more than seeing an elderly Black woman being pushed in a wheelchair. It was hard to navigate the city that day. Police had closed off many of the streets, even to foot traffic. As I approached this woman, I could see that her companion was having trouble pushing her chair over the grassy area, which was the only way they could go since the sidewalks had been cordoned off. For me, she was a symbol of the generations before me who had suffered through indignities and hatred and yet still hung on. They hung on and fought long enough to make this day possible.

I used my press credentials, and with a little help from two brothers on the DC police force, we were able to get that woman a prime spot to watch history. She was moved to tears. I thanked the officers for helping me pay back a small fraction of the debt we owed the generations before us, the debt that had afforded those officers, Barack Obama, and me a chance to live out our dreams.

Black voters were inspired by the man who would become president. According to the Roper Center for Public Opinion Research, Barack Obama won a whopping 95 percent of the Black vote in 2008 when he defeated Republican John McCain and 93 percent in 2012 when he defeated Mitt Romney.

Black America made sure that Obama's first victory was no fluke. He left office in January 2017 as one of the most beloved figures in African American history. In fact, President Obama earned a place in the Black people's Hall of Fame: his photo now occupies a spot next to photos of Jesus, King, and Kennedy in Black homes all over the country.

The infatuation with President Obama and his family has waned little since he left office, and in fact, many have dubbed him their "Forever President." A more objective look at the Obama presidency raises some fair and complicated questions. With the unwavering and staggering support he received from the Black electorate, did he pay his debt to this loyal base? Was the political quid pro quo met, or was his historic victory enough?

WAS LIFE REALLY BETTER FOR BLACK PEOPLE DURING OBAMA'S PRESIDENCY?

ERIC HOLDER: By almost any measure, Black people were better off by the time Obama left office in January 2017. If you compare those eight years, Black folks were better off economically, they were better off with regard to health care, and measures were taken with regard to criminal justice reform. That doesn't mean over the course of eight years Barack Obama reversed all that Black folks in this country have had to deal with since 1619, but substantial progress was made.

On December 1, 2008, Barack Obama announced Eric Holder to be his nominee for the attorney general of the United States. Holder would become the first African American to hold that position when he was confirmed by the Senate on February 2, 2009, by a vote of 75 to 21. Three years later, the Republican-controlled House of Representatives would hold Holder in contempt of Congress during an investigation of an ATF gun scandal. He was cleared by the Justice Department's inspector general. Holder resigned in April 2015 to return to private practice.

BAKARI SELLERS: He did yeoman's work for the Black community. He increased the wages of Black folks, medically insured Black folks; the steps he took with criminal justice reform, the executive acts, task forces on policing—all of those things were strides that directly helped to lift up targeted Black communities. The problem is he had to do this with Mitch McConnell—who at that time was arguably the second most powerful man in the world—saying that he was going to do everything he could not to help Obama succeed.

MARC MORIAL: The National Urban League did a report on President Obama and found that one of the things we struggled with was the standard by which we evaluate Barack Obama. Do we evaluate him in comparison to what I call the mythical super-Negro, super-politician, superman standard? Do we evaluate him in comparison to, let's say, the three previous presidents? How do you evaluate him?

We looked at Barack Obama from a standpoint of evaluating the conditions that Black people and the country were in the day he took office and where the country was the day he left office. We concluded [that] his presidency was good, not excellent. Joblessness, Black graduation rates, the status of health care, all improved from day one to the final day. Home ownership, no real progress. Civil rights enforcement, good to excellent in terms of the Justice Department.

So I give the president good marks, and understanding the partisan battles he had, I shy away from the norm, that the first African American president somehow should have an *S* on his chest.

VAN JONES: All of us are quite proud that Obama not only did Black people proud, he did America proud. But at the end of the day, the backlash against him—the carefully engineered and orchestrated backlash against him—stopped him from doing more. It's hard to imagine any subsequent president or government doing a whole lot more under [those conditions and in the] present environment.

MAXINE WATERS: He was working uphill, swimming upstream all the time. That prevented him from doing maybe everything he wanted to do or could have done. He was being scrutinized in ways that caused him to back up from certain efforts.

AL SHARPTON: I don't think he gets enough credit for health care. Nobody had been able to push that through, and it's vital. Bad health, sickness, illness comes in our families and wipes out everything we have. That was one of the most important things that could happen to Black people. Second, his administration fought aggressively for voting rights. All of what Eric Holder did to combat voter suppression was viable. And that was when they [Republicans] started setting up everything that they're doing now with voter ID and moving districts around.

HAKEEM JEFFRIES: Well, during eight years of his presidency, Barack Obama also turned the economy around, which significantly benefited the African American community, and began the process of changing our criminal justice system through passage of [the Fair Sentencing Act of 2010], which struck a blow against the mass incarceration epidemic. President Obama also diversified the federal court system in a way that has served, to some degree, as a firewall against President Trump's current efforts to flood the system with right-wing judges. No one can totally transform the country in an eight-year period, and it's important to keep in mind that because of the midterm elections that occurred in 2010, the majority of President Obama's time in office was spent with an obstructionist, Republican-controlled House. Notwithstanding that fact, he has left the country and the African American community in a much better place than where we were before he took office.

Congress passed the Fair Sentencing Act of 2010, which reduced the sentencing disparity between offenses for crack and powder cocaine. Prior to passage of the act, people faced longer sentences for offenses involving crack cocaine than for offenses involving the same amount of powder cocaine. The majority of those arrested for crack offenses are African American. Because of the sentencing disparity, African Americans served, on average, as much time in prison for nonviolent drug offenses as Whites did for violent offenses.

* * *

Being the first carries a burden, and that burden certainly was shouldered by President Obama. So much hope came with his victory that many clung to the belief that he, his political deeds, and his ability to enact legislation would supersede or at least match the historic significance of his win. More misguided was the notion that all of this would happen quickly and without substantial pushback.

I recall talking with Nelson Mandela in 1994, right before he took office as president of South Africa. I asked, "What would be your number one task as president of South Africa?" Without hesitation, he said, "Managing expectations." He told me that he must show that he wasn't there to seek revenge for what Whites had done to him and other people of color, and that Blacks must know that their conditions would not change overnight once he took office.

WHAT UNIQUE OBSTACLES AND BURDENS DID OBAMA FACE AS A BLACK PRESIDENT?

STACEY ABRAMS: We have to recognize, as a people, that the presidency is not a magic wand, and that is one of the reasons it's so important for us to pay attention to the elections at every level. We ascribe so much power to a single job that when [the occupant of] that job fails to meet those expectations, it diminishes our belief not only in the job but in the job holder, and that is inappropriate. His presidency was an extraordinary gift to our country. Certainly, juxtaposition with his successor shows that the brilliance of President Obama continues to shine through.

JEMELE HILL: Just being politicians, [there are] different expectations. That being said, why should a Black president have to feel the burden of shaking hands with people who hate him and try to delegitimize him? There are times where I wish that some of the ugliness that he and we are exposed to would be returned in kind. Maybe not in the same way, but maybe just letting people know [the effect of what they're doing] and [making them] live with the uncomfortable notion that they are not forgiven.

From where I stand, high expectations and the conciliatory nature of President Obama made for an interesting mix. Black America wasn't always in lockstep with President Obama. There were some fundamental policy issues that his administration did not always address that dealt with the larger needs of a majority of Black Americans. Obama knew that he had to convince White voters he would not overlook their needs and wants. Some critics say he went out of his way at times to prove this. The unanswered question is, were these counterintuitive differences ideological or political? If the latter, his motive to satisfy White America could have been to the detriment of his base.

ED GORDON: What were Obama's biggest missed opportunities?

MARC MORIAL: The biggest missed opportunities were in the economic arena and that the president was not always well served by an overwhelmingly White set of economic advisers, who may have had an intellectual understanding about some of these problems but were not open to, in a big way, suggestions from Black economic policy experts about steps that needed to be taken.

D. L. HUGHLEY: If Obama had not assumed that Hillary was going to win [in 2016], and had done something actively about the Russian infiltration of our election system, we'd look different today. [If he had done something sooner about trying to secure his Supreme Court nominee Merrick

Garland on the Supreme Court], we'd have a different result than we do now. But we don't—all because we thought something would happen just by happenstance.

ANGELA RYE: If we would have known we were going to end up here, would we have taken a different approach? I remember there were grumblings about where the bench [would be] post-Obama. Would we have spent more time focusing on getting the administration to help build a bench to develop infrastructure? Not just within the Democratic Party but within our community?

BRITTNEY COOPER: There were some moments, particularly in the middle of the Black Lives Matter movement, when he cared more about appeasing the American public than about taking care of Black folks. He was the first Black man in history who had a considerable level of power, who could take care of us. And I was deeply disappointed in him for that.

AL SHARPTON: I didn't agree with him on Gaddafi and Libya. Sometimes, he would publicly be too much of a healer without dealing with the injured. He tried hard to work with the Republicans. And it took him a while to understand that it didn't matter what he offered them.

> The Obama administration helped design a UN resolution to take military action that resulted in a US-led NATO intervention in Libya. The country's leader, Muammar Gaddafi, was eventually killed by rebels. There was no real plan for the aftermath of Gaddafi, and the nation fell into a bloody civil war. Obama would later call this the "worst mistake" of his presidency.

*　　*　　*

Given the magnitude of Obama's job, he could change the world's balance with just a few words or the shift of a position. Even with all this power, I believe, fundamentally, race remained the biggest hindrance for Obama. The extra burden, the "Black tax" that all African Americans have to metaphorically pay, is still charged, even when you become president. Often, when issues of race came up, many wanted the president to take a more aggressive approach, but that was not how he won the White House. He was not race-neutral, but at times he was race-lite. A number of high-profile racial incidents came up—from dealing with controversial comments by his former pastor, Jeremiah Wright, to the infamous White House Beer Summit after famed Harvard University professor Henry Louis "Skip" Gates was racially profiled at his home by a Cambridge, Massachusetts, police officer—these incidents and others gave Obama a chance to send a firm message about tolerance and race. Many felt his message was tacit at best. But he could also be compassionate about race, as he showed at the memorial service for Clementa Pinckney, Democratic member of the South Carolina Senate and pastor of Mother Emanuel AME Church in Charleston, South Carolina.

On June 17, 2015, a twenty-one-year-old White man entered the house of worship and went on a killing spree during a prayer service. The shooter took nine lives, including that of Pastor Pinckney. The president struck all the right healing and compassionate notes that day. Some wanted those notes to be heard elsewhere, including when circumstances called for a sterner message about race—a stronger rebuke after unjustified shootings of Blacks by law enforcement or a more pointed stance on racism in America. Throughout most of his time in office, the president was able to strike the delicate balance of showing Whites that he had been inculcated to their ways enough to make them feel comfortable yet still remaining "Black" enough to feel comfortable in his skin. It is another one of those burdens that Blacks have had to carry—a grudging cultural appropriation, done more out of survival than envy. Obama is a master of balance in this area. His makeup is not to burn down the house; he was never going to be a race rabble-rouser. He was more Drake than Tupac.

WAS OBAMA BRAVE ENOUGH?

MICHAEL STEELE: I've had numerous conversations with people whose sense was that there were times [when] Obama was, and I'll use the word, "afraid" to use his Blackness on their behalf. And to say, "Yeah, I am the president of everybody, but I'm also looking at the ills of this community, and I identify with that, I connect with that, and we've got to do something about that."

ANGELA RYE: I remember being executive director of the Congressional Black Caucus, and we regularly found ourselves at odds with President Obama. I believe him to be the greatest president in my lifetime, no question. But that didn't mean he couldn't have been greater on issues that we have. I don't think that the criticism bestowed on him squarely belonged to him. We had expectations of our civil rights leaders and members of Congress. There would be a lot who talked big, and then once they got in the room with President Obama, they were just happy to be there.

DERAY MCKESSON: We met with Obama twice. What I'll never forget about one of the meetings was that before they walked in, almost all of the civil rights leaders had big talk: "We gotta tell Obama this, we gotta tell Obama that." When he walked in, literally, one by one, they thanked him. And I was like, "What are you thanking him for?" It was really wild to watch these leaders just walk in the room and congratulate him because he was the Black president. I walked out not even being really mad at him, because he could walk out of that room and be like, "They didn't push me," and that would have been honest.

AL SHARPTON: Obama is not an activist. Obama is Obama. I took some heat for working closely with Obama from some Black scholars who had worked with Bill Clinton, who [by the way] passed a crime bill that locked up a half a generation of Blacks and a welfare reform bill that did the same! So even if you don't want to give Barack Obama credit on health care, credit on the voting stuff, explain to me what bill he put through that hurt us.

The Violent Crime Control and Law Enforcement Act of 1994, referred to as the Clinton crime bill, became law in 1994. The act provided for one hundred thousand new police officers, broadened federal law in a number of ways, and included a section banning assault weapons. Other parts of the act were more controversial, including a greatly expanded federal death penalty, new classes of individuals banned from possessing firearms, and a variety of new crimes defined in statutes relating to immigration law, hate crimes, sex crimes, and gang-related crime. A number of the provisions were seen by some as disproportionately targeting people of color, in terms of unbalanced sentencing and engagement with the judicial system.

*   *   *

People understood the pressure Obama was under. The added element of race—and the undue burden of having to prove to White America that he was capable—was something that Blacks understood. It was something that was commonplace to us. The community didn't want to add pressure or heap on too much public scorn and add another encumbrance to an already difficult balance. We didn't want to fuel those who were putting everything he did under a microscope to find flaws. However, we did want him to be accountable to a community that was standing beside, behind, and in front of him when needed. The legendary entertainer and activist Harry Belafonte had been here before. He was front and center with Martin Luther King Jr. during the height of the civil rights movement. In the late 1950s and early '60s, when he was one of the top entertainers in America, Belafonte chose to put his career at risk and lend his public support and his money to a cause he saw as just. He understands the concept of making a calculated moral decision.

SHOULD OBAMA HAVE BEEN A MORE MILITANT ACTIVIST FOR THE BLACK COMMUNITY?

HARRY BELAFONTE: Obama gave Black America a very passionate and polite environment in which to reveal itself, although he fell [far] short of what he could have done and the legacy he could have left us if he had been more militant about Black interest.

ED GORDON: So, should he have been more militant?

HARRY BELAFONTE: He should have been! S-H-O-U-L-D!

SHERMICHAEL SINGLETON: When you see what Obama's administration did for the LGBTQ community and DACA for the Hispanic community, those are tangible things that those communities can point to. Where are the tangible things for Black people? That disappointed a lot of Black people. They may not say it publicly, but I know my family and friends talk about it, and these are people who love Obama. They say, "I was hoping for a little bit more."

TAMIKA MALLORY: That's true. But he was very limited in terms of what he could do, and we know that Black people deal with that at every level, even being president.

MALCOLM D. LEE: He was what you want a reasonable leader to be. "Let's work together here." As a Black man, he could never just be like, "F*ck this, I'm doing what the hell I want to do!" That wasn't who he was. He tried to be the "Great Uniter."

SHERMICHAEL SINGLETON: I am not trying to excuse Republican obstructionism at all, but I still think there were areas where, through executive action, the president could have used his signature to get some things done that would have directly benefited African Americans. His administration didn't because they knew Black people would be reliable supporters of Obama no matter what.

Among other immigration changes, President Obama announced a policy that allowed certain immigrants to escape deportation and obtain work permits for a period of two years—renewable upon good behavior. To apply, immigrants had to be younger than thirty-one on June 15, 2012, must have come to the United States when they were younger than sixteen, and must have lived in the United States since 2007. He would fight vigorously for the children of undocumented immigrants who were born outside the United States. In 2014, President Obama announced his intention to expand his Deferred Action for Childhood Arrivals policy. A number of states sued to prevent the expansion, which was ultimately stopped by a 5–4 vote in the Supreme Court.

TAMIKA MALLORY: In terms of his politics, he played it very safe. We need leaders in this moment who are somewhat similar to Trump, not as hateful but willing to say, "I don't give a damn. I'm here to feed the hungry and to free the poor." We really need that.

ANGELA RYE: I had friends who worked in the [Obama] White House who would say, "How could you criticize the president?" I'd say, "Because there are still Black people hurting, and we know when he's gone, this issue's over."

MAXINE WATERS: Sometimes, cover is needed. In the case of Obama, because he was a Black man, the right wing was furious. The [White] supremacists were furious. They slept on his first election, and by the second election, he had gained enough power and was able to raise tremendous sums of money to get everything out of the election that could be gotten. We were not about to, in general, point out any misgivings or mistakes or criticism, because we didn't want to hurt the fact that this Black man was now the president of the United States.

*   *   *

The Black community often went out of its way to shield Obama, but did he do the same? Some believed him to be paternal and condescending at times. Critics said that when he spoke at galas or events, Obama often lectured or rebuked Blacks about how they needed to improve. His detractors characterized this as victim shaming, once again trying to distance himself from what he saw as questionable behavior that might be interpreted by Whites as demeaning and somehow reflect on him. His supporters saw a caring president who only wanted the best for his people and was offering a road map for a better, more fruitful life.

DID OBAMA DO ENOUGH TO PROTECT THE BLACK COMMUNITY?

ALICIA GARZA: This has gotten me into trouble, but I'm going to say it anyway because it's true. In many ways, Obama believed that there were a lot of problems that Black communities faced that were the fault of their own. Here's an example: After Trayvon Martin's death and subsequent protests ensued—this was before George Zimmerman was acquitted—Obama was relatively silent. It was a protest that actually got the district attorney, Angela Corey, to even press charges. George Zimmerman would have walked free had it not been for the Dream Defenders, or Sybrina [Fulton, Trayvon Martin's mother] and her family putting pressure on the district attorney to press charges. When George Zimmerman was acquitted, protests ensued across the nation, and Obama tried to find a middle ground. He tried to establish himself as Black with his comments like, "If I had a son, he would look like Trayvon." That was essentially the same thing as saying, "See, I'm Black, right?" But then he also called for systems to work. That was really a bath of ice water for protesters.

AL SHARPTON: Yeah, but he did stand in the Rose Garden and said things that he didn't have to say about Trayvon Martin, and came back with Eric Garner, and worked with those of us in the fight when he knew others didn't want him to. Don't forget: he went every year to the Congressional Black Caucus; he came as president twice to the National Action Network Convention. Clearly, his actions spoke a lot more than his words. I had the advantage of talking to him a lot, and I understood he couldn't come out and say what I would have to say, which is why he gave me access to say it.

ERIC HOLDER: Take a look at the treatment of young Black men by people in law enforcement that, in some ways, was potentially brought to the fore by the increased consciousness that his election brought about. People need to understand this. I always ask: Do you really think that there were no Black people killed inappropriately by people in law enforcement before Barack Obama was president? Do you think the situation is worse now—or in 2009, or 2012, or 2014—than it was in 1950? With the election of the president, and frankly having a Black attorney general, the thought that there was the possibility that something could be done about that, people's consciousness was raised, and that's a good thing. It shone a light on things that had been going on in the past.

MICHAEL ERIC DYSON: Barack Obama was great in many ways, but as you know, he went around the country doing "Bill Cosby" lite, and he told us why parents shouldn't serve cold chicken for breakfast. All right, that's fine in itself, but in the context of a White culture that is listening to you scold Black America and scorn Black behavior, then that reflects a kind of White supremacist logic and an anti-Black sentiment that has to be called out. So, I would argue that both with Bill Cosby and Barack Obama, some of what they were chastising the community about was rooted in the truth. Yet, in the cases of Cosby and Obama, they ain't had nothing to say about the White man. In fact, they let the "White man" off the hook. Barack Obama depended upon Black solidarity to buffer the legitimate critique that he endured. Black people do have to be held to account, but when you perform that excoriation of Black people in public, make sure you don't make it seem like White folk ain't got some of the same problems.

Michael Eric Dyson is a renowned scholar who has been a staunch supporter of President Obama, understanding the delicate balance the president had to strike, along with the tremendous onslaught he faced from the right wing his entire presidency. He has also been a harsh critic of him at times, feeling Obama had abdicated his base for political expediency.

ED GORDON: What has Obama's legacy left us with?

VAN LATHAN: The reality is that President Obama is, no matter what happened in his eight years, the most significant African American who ever lived besides Dr. King, maybe even more significant than Dr. King.

HAKEEM JEFFRIES: In the African American community, we had our Jackie Robinson moment at the presidential level when Barack Obama was elected in 2008. That was a beginning, not an ending. So, it's important to recognize that President Obama, who did a phenomenal job, opened up the door of opportunity to create a better place for us in the United States of America.

D. L. HUGHLEY: There are children right now who literally believe they can be president. There are children right now who literally believe that they can ascend to heights that their parents could never have imagined. Even if he did nothing else but plant a seed in children that will bear fruit that I'll never see, he did an amazing thing. Was he limited? Yes. Did he do things that I wouldn't have done? Yes. But the idea that now our children have an aspirational figure they can point to that no one can knock down. Wow! America dated a Black guy, and she liked it. [laughs]

> *There are children right now who literally believe that they can ascend to heights that their parents could never have imagined.*

ERIC HOLDER: History is going to be very kind to Barack Obama, and Black history is going to be very kind to the Obama administration.

*   *   *

Obama's victory showed not only the power of the Black vote but also the precarious position that Blacks who ascend to political heights are forced to place themselves in. Like many who've navigated uncharted waters, Barack Obama sometimes had to find his way through rough tides, while others stood on the shore telling him how he should get back to dry land. President Obama never said that he was unquestionably confident in his direction and that the "wants" of brothers and sisters would have to wait. He accepted the only road there was to the White House. He understood the needs of the community and weighed the options to find the best way to respond to them. He fought through arguably the most divisive and partisan Congress any president has ever faced. Political calculation was his strong suit.

His place in history was fixed the day he won the Democratic nomination, and he was catapulted to almost mythical heights when he won the Oval Office. Presidents are best judged with a historical lens that takes time to calculate what they've done. The grand scale of a decision or policy is sometimes so complicated and complex that its fruition and the impact of that action won't be fully recognized for years.

Some wanted a protector, a militant president, one who was more aggressive in his demands and approach, but that is not how Obama won the presidency.

By reflecting on the challenges of Barack Obama's presidency, we have a stronger vision of what we want from future leadership and institutions and how we should operate ourselves. How much cover and leniency should we allow? Asking these questions of ourselves and each other is vital to our growth. President Obama, HBCUs, and civil rights leaders and organizations are among those whom some deem to be publicly "untouchable" because of their importance to our legacy. An "immunity" of sorts is often granted to them. They are off-limits when it comes to public debate about their performance.

We understand the pressure President Obama was under. Many of us experience it at work and in our daily lives, but it's not on public display. Our actions aren't going down in history. The undue burden of feeling that you have to prove to White America that you are capable is something that

Blacks know all too well. Obama knew this before he became president. As Black Americans, we didn't want to add another set of eyes to the microscope he was already under, picking apart each and every one of his flaws. However, we did want accountability. We wanted him to stand fully beside, behind, and in front of us when needed. Regardless of his legacy, the most important takeaway here is that we now know what we want and what to look for in our leadership as we move forward.

At the end of the day, President Obama has shown great dignity in the face of all this criticism, and Americans should be most proud of that. He rose above the muck to personify an adjective that history had not, up until that point, ascribed to the president of the United States: Black. He was, in the best way, presidential.

STARTING YOUR OWN CONVERSATION

- How did the quality of life for Black people change—in your town, your state, the country—during Obama's presidency? What were the most noticeable improvements or significant drawbacks?

- In what ways must Black leaders account for their race that other leaders aren't forced to deal with? How did Obama do this, and in the end, did he succeed?

- What was the debt that Obama "owed" to the Black community, and was he successful in paying it back?

- What legislative and administrative achievements from Obama's presidency had the most lasting positive impact on your community? How can we ensure that this progress continues?

- What did Obama's presidency change about the way you will view future political candidates? What would you like to see more or less of from future Black leaders?

TRUMP
MAKE AMERICA HATE AGAIN

STACEY ABRAMS	Politician & Author
WILLIAM BARBER	Minister & Activist
HARRY BELAFONTE	Entertainer & Activist
LAURA COATES	CNN Analyst & Radio Host
TIFFANY CROSS	Managing Editor of *The Beat DC*
ERIC HOLDER	Former US Attorney General
D. L. HUGHLEY	Comedian & Author
TAMIKA MALLORY	Social Activist
MARC MORIAL	President & CEO of the National Urban League
ANGELA RYE	Attorney & Political Analyst
SHERMICHAEL SINGLETON	Republican Strategist
MICHAEL STEELE	Former Chair of the Republican National Committee
MAXINE WATERS	US Representative from California

It was the morning of November 8, 2016, and I was on the *Steve Harvey Morning Show*, talking about the importance of voter turnout in scoring a Democratic victory and specifically how certain states would be key to propelling Hillary Clinton to the Oval Office. As the morning went on and producers took somewhat unenthusiastic calls from people planning to vote that day, I couldn't help but notice that the excitement meter was much lower than it had been during the previous presidential election. I wondered if this was a harbinger of things to come.

As the show wound down, I was asked for my prognostication. Who did I think would win the election? The seven-year-old me, who never thought he'd see a Black president, had been wrong. Now I was faced with the question of whether there would be a woman in that position. From what I knew about Clinton's history, surely she could emerge victorious—but I cautioned America that Trump might still win. Nephew Tommy, one of the cohosts, laughed at me. "Come on, Ed, you don't really think he can win, do you?" I hoped that I would be wrong again.

It became clear fairly quickly in the evening that there was a real possibility that Trump could defy most of the cable talking heads and oddsmakers and make a real race of it. Before 11:00 p.m. EST on Election Night, it looked like Trump might win the White House. Between 11:00 p.m. and midnight, key states started to go Trump's way. My wife, who had been watching the coverage with me, angrily went to bed. She couldn't bear to witness the unthinkable come to pass. I continued to watch; like the proverbial train wreck, I couldn't turn away. By 1:30 a.m., Clinton's "firewall" states began to fall. By 2:00 a.m., Clinton's team was hoping against hope. By 2:30 a.m., Trump had enough Electoral College votes to put him over the top. Slightly afterward, Clinton conceded. A reality TV huckster had won the presidency. His base, many of whom were voting less for his political ideology than for his divisive rhetoric, had come leaping from out of the shadows. His campaign had taken a page out of the Republicans' old playbook and put it on steroids.

Between the late '50s and the mid-'80s, Republicans saw Jim Crow laws descending and the civil rights movement ascending. African Americans and other minorities were making real advances in society. Over this time, in one form or another, Republicans engaged in a plan dubbed the "Southern strategy." It was a plan to use hate and fear to motivate southern voters to support the White candidates who would preserve their "way of life" by stemming the growing tide of integration. Black progress was considered the problem in the South. The nefarious plan was cloaked in political rhetoric to legitimize its insidious agenda. The first step was to shift attention to states' rights in order to gain control of the federal government, which was, in their eyes, giving African American citizens too much freedom. Half a century later, Trump revived the fearmongering and played on prejudices to find common ground with voters who felt integration and other post-Obama progress threatened to upstage the America they had grown up longing for: a White America.

Trump resurrected and continues to use the old Republican Party Southern strategy tactics today. His racist dog-whistle politics and blatant hate-mongering speech are unrestrained and unapologetic. He adopted the campaign slogan "Make America Great Again," which was itself a simple variant of conservative icon Ronald Reagan's slogan, "Let's Make America Great Again," which he employed during his successful presidential run in 1980. Trump is more fearless and unencumbered than conventional politicians; he entered his first race not owing political chips to anyone. He is a true maverick, choosing to buck convention and win "his" way. And, by all accounts, as president he doesn't waver. That is rare, and dangerous, to both the left and the right. From day one, the Republican Party had little leverage and, consequently, were at the mercy of this outlier. "I could stand in the middle of Fifth Avenue and shoot somebody, and I wouldn't lose any voters," Trump once said. When Republicans got over their embarrassment and realized that Trump could be turned to their advantage, his lies gave cover to the Republican obstructionists who had tried to stymie Obama at every turn. Before Trump, they would block Obama's progressive agenda but say little, perhaps adding a wink and a nod. Now they had a publicity-hungry loudmouth who would say all the things many of them were still too diplomatic to say out loud. They had the figurehead they needed to mount their attack to turn the clock back and regain the power they erroneously believe is exclusively theirs as White America.

Whether or not he readily admits it, Trump is the mouthpiece for this White power structure. Most polls depict the composite voter in the Trump base as a White man over fifty years old who lives in a rural area. He is a non–college graduate, an evangelical, with an annual income of over $50,000. During his campaign rallies, Trump often uses phrases like "the good old days" and "those people," referring to times when violence was used to intimidate Blacks and other minorities. Trump has created an environment that empowered those who latently held racist beliefs, and now he can comfortably play out his own biases in public.

Conservatives have found their carnival barker. Now it's time for us to play hardball to thwart their attempts to curb any further advancements in civil rights. In his song "B-Movie," Gil Scott-Heron captured this sentiment perfectly when he wrote the tongue-in-cheek lyrics, "First one wants freedom, then the whole damn world wants freedom. Nostalgia, that's what we want—the good ol' days." Unfortunately, if we do go back to those "good ol' days," the consequences for African Americans and this nation will be devastating.

*   *   *

Former attorney general Eric Holder was the defendant in a 2013 Supreme Court case, *Shelby County v. Holder*, regarding the constitutionality of two provisions of the Voting Rights Act of 1965.

The Voting Rights Act was a landmark piece of federal legislation that prohibited racial discrimination in voting. Up until that point, many discriminatory practices in local elections were still technically considered legal. Yet without political clout, Blacks and other people of color would never be able to muster enough power to change the laws that made it legal to withhold or hinder the rights of some citizens. The law constitutionally guaranteed this right to minorities. This act is considered by some legal scholars to be the most important piece of federal civil rights legislation ever enacted in America.

In 1965, Black America and its allies understood the gravity of the Voting Rights Act and fought hard to ensure its success, not just in the courts and on Capitol Hill but also in the streets. The monumental Selma-to-Montgomery marches, three in all, demonstrated the powerful public support for Black citizens' constitutional right to vote. The intractable posture taken by those who opposed the changing voter laws was marked by deadly confrontations. A whirlwind of violence occurred between February and March of 1965: activist Jimmie Lee Jackson was killed by an Alabama state trooper; future US representative John Lewis and other protesters were tear-gassed and beaten unconscious by state troopers on "Bloody Sunday"; James Reeb, a White pro–civil rights minister, was severely beaten by segregationists and later died of his injuries. With mounting pressure, the courts and the federal government were forced to intervene. By March 15, 1965, President Lyndon Johnson told a joint session of Congress that Selma was a "turning point" and that the nation must overcome "the crippling legacy of bigotry and injustice. And we shall overcome." Soon after, in August 1965, the Voting Rights Act was passed by Congress and signed by Johnson.

Over the years, attempts have been made to weaken or even gut that law, including the recent *Shelby County* case, where the Supreme Court struck down these two key provisions in the Voting Rights Act. This ruling may have severely weakened the cause of civil rights by allowing states to make it more difficult for Blacks and other minorities to vote. Since the ruling, we've seen states imposing much stricter regulations regarding voter IDs as well as closing or changing polling places in predominantly African American areas.

WHY IS IT SO IMPORTANT TO UNDERSTAND AND PROTECT VOTING RIGHTS?

ERIC HOLDER: We need to be conversant with history and understand that we can't build a future without understanding the past. We need to understand the full range of Black experiences from 1619 to the 1960s. It's absolutely necessary, and those people who

History is the foundation upon which progress is made.

would characterize it as trite or will try to "use" it in that way are really doing a disservice to the ongoing struggle. You can't think about voter suppression without understanding what went into the creation of the Voting Rights Act. You can't understand how the gutting of the Voting Rights Act, in the *Shelby County* decision, was such a disastrous and wrongheaded thing without understanding the implications and how it is operating in the present. History is the foundation upon which progress is made.

WILLIAM BARBER: America is going through the birth pains of a third Reconstruction. The history of Reconstruction is always surrounded by the issue of race. Whether it was the first Reconstruction that took place from slavery up until around the 1890s, or the second Reconstruction from 1954 up until around 1968. Post-2007, the electorate that produced President Obama broke through in the South and showed that the Southern strategy was vulnerable, had holes in it. We saw the beginnings of a possible third Reconstruction. It had the possibility of addressing issues of race and poverty, and we've seen the reaction to that ever since. The Supreme Court has been an accessory to the crime of racist voter suppression. But we have power. People of color are 40 percent of the population in the South.

> *People of color are 40 percent of the population in the South. . . . If you break through in the South, you break the whole political process open.*

If you registered 10–30 percent of the unregistered voters in the South and they voted, you could fundamentally break through in the South, and if you break through in the South, you break the whole political process open.

ANGELA RYE: In the first year and a half after Trump won the November 2016 election, I was politically depressed and thought, *How am I going to encourage people to vote and to get involved when this has challenged my belief system at its core?*

MARC MORIAL: The National Urban League's "State of Black America" report has a complete section on foreign interference in the 2016 election relating to Black voter suppression. The Russians infiltrated the Black Lives Matter movement online [and] created thirty to forty trolls, sending messages like "Don't vote for Hillary Clinton, all leaders are sellouts." It was done to promote friction and division in the community. I saw an article that said on Election Day in 2016, [the Russians] may have posted 1,300 videos. Social media allowed for fakers, takers, trolls, and manipulators to infiltrate the community and start posing as young activists. It was stunning in its breadth, depth, and sophistication, and it was all targeted at trying to suppress African American voters.

ED GORDON: Blacks must worry about future interference. Mitch McConnell is the personification of an obstructionist. He was once seen as a moderate and is now one of the leaders of the political right. He often pushed his colleagues to withhold Republican support for major presidential initiatives during Obama's presidency. He blocked an unprecedented number of Obama's judicial nominees, including Supreme Court nominee Merrick Garland. He has also obstructed legislation on civil rights and criminal justice [reform].

ERIC HOLDER: The Obama administration faced principal opposition in Mitch McConnell and Republicans in the House, but the president also used his executive authority, and he got a lot of criticism for signing executive orders. The things we try to do in the Justice Department [are that we] try to build up, deal with that trust gap; [we try] to reform police practices, to record numbers of consent decrees. People have to focus on what Jeff Sessions [did] when he got there. One of the first things he said was "We're not doing any more consent decrees," and [he] basically tried to reverse the use of all the techniques that we had during the time that I was at the Justice Department.

LAURA COATES: We are in a time when civil discourse seems to be in the rearview mirror; however, if returning to civility means that we gladly accept a plate full of dirt to eat, then I think we need to make demands which we are already entitled to receive, and we make people accountable for giving it to us late.

People may say, "I miss when so-and-so was in office, because it was a nicer time. People were kinder to each other." Well, it didn't mean that White supremacy and White nationalism weren't training while the lion slept. They were getting more and more bold. And then, when there was a window of opportunity for them to show their true colors, you saw people marching through the streets, no longer having to put a sheet on because they were that empowered. When we look at where we are now, especially in the Trump administration, we do it not with an eye to returning to a past time but to becoming expectant of opportunity and equality now and active about demanding our rightful place.

* * *

Our demands for opportunity and equality under this administration are falling on deaf ears. Trump's White House shows very little concern about minority communities. Many African Americans feel that is, with varying degrees, a continuing trend of GOP administrations. Republicans have refuted that, saying theirs is a wide tent. During these discussions, they will remind you that Abraham Lincoln was a Republican. Who better than the man who signed the Emancipation Proclamation to prove their openness? There is no denying Lincoln's monumental contribution to the nation's racial advancement, but if Republicans have to go back 157 years to highlight their contribution to civil rights, they have a problem. If Lincoln is the example of the White savior of a nation walking a moral path, then Donald Trump is the antithesis of that. He has chosen to appeal to the lowest common denominator—race—to further divide our union.

Donald Trump claimed 8 percent of the African American vote in 2016—two more percentage points than Republican candidate Mitt Romney in 2012.

HOW HAVE THE INTERESTS OF THE BLACK COMMUNITY CHANGED DURING THE TRUMP ERA?

MICHAEL STEELE: In the GOP, there is very little interest in addressing the ideas, situations, and conditions of our community. Who do I take my list of grievances to? Who do I take my list of concerns to? There is no one inside the administration who looks like me, who is in a position to receive agendas to try to move forward. There are definite attempts at the edges to do certain things; there's the "Oh, Black unemployment is the lowest it's ever been." Well, that's a load of crap because those numbers started dropping two years before he even became president. What the Black community sees from this administration is an embracing of White nationalism, embracing of the KKK. The deriding of our homeland as a sh*thole and a host of other things that says to them, "Not only do I have no interest in who you are and what you represent to the country, I'm not even going to pretend I have [any] interest."

Michael Steele is a history-making Republican. From 2003 to 2007, Steele served as lieutenant-governor of Maryland. This victory made him the first African American elected to statewide office in Maryland. In 2009, he became the first African American to serve as chair of the Republican National Committee. He held that position for three years, but not without rancor. Some in the party believe his win was a knee-jerk reaction to the Obama victory in 2008 and that Republicans needed a face of color to counteract the newly elected Black president. But Steele has never been delusional about the challenges for Blacks in the GOP, nor has he blindly followed party lines. He has even been critical of the Trump administration.

SHERMICHAEL SINGLETON: Trump's presidency uncovered this naiveté about how much progress we've made, and we certainly have made progress, but there are people who are on the fringes who, as a result of Donald

Trump and some of his more controversial pronouncements, now feel they are no longer on the fringes. They now feel they have a place, and even when Trump's gone, those people will still be here. It's incumbent [on] both political parties to let them know they shouldn't be fearful of a more multicultural society. There is a tendency on the Democratic side to ignore these people, to not talk to them. That doesn't help anything. These people are still going to be around, these people are having children, they are working in schools, [they] are in law enforcement. Some of these people are politicians making legislation. To ignore them does a disservice to the people who will be impacted by these types of people. Trump revealed what we'd swept under the rug. After we elected Obama, there was this Kumbaya moment, and we sort of forgot about all of these ills in society that have just been lingering.

TIFFANY CROSS: I don't think there was a single Black person out here surprised at the amount of vitriol that has been unearthed. For us, it never went away. We always saw it. Obama didn't absolve anybody from being a racist. You can certainly vote for Obama and still be a racist.

TAMIKA MALLORY: Donald Trump was a necessary moment for Black America. If Hillary had been elected [president], we would be dealing with some of the same issues that we faced with Obama. She had enough Black people [who] were close to her who would have helped to quiet down some activists, some of the more radical areas of our movement. I think Trump was something we just needed. We needed it to bring folks together, communities together that had not traditionally seen themselves as allies. We needed it to open up doors and rooms that we thought were cleaned out. Now we have the opportunity to see those things. There were some folks who were already sounding the alarm, saying things are not as good as we think, and now it's in our faces and we have an opportunity to work on it. Sometimes things have to be completely torn down in order for them to be rebuilt, and that's what's happened.

A 2016 election eve poll by the African American Research Collaborative showed 48 percent of African Americans labeled Trump a racist who is deliberately trying to hurt minorities.

ED GORDON: Do you think this racial animus will live beyond Trump?

MICHAEL STEELE: Yes, I think it [will]. If Trump is not reelected, be prepared for a significant portion of his supporters to say the election was rigged, and [his opponents] wanted to get rid of him.

STACEY ABRAMS: But we've always been divided. This isn't new. Political polarization, racial polarization, these have been constants that are baked into the DNA of America. And before we decry that we are further apart than we've ever been, I think that we have to read our history. Trump is a racist, xenophobic, homophobic, sexist demagogue who has very little concern for the people he was elected to govern. And that plays out in his domestic and foreign policies but also in his treatment of the most august rules and responsibility we have in this nation. There's going be a fight, regardless. And if he does get reelected, just strap in. He will make these four years pale in comparison to what will come.

MAXINE WATERS: The president, in so many ways, has made it okay for the right wing to resurface, for the White supremacists to resurface, for the KKK to resurface, and it is absolutely one of the most destructive things that a president can do. He is a separatist. He is a racist. And he is sending signals and dog-whistling to the White supremacists, saying, "You're right, the Blacks have gone too far, minorities have gone too far, these Mexicans are coming over the border, these murderers are coming into our country, and we're going to stop that. We're going to take our country back because they have gone too far; they've done too much and they're doing too well."

ERIC HOLDER: I want to know, in Trump's mind, when did he think America was at its greatest? My guess would be he'd pick sometime in the

'50s. If you look back now, women were treated as second-class citizens, denied opportunities that women now have; obviously African Americans were living in an American apartheid system; folks in the LGBTQ community didn't have nearly the rights that they have now. It was a nice quiet time for people like Donald Trump. I think he thinks America was great then, and America *was* great then, but it was imperfect.

D. L. HUGHLEY: White people right now love Trump because they want to preserve who they are, and they will fight to do it. They fight to do it [now]. They'll rewrite what they call "justice" and "patriotism" and American pride. They'll rewrite it just to survive.

Trump is the notion of America. An unqualified man who is craven and unscrupulous. You know what's funny? If you took eight years of Obama, and you put a report together on the list of his scandals, it would go on a Post-It note. Two years of Trump, we got two volumes and five hundred pages. That's a lot of trees. America, we can't grow enough trees to keep up with the bullsh*t.

HARRY BELAFONTE: I don't believe that, in today's climate, with Trump and what's going on with him all over the place, including these investigations, the Black community is aggressive enough and loud enough in its participation in the process of pointing out [that] this president is unacceptable and that the policies that exist today, in relation to race, need more vital analysis and participation into its elimination.

ED GORDON: Should Black America be afraid of future leaders like Trump?

MAXINE WATERS: Well, first of all, the really, really scary thing is if [Trump] is able to use so-called executive power as he has redefined it—in any way that he wants to—and he can stop his cabinet people and others from coming before the constitutionally mandated committees of the House of Representatives and the Senate—if he's successful with that, *game changer!* Absolutely, a game changer. There will be those who follow in his footsteps who will do the same thing since he will have established the precedent.

ED GORDON: No matter what happens in 2020 with the election, when you look at this presidency and all the attempts to move America backwards, what do you think is the biggest concern that we should be looking at? Is there a singular issue that we should be focused on?

ERIC HOLDER: Ed, that's an interesting question. I'm not sure there's any one thing [we should push back against]. There's a whole range of things. It sounds kind of trite and maybe even a little naive, but this retreat from American values and norms is really a descriptor for what is *most* dangerous about the Trump presidency.

Then there's a whole range of things that are more specific that fall under that, like the way in which the White House interacts with the Justice Department, the president interacts with the attorney general—he's broken all kinds of norms and traditions. There's a whole range of things that we simply never expected an administration to do. Disregard of precedent, disregard of facts, you base policy on ideology as opposed to evidence, and as a result, if you're not fact-bound and if you have no sense of shame, that gives you free rein to come up with policies that benefit the few and don't ultimately serve the nation.

MICHAEL STEELE: At the end of all of this, there is an unvarnished truth that smacks hard in the face of White America. In a few short years, the majority of the population in this country will not be White. It will be African American, it will be Hispanic, and that is, for White America, concerning. Because that new majority will then begin to have the power to change the economic, political, and social dynamic.

*   *   *

Donald Trump's presidency has been a circus of unconventional political chaos wrapped in lies and hatred. Seemingly without a bit of compunction, he has used race as his battering ram to scare and divide America. People of color have clearly been deemed expendable fodder to keep his base fed and himself in power. I have covered presidential elections since Bill Clinton's first victory, and I have seen up close what it takes to win that office. Groups are often used as chess pieces in order to gain the Oval Office, but what Trump is doing goes beyond political gamesmanship. He has uncovered a racial uneasiness that was just beneath the surface that many believed to be buried much further down.

The unseen danger that his presidency brings is the political offspring that will surely arise from his time in office. There are those misguided people who take his ego-latent moves as righteous, as self-affirming to their own prejudices that were often kept in secret. It will take serious-minded opposition to stop this threat. Once again, people will be called to participate in a system that hasn't always been equitable to people of color. Voter suppression and some argue outright chicanery have been thought to steal elections away from minority voters and those who support their views and agenda. We must understand that casting a ballot against Trump is a better "risk" than another four years of him as commander in chief.

People often ask me, "Will Black America survive the Trump presidency?" My answer is, of course we will. We have survived far worse times in history and certainly far more cunning adversaries. Yes, we will survive Donald J. Trump—the reality show star huckster who was not even elected by a majority—and we'll do it "bigly."

STARTING YOUR OWN CONVERSATION

- How politically engaged is your community now compared to how it was during the Obama era?

- What factors do you think dissuade Black people from going to the polls? What resources are needed to overcome those factors?

- What effect has social media had on political engagement and voting in the Black community?

- Which issues are more politically motivating for younger Black voters in your community? For older Black voters? Which issues are motivating regardless of generation?

- Which politicians of color today seem the most engaged with the issues that matter to you, your family, and your friends? What do these political leaders need to help them combat any opposition from empowered White supremacists that comes their way?

STAY WOKE...AND STAY ACTIVE

THE NEW BLACK VOTING MUSCLE

STACEY ABRAMS	Politician & Author
CHARLAMAGNE THA GOD	Radio Personality & Author
LAURA COATES	CNN Analyst & Radio Host
BRITTNEY COOPER	Academic & Author
TIFFANY CROSS	Managing Editor of *The Beat DC*
BEN CRUMP	Civil Rights Attorney
SYBRINA FULTON	Mother of Trayvon Martin & Activist
ERIC HOLDER	Former US Attorney General
HAKEEM JEFFRIES	US Representative from New York
DERRICK JOHNSON	President & CEO of the NAACP
VAN JONES	Commentator & Author
TRACY MAITLAND	President & CEO of Advent Capital Management
ANGELA RYE	Attorney & Political Analyst
BAKARI SELLERS	Attorney & Political Commentator
AL SHARPTON	President of the National Action Network
MICHAEL STEELE	Former Chair of the Republican National Committee
T.I.	Rapper & Activist
MAXINE WATERS	US Representative from California

As I grew up, and went from a boy to a man with a voting status, the refrain I heard from my elders was this: "People died for your right to vote." That declaration has been passed down from generation to generation as a reminder of just how important the exercise of voting is. Voting can influence and impact many sectors of your life. Your employment and economic well-being can be impacted. So can your ability to gain quality education and housing, and your quality of life or even the existence of life (should the case of abortion, for example, be determined at the ballot box). These decisions can be of great generational import and can define the fate of our families for years. Supreme Court appointments, for example, set America's outlook and direction for decades. After Trump's victory, the high court has become increasingly right leaning. He has placed more than one hundred judges in federal seats, all of whom skew conservative. Casting your ballot often has multiple implications that have far-reaching ramifications. Your vote goes far beyond the politician or propositions of a single election.

African Americans wield a tremendously potent voting bloc, led by Black women, whose votes, as we've seen in recent elections, can tilt the balance of power. They have ensured the margin of victory for some elections and put up firewalls in others, including shutting down Republican Roy Moore's bid for a Senate seat in Alabama. Moore had a checkered history of making racially insensitive comments, and a number of women have accused him of sexual harassment, including some who were minors at the time of these alleged incidents. Exit polls of the race showed that 98 percent of Black female voters cast ballots for his opponent.

From local elections, which far too many voters falsely assume have a minimal impact on their lives, to presidential elections, where, according to the United States Election Project, an estimated 56 percent of the voting-age population turned out in 2016, each election can be life-altering on many levels. That is why we see such a strong fight by and for Trump. The winds of change were blowing under Obama. Frightened by Obama's election, the opposition ramped up efforts for voter suppression.

However, since the election of Donald Trump, we've seen people of color become more motivated to build coalitions and create initiatives to combat the onslaught of voter suppression and intimidation. In some cases, these tactics have arguably cost candidates of color election victories. After a skillful campaign, Stacey Abrams lost her election for the governor's office in Georgia by less than a percentage and a half. The race was fraught with questions about voting irregularities and abnormalities. Many saw that election as the prime example of recent efforts to roll back voting rights for minorities.

WHAT DOES THE FUTURE OF BLACK POLITICAL LEADERSHIP LOOK LIKE?

STACEY ABRAMS: A component of what precipitated me launching the New Georgia Project, Fair Fight, and now the Fair Count project is making people have a belief in believing. Letting them see actual change. People need to see that change is possible, and they need to know something is being done. The three organizations we launched were designed to bring community into the process. If you want people to believe, they need to see things being done.

When it's a person or an entity doing things for you or to you, then you are exempted from responsibility, more than it being a third party doing things, people need to be engaged in their own success. One of our opportunities is to say, "Yep, this is a fight, and we need you to fight with us." People believe when they're in the mix! That's a real space that we haven't fully exploited since the 1960s.

BAKARI SELLERS: I've founded an organization to do something similar. We robbed and duplicated what my friend Stacey Abrams did in Georgia, and we're trying to do it in South Carolina, one precinct at a time. Not just registering new voters but also going and touching those inactive voters, those voters who just haven't shown up in the past few years. We're also doing training so we can have people run for office. I was very pleased with the number of new mayors that we have, from LaToya Cantrell in New Orleans to Frank Scott in Little Rock, Randall Woodfin in Birmingham, and Vi Lyles in Charlotte. And Atlanta has a mayor named Keisha!

* * *

As the important 2020 presidential election approaches, Stacey Abrams; Andrew Gilliam, who lost his race for Florida's governor's seat amid questionable circumstances; and others have formed organizations and campaigns to help ensure that there is more scrutiny of future elections. Voter turnout will be critical, and the Black vote could very well determine who sits in the White House. Minority voters need to be engaged, motivated, and believe that when they cast their ballots their votes will count. The Obama presidency has inspired a new generation, especially young people of color, to enter politics, to seek office, and to do things differently. His historic wins and the backlash that followed have caused an electorate to wake up!

HOW HAS VOTING CHANGED IN RECENT YEARS?

SYBRINA FULTON: I learned that it's not only important that everybody wants to do the best voter registration drive. You've got to go to the next step, and that is actually voting and learning who's on the ballot prior to the election.

Sybrina Fulton was motivated to jump into politics and is running for a seat for the Miami-Dade County Board of County Commissioners. Her motivation was greater than being spurred on by President Obama's victory; it was motivated by her son Trayvon Martin's murder.

TIFFANY CROSS: Without Obama, we wouldn't have Congresswoman Lauren Underwood [D-Illinois], the youngest Black woman elected to Congress. She beat a Tea Party incumbent. We have Congressman Ro Khanna out of California, who is South Asian, one of the fastest-growing populations in the country. Michael Blake, who is an elected official, just became public advocate in New York.

MAXINE WATERS: This new group thinks differently. Take socialism, for instance—they're not afraid of it. They look at what's happening between the haves and the have-nots as a responsibility of government. If socialism pays for a college education for all people, that's fine with them. If you talk about how they get a loan or how they become entrepreneurs, if government or the private sector plays a role in that, that's fine by them. They don't define socialism the same way that it has been defined in the past. That's why Alexandria Ocasio-Cortez, who calls herself a Socialist Democrat, has such an attraction. Because the cause, socialism, for them means a fairer society that looks out for each other and provides resources for those who need it.

LAURA COATES: Look at someone like Keith Ellison, [who] recognized the fact that while it may be wonderful and extraordinarily prestigious to be a congressman, being a member of Congress [is] not powerful enough to actually make a day-to-day impact. He left being a congressman, a very comfortable seat, to become a state attorney general. Now, a lot of people look at that as a move down on what they perceive as the power structures. In reality, he was so sharp to understand that the power of the attorney general and the power of the state were going to be infinitely more influential on what he and his community were grappling with. I hope that people [move] away from the idea of "Okay, I'm going to focus every four years on who is going to be the president" and instead focus on the people who make a day-to-day difference.

Keith Ellison was a US representative from Minnesota, the first African American elected from the state. He served from 2007 to 2018. He also served as deputy chair for the Democratic National Committee from 2017 to 2018. Ellison decided to run for the post of Minnesota's attorney general in 2018. He won the office and became the first Muslim person to win election to a statewide office in the United States and the first African American elected to statewide office in Minnesota.

DERRICK JOHNSON: One of the things that I absolutely commend [Stacey Abrams] on is she worked really hard over a period of five-plus years to build the political wherewithal to be taken seriously in her race. She actually won that election, but it was stolen. How? One, she didn't accept the advice and the commentaries from the consultant class, who would limit one's view on what's possible. Secondly, she did it in a way in which she didn't just speak to a shrinking base; she increased the base by going out and registering people to vote who simply were left off the table, to enlarge the playing field. She didn't fall for the narrow talking points in ways that would've excluded her from even winning the primary.

Lastly, and most importantly, she was able to communicate across communities, because if you get away from the rhetoric that's on television and you talk about basic issues that people care about, and you're able to do so in simple language, you break through over time. And that's what she was able to do. A tremendous turnout in African American and Latino communities, and a huge crossover vote among working-class White folks who simply have nowhere to go and no one is talking to them. Elections are nothing more than popularity contests. The real question is, can you govern?

*　　*　　*

In many federal, state, or local elections, the African American vote has become the most coveted in the Democratic Party. The question for 2020 is, what will that constituency get for their support? It's no secret that Blacks have been taken for granted politically for years. Republicans never really cared about inclusion, and Democrats knew they had the votes. After elections, traditionally Democrats have either seen Blacks as scapegoats, blaming them for not turning out in large enough numbers to "ensure" victory, or taken them for granted and immediately ignored them after the election. However, this might be changing. A great wave of political awareness is moving through Black America right now.

HOW HAVE BLACK CONSTITUENCIES CHANGED?

T.I.: I see more gangbangers, drug dealers, and street dudes congregating, having conversations about politics and current events that affect our communities, more now than ever. Before, in order to hear about politics, city council, elections, and the positions of certain candidates, you had to go around "squares." It wasn't nobody in the 'hood talking about that kinda stuff, and now in gambling houses, traps, and pool halls, you hear these people talking about politics and consciousness. That didn't happen before. The word is spreading, and the interest is growing. The seed has been planted; it just hasn't beared the proper amount of fruit that is necessary for us to take significant steps toward some progress.

TRACY MAITLAND: Our people have got to understand that there's a lot of power in politics. It can control our destiny, it can control our economics, and I don't think we fully understand that. Because it hasn't worked as well as we would've liked it to over the years, people just dismiss it, saying, "It doesn't matter." It does matter! Who the president is matters, who the mayor is matters, [and] who the local school superintendent is matters. We need to be fully engaged, because it really matters.

TIFFANY CROSS: I worked on a campaign where people who were formerly convicted came together and used their political clout. Maryland has an overwhelming number of citizens who are released from federal prison entering society again. The state has forty thousand of them, around twenty thousand of whom are from Baltimore. They would host debates; they would have roundtable discussions. All people who were once prisoners and who are now returning citizens said, "Yeah, we want to know what you're doing for us." And everybody who was running for mayor in that election made a point to go and speak to that group.

> *Maryland has an overwhelming number of citizens who are released from federal prison entering society again. The state has forty thousand of them, around twenty thousand of whom are from Baltimore.*

When you come together and link your power with each other and lock arms and march [in lockstep], people pay attention. Even if your interests may be different. Even if there are subtleties in your political asks, there's still power in saying, "You have to get through *us*." And we see that at [both] the local and the federal level. You have to become a part of the system to disrupt it. You can either impact politics or stand on the sidelines.

ED GORDON: What does it mean to be truly "woke" in politics today?

ANGELA RYE: Awareness is nothing if it's never applied. I started saying "Work *woke*"—that's a hip-hop version of "faith without works is dead."

MICHAEL STEELE: Yeah, you can be *woke*, but there are people who walk in their sleep. There is no sense of being up and about and moving and functioning but still being clueless and unaware. Self-awareness is a big part of it, and self-awareness starts within your own home, within your own community.

ANGELA RYE: At some point, you know what has to be applied to change your circumstances, or the circumstances of your neighbor, at least ideally. Imagine what we could do if there were more of us engaged. We need to see hope in our unity, and if we all really come together and engage, how powerful that would really be?

MICHAEL STEELE: I have to know and appreciate what my condition is before I can change it, and I sure can't go to someone else and tell them that they have an obligation to change it or help me change if I'm not even aware of just how severe the change is that is required or how difficult the position I'm in truly is.

VAN JONES: We're in the post-Obama, reality-check moment, in which I think we're starting to figure out [that] there's only so much help we're going to be able to get from the government, from the broader society, and that we need a new strategy. Really, from the 1950s through 2008, African Americans were forced to look toward the government for solutions because of being locked out of the democracy, being redlined when it came to capital. You had Thurgood Marshall going to the Supreme Court, you had Dr. King marching on Washington, you had the election of a bunch of Black mayors and the Congressional Black Caucus and before that, the Civil Rights Act. So, it was a two-generation project trying to figure out [how we could] get the government to give us some relief, give us a redress, force open the doors of opportunity, et cetera.

ED GORDON: What's in it for individual voters?

AL SHARPTON: We are going to have to show people that their vote matters. Because unless you have a Maxine Waters, somebody who really goes in there and fights, we don't see muscle demonstrated because it's too invisible. We need to know "Oh, that's what this is about." Maybe I'm spoiled because, when I was growing up, we had an Adam Clayton Powell Jr. and a Shirley Chisholm, so we understood what it was about. I think a lot of our political figures do not know how to rally and do the consensus building with legislators at the same time.

Adam Clayton Powell Jr. was a Baptist pastor who became the fourth African American elected to the US House of Representatives. Powell represented Harlem, in Upper Manhattan, from 1945 to 1971. Powell was a flamboyant and powerful figure who fought, among other issues, for American support of emerging countries in Africa. In 1961, Powell became chair of the Education and Labor Committee, making him the most powerful African American in Congress. His later career would be shrouded in controversy and scandal. Powell would lose his seat. He lost reelection in 1970 to Charles Rangel.

HAKEEM JEFFRIES: We have to build upon the progress made during the eight years of Barack Obama's presidency. We have to continue to vote with the same level of intensity as if Obama's name still appeared on the ballot. If we don't, that opens the door for people like Donald Trump to walk on through and work to roll back the gains that have been made.

*   *   *

It keeps coming back to voting. Black America hasn't shown up at the polls in the same numbers as when Obama first ran for office. In fact, in 2010—the first midterm of President Obama's presidency—Republicans won major victories in state and local races all across the country. Republicans gained a majority in the US House of Representatives and six Senate seats. It was one of the largest party shifts in US history. While typically not this large, midterm party shifts do happen. Traditionally, overall turnout is lower for midterm elections. In 2010, there were various reasons that African Americans stayed home, including the feeling among some that Obama had reached the pinnacle of American politics and their voting responsibilities were done. Black voter turnout that year was around 42 percent, which certainly contributed to the overwhelming defeat that the Democrats suffered that year. To be clear, Blacks didn't owe Dems anything, considering the years of neglect they saw from the party, but did Black voters owe Obama? The crushing defeat Democrats suffered made it virtually impossible for the president to move legislation and programs through Congress. Had Blacks voted in greater numbers during the 2010 midterms with the same zeal that we used to usher him in, Obama probably would have had a very different presidency.

HOW IMPORTANT IS IT TO REACH ACROSS THE AISLE? CAN POLITICAL PROGRESS BE MADE WITHOUT YOUR POLITICAL "ENEMY"?

HAKEEM JEFFRIES: John Boehner and Mitch McConnell repeatedly made clear that their primary objective was to stop Barack Obama from getting things done, and as a result, they hindered his ability to make more legislative progress on behalf of the American people. Thankfully, during President Obama's first two years in office, he had a cooperative House and Senate, and as a result, important pieces of legislation on health care, criminal justice reform, the economy, consumer protection, and regulating the financial services sector were put into place.

BAKARI SELLERS: A lot of the onus is on the candidate or the party [itself] to make sure that you are interacting with [your constituencies] more [often] than on an every-other-year basis. It's about candidates showing that they are talking about our well-being and actually spending time with these voters. The Democratic Party has to do a much better job in meeting people where they are. The culture that we've created is not conducive to being successful over the long haul. We literally need to meet people at the football games in their communities, in their homes, on television, and on radio, and we have to sustain that contact.

* * *

One of the aftereffects of the Obama presidency is what I called the "Obama Hangover." The cause of this political affliction was electing a Black candidate from central casting; he was actually a better president in real life than Morgan Freeman was in the movies. Anyone following Obama would be a bit of a letdown. Many Black voters now wanted someone they could have a true attachment to, someone who would make a discernable difference for them. That didn't mean the candidate had to be Black, but that would have certainly been a bonus.

When Hillary Clinton ran in 2016, she was a known commodity. Her husband had formed a relationship with Black America over the course of his eight-year presidency, although it was at times shaky. The man some called "America's first Black president" understood the dynamic of Black America as much as any White man can. In fact, in 1992, Bill Clinton said to me, "I know Black America wants a Black president, but right now I am the closest you're going to get." However, I never felt he was "Black," but I did feel he was genuinely comfortable around Black people; his wife didn't have the same connection, and that cost her. Black folks liked her enough, just not enough to run to the polls. Eleven percent of those who voted for Obama in 2012 didn't vote at all in 2016. Presumably, for many of those voters, Clinton didn't speak to them, nor did she try, believing that selfies with Jay and B and stage appearances with LeBron James and her husband were enough to pull out the Black vote. They weren't. Nor should they have been.

Even if you didn't love Hillary Clinton, there would have been progressive federal appointments, an ally in the White House to fight against voter suppression, a more sensitive immigration policy—all these things would have been different with a Clinton victory. Many of the extensions of voting aren't calculated when a person decides to stay at home, but they should be. Potential voters don't always consider Supreme Court appointments when they opt out of voting in a presidential election, but they should. Even those who didn't like Hillary must be asking now, "Was my disinterest worth multiple seats on the high court?"

HOW IS THE POLITICAL SCENE FOR BLACKS DURING THE TRUMP ERA DIFFERENT FROM WHAT IT MIGHT HAVE LOOKED LIKE UNDER HILLARY CLINTON'S LEADERSHIP?

BEN CRUMP: Some people said [the choice] didn't matter between Hillary and Trump. Well, we have empirical evidence that it matters greatly. The presidential election is important, but the people who are gonna stand directly in control and have some say-so [on] whether your son or daughter is killed in the street or killed in the courtroom with trumped-up police charges will be your local district attorney. Your mayor and city council are gonna select who the chief of police is going to be.

ERIC HOLDER: Republicans are not just trying to dismantle [what] Barack Obama did; they are trying to go much further back. They are trying to dismantle, in many ways, the gains that were made during the civil rights movement. The *Shelby County* decision isn't an anti-Obama decision; it is trying to gut the Voting Rights Act, which is the pearl of the civil rights movement. It's a raw political move. They understand that their ideology is out of step with the times; they understand that there are demographic changes of the likes this country has never seen before. They're trying to cement their hold on power, and a lot of the things that they are doing are antidemocratic. Whether it is doing away with the protections of significant portions of the Voting Rights Act, voter suppression, or gerrymandering, this is all a way in which Republicans, who are increasingly becoming a minority party, can exercise majority power, and they're not ashamed about that.

They're [also] not shy about what their intentions are. Mitch McConnell and Republicans in general are using raw power to ensure they leave a system in place that won't be responsive to the change in demographics and a change in the way the nation views itself. We [have] often identified as a center-right country, and I think this country is drifting to the left. That is something that's inconsistent with Republicans' retention of power, so they are doing everything they can to make sure that they institutionalize their hold on power.

BAKARI SELLERS: The problem that we have is that, on the larger level, the Congressional Black Caucus and the Republican Party have an unholy alliance, which is where [we see] a lot of the hyper-partisanship we have through gerrymandering. The CBC believes they need more Black folks in their districts, and the Republicans are happy to give them as many Black folks as they want. But what that means is there aren't enough minorities to make other districts competitive. That's some of the stale thinking that has to be challenged and some of the status quo thoughts that have to be pushed back against.

*　　*　　*

Black women didn't wait to be handed power; they took it. The power that they have displayed in the political arena has been astonishing—and it's still maturing. The political muscle this group has formed is spawning brand-new political action committees, record numbers of female candidates, incumbents with strong backing, and arguably the most progressive and reliable voting bloc Democrats have. Women of color are also some of the most powerful and vocal political figures on the scene today.

Congresswoman Maxine Waters heads the powerful US House Committee on Financial Services and is one of the most influential people on

Capitol Hill. California senator and 2020 presidential candidate Kamala Harris and former Georgia gubernatorial candidate Stacey Abrams are fast-rising stars in the Democratic Party. Strategists and advisers like Angela Rye and Symone Sanders are some of the most influential political voices in our country today, and White House correspondent April Ryan is one of the most vehement members of the White House press corps.

Roadblocks are still in place for women, but their political clout cannot be ignored, and their issues will have to be addressed.

HOW ARE BLACK WOMEN SHAPING OUR CURRENT POLITICAL CLIMATE?

STACEY ABRAMS: A Black woman is running for president; you've got Black women running campaigns. Women are handling pivotal parts of campaign infrastructure. These are all emblematic of the evolution of where Black women stand. Fundamentally, Black women engage in politics because we care about community and we care about family. Until our family, our faith, and our opportunities are secure, the work will continue.

MICHAEL STEELE: The emergence of the Black female voice has been phenomenally important and will be transforming the country going forward. It is not necessarily manifested in one individual. Folks like Stacey Abrams or Ayanna Pressley, for example—they are representative of an enormous groundswell of civic and political engagement by Black women. The role that they play will be profoundly important for the community as a whole. It's consistent with our history because, at the end of the day, it has been the Black female who has been the stabilizing force of what constituted the Black family, given that our narrative about families is very different from [that of] White folks (they broke our families up, so).

BRITTNEY COOPER: Black women are the most committed voting constituency in the Democratic Party. As we think about the future of progressive politics, Black women are really at the fore of that conversation. Any of the political possibilities that we had, both in the Obama era and the

Trump era, have come from Black women. Black women are the reason that Barack Obama was reelected in 2012. We had a surge of new Black women voters who came out to ensure that President Obama got a second term in office, and then we also came out heavily in support of Hillary Clinton and supported her to the tune of 94 percent.

Then there was this narrative about "low Black voter turnout." No, Barack Obama and Hillary Clinton are the candidates who had gotten the most Democratic votes in history, and Black women were huge drivers of that.

We had a surge of new Black women voters who came out to ensure that President Obama got a second term in office, and then we also came out heavily in support of Hillary Clinton and supported her to the tune of 94 percent.

TIFFANY CROSS: The path to the White House leads straight through Black women. It doesn't work without us. And remember: all Black women don't feel the same way. All Black women aren't in the Stacey Abrams camp or the Kamala Harris camp. You look at the things that Alexandria Ocasio-Cortez has done. You look at the things that Ayanna Pressley has been able to do and Ilhan Omar out of Minnesota. They had problems with the way that they saw government working, and [so] they became part of it. They are becoming political superstars.

BRITTNEY COOPER: We've got a Black maternal mortality crisis in the country and a Black infant mortality crisis in the country. We're seeing Black women die in childbirth [at a disproportionate rate compared to] their White counterparts. And that's something that should be at the fore for the Democratic Party's platform, where we talk about health care for them. If we're talking about health care, what does that mean to make Black women's lives safer? We're talking about reproductive justice that's not just about the right to determine whether one carries a pregnancy to term. It's also about when your children actually get here; are they going to be shot down by the police, or will you have the opportunity to raise them into thriving, productive adults? Those are all questions that have to be at the fore of progressive policy making and that Black women can be drivers of.

*　*　*

For all of the advancement that Black women are making, some see minuscule overall advancement of African Americans. Part of that stems from the disparate political issues within Black America. Years ago, there were more centralized issues that blanketed the entire community. Today, economic, geographical, and social differences between Black people have created factions with different vested interests. Creating a common Black agenda is a harder task than in the past. Scholars debate if there ever even *was* a Black agenda.

The real power of politics doesn't come from politicians; as Frederick Douglass said in 1857, "Power concedes nothing without a demand." It is now Black America's time to demand. It is Black women's time to demand. Our votes should come from a more authoritative position, commensurate with the importance of our participation.

Congress members will have more weight on the Hill if they have an active and vocal constituency. And being vocal isn't just about complaining when things go wrong. Our Congress members want proactive support. They want their colleagues, especially those across the aisle, to understand that they have the means to mobilize and push. Participation beyond Election Day is paramount for political wins of all kinds.

In return, politicians need to create a contemporary political agenda with alliances that have purposeful goals. The lack of such an agenda continues to hinder the modern-day fight for equality. History shows that any substantial wins in civil rights and equality have come with an ad hoc plan and strong coalitions. Young White college students who joined the marches and freedom rides in the '60s brought new attention and empathy to a cause that, until then, had been seen by many as only a Black fight rather than a fight to make a better union. When people started to view civil rights as an all-encompassing battle, the movement accelerated, making way for real change.

The best political gains have always been rooted in cooperation. Blacks need to lead these efforts, men need to vocally support these women, and Whites need to see that they have skin in this game too. A divided nation is a weaker nation for all. While not numerous, there have always been alliances between groups with separate interests. Integrated efforts are always stronger and more effective. By integrated, I don't mean just racial or ethnic groups but also those united because of a common cause, a singular rallying cry. As Bishop William Barber suggests, it is best when morality is the bond.

Conservatives will use race as a way to cloud and camouflage the difference between right and wrong. The biblical phrase "iron sharpens iron" describes the real path to victory. The idea of a truly diverse electorate and government is not only for those who are the minority—it is for the nation as a whole. Diversity and unity serve to make that iron as strong as it can possibly be. Sometimes we muddy the waters looking for complex solutions to complex problems when the most sensible solution is often simpler than we think. In this case, we all must pursue actionable items. Doing as much as you can to make sure that you, your family, your neighbor, and your community are engaged, registered, volunteering, donating, voting, and demanding action from elected officials after elections is the best way to victory and the least complicated path to controlling more of your life and your future. African Americans need to believe in the power of their vote, exert that power, and reap the benefits of giving their vote to a party or a candidate. Although the bulk of the Black vote has historically gone to the Democratic Party, it might not always be that way. Education is needed to understand how to evaluate what and who we are voting for. Looking beyond party affiliation or the charisma of a candidate, voters must become better versed in each party's platform and every candidate's stance and how they align with that voter's beliefs. Educated voters make sure their concerns are being addressed and understand that real engagement with a candidate begins in earnest once a candidate is elected and takes office.

STARTING YOUR OWN CONVERSATION

- In this chapter, we talked briefly about how we used to be a more centrist nation, and now we're leaning more to the left. What indications do we have that the political needle is shifting?

- Which candidates today strike you as particularly engaging or open to engagement with their constituents? How have they demonstrated their openness to serving the needs of their community?

- How might other candidates better engage with your own community?

- We also talked a lot about accountability in this chapter, particularly after candidates are elected. What do public servants owe their constituents—particularly large demographics of voters who elect them to office?

- Given that Black women are such an important demographic in modern elections, what issues do you think matter most to them? How have candidates historically addressed—or neglected to address—these issues? And which issues do you think might become more important in upcoming elections?

IT'S THE GENERAL'S WAR... BUT THE SOLDIER'S BLOOD

THE CHANGING FACE OF BLACK LEADERSHIP

5

STACEY ABRAMS	Politician & Author
WILLIAM BARBER	Minister & Activist
HARRY BELAFONTE	Entertainer & Activist
TODD BOYD	Academic & Author
JITU BROWN	National Director of the Journey for Justice Alliance
CHARLAMAGNE THA GOD	Radio Personality & Author
TIFFANY CROSS	Managing Editor of *The Beat DC*
BEN CRUMP	Civil Rights Attorney
RICHELIEU DENNIS	Founder & Chair of Essence Ventures
MICHAEL ERIC DYSON	Academic & Author
SYBRINA FULTON	Mother of Trayvon Martin & Activist
ALICIA GARZA	Cofounder of Black Lives Matter
JEMELE HILL	Journalist & Broadcaster
ERICKA HUGGINS	Activist & Educator
D.L. HUGHLEY	Comedian & Author
DERRICK JOHNSON	President & CEO of the NAACP
VAN JONES	Commentator & Author
KILLER MIKE	Rapper & Activist
VAN LATHAN	Television Producer
TAMIKA MALLORY	Social Activist
JULIANNE MALVEAUX	Economist & Author
DeRAY MCKESSON	Social Activist

MARC MORIAL President & CEO of the National Urban League

ANGELA RYE Attorney & Political Analyst

AL SHARPTON President of the National Action Network

MICHAEL STEELE Former Chair of the Republican National Committee

SUSAN TAYLOR Former Publisher of *Essence* & Founder of the National Cares Mentoring Movement

T.I. Rapper & Activist

MAXINE WATERS US Representative from California

D oes America have a Black leader? It seems that ever since Martin Luther King Jr., many have asked that question. In fact, much of America saw King as the voice that spoke for all Black people (as if one person could ever do that).

Since Dr. Martin Luther King Jr.'s death in 1968, there has been a considerable amount of revisionist history when we look back at the civil rights era. Dr. King is celebrated as one of the world's greatest figures, and his contributions to humanity are incalculable; however, his was never the singular voice for African Americans. Some scholars have argued that civil rights and labor leader A. Philip Randolph was the real leader of the movement and that Dr. King was just a better orator and a media magnet. It can be argued that at the time of his death, Dr. King was a fading voice in some corners of the Negro community. There are those who felt his nonviolence message was passé or his stance on ending the Vietnam War was too controversial. His assassination brought an elevated status to his legacy and perhaps put his greatness back in focus for those who had grown tone-deaf to his agenda. Since then, people have searched for an individual to fill the void that King's death created—the new "official" voice of Black America.

As a child, I remember attending the NAACP Freedom Fund dinners and listening earnestly to those larger-than-life figures on the front lines of the civil rights movement deliver speeches and wage the righteous fight: Ben Hooks of the NAACP, Dorothy Height of the National Council of Negro Women, and Joseph Lowery of the Southern Christian Leadership Conference, to name a few. There was Stokely Carmichael and Louis Farrakhan, who, among others, were more aggressive and more controversial than other Black leaders. Andrew Young and John Lewis would go on to be well-known, respected veterans of the civil rights movement. Jesse Jackson was the closest to becoming the post-King voice of Black America, but as years passed and times changed, the desire and expectation for someone to fill that void waned. Wearing the heavy crown of Black leadership can be taxing. Once, while I was sitting with Jesse Jackson in his hotel room late one night after spending a nonstop day with him, he quietly admitted, "I am tired." It was spoken not in the context of that day but more in a general sense. It felt as if he had spoken those words less to me than to the universe.

The next morning, I'd bet he probably didn't even remember his utterance. He was back out there, on the grind.

Leadership is often a lonely road that leads to an uncertain ending. In many cases, it is a difficult life path for those who choose to pursue it. For some, the passion of being a changemaker never dies, but for others, the light dims over time, especially as the spotlight grows harder and harder to keep, alongside the inevitable generational shift of power and influence.

WHAT DOES BLACK "LEADERSHIP" LOOK LIKE TODAY?

TODD BOYD: That old-school belief of the Black leader being one person or a small handful of people is outdated. There was a time when Martin Luther King was seen in that light. Malcolm X was for some people. In the '80s, when Jesse Jackson ran for president, there were people who regarded him in that light. Remember, Obama became president of the United States; he didn't get elected "president of Black people." If Barack Obama had been vying for that symbolic title, he would've lost.

We can't depend on one march, one moment, one president, to lead us up out of four hundred years of problems.

JEMELE HILL: It's just the way the world works now; we can't depend on one person or one body. Black people face such wide-scale problems, they have to be addressed in a number of ways. From the national level and beyond. It has to be a full-pronged attack. We can't depend on one march, one moment, one president, to lead us up out of four hundred years of problems.

VAN LATHAN: There's been a void in the leadership that we had from times gone by. Things move a little bit differently now. We all have to open our minds to see how things have changed. The leaders when I was a kid—Martin, Malcolm, Fred Hampton, Angela Davis—those people were resolute in what they were doing. Many of them paid the ultimate price, and because they did, we never got to see the evolution of their mind-set—where they would have taken future societies of Black children, Black men and women.

DeRay Mckesson: How do I say this gently? There is an industry that is built on exploiting. There are a lot of people who weren't with us in St. Louis [at the protests following the death of Michael Brown at the hands of the Ferguson police], who did not do any of that work that allowed the protest to continue or sustain, and they have deemed themselves leaders in these moments. When you ask, "How do we execute an outcome to change the system?" they don't have any [ideas]. It's a lot of hot air and a lot of talking, and I understand people's frustration because there are way more of those people than not.

T.I.: Leadership is diluted because everybody wants to be the leader of something, but everybody ain't fit to lead. Everybody wants their idea to be the best idea and their strategies to be the most effective strategy. But everybody ain't made the sacrifices or took the necessary steps to be in a position to do so. It's not that they aren't passionate or capable; they just haven't taken the necessary steps to be in the position that one must be in to qualify as a leader.

Susan Taylor: Too many of us want to be in the light and don't know how to be a part of the army. Not all of us need to lead the army. We have to know when to step forward and when to step back. I think it's primarily saying, "Ego, get behind me."

Richelieu Dennis: The pressure of oppression has occurred for so long and [been] so [intense] that our leaders have just simply had to lead us to survival, and keep us from becoming extinct.

*   *   *

Racial injustice still casts a shadow over people of color—no matter what your pedigree, wealth, or fame. Whether it's a brotha doing time on Rikers Island in New York, a sista in her sophomore year at Spelman, or a billionaire like Robert Smith, we're all lumped together by race. Over the last four years, we have learned that this kind of thinking is more pervasive than most people thought. America is once again learning that racism is not confined to the South or the Midwest. Racism is alive and well, from sea to shining sea.

It will take a much stronger, more definitive political agenda to ensure that change is not just anecdotal but has a legal redress. Over the years, there have been Black political meetings and summits designed to form a blueprint to achieve justice, but nothing comprehensive or formal has come out of these gatherings for decades.

WHAT DO BLACK LEADERS NEED TO DO NOW TO MOVE BLACK AMERICA FORWARD?

ANGELA RYE: Every year until the Emancipation Proclamation, Black people met to formulate an agenda. Mostly around our freedom, but we still—if we are clear on it—are truly not free. The last time we had a political agenda was during the National Black Political Convention in Gary, Indiana, in 1972. Some people may argue that the Covenant with Black America [events were] one. Some people may argue that the National Urban League's State of Black America Report every year should function as an agenda. We may disagree slightly on the means, but we can come together enough to show this is what we want these presidential candidates to answer to. If they can't sign this pledge or do this thing, they don't have our support.

> The National Black Political Convention took place in Gary, Indiana, in 1972. Ten thousand African Americans gathered to discuss economic, social, and political agendas for Black America. Part of the objective was to increase the number of Black politicians elected to office. Participants included Gary mayor Richard Hatcher, civil rights leaders Jesse Jackson and Coretta Scott King, Black Panther cofounder Bobby Seale, and boxer and political activist Muhammad Ali.

SUSAN TAYLOR: In 2008, during the Democratic National Convention where President Obama was being nominated, I was given ten minutes to speak to all of the African American leaders who had gathered for a breakfast. I asked the group to come up with a three- or four-point plan to include education, health care, economic development, or housing. Whatever they felt was important. We would then have assignments for our organizations and just try to move that forward. We'll make sure that [the National Association of Black Journalists] is aware of it. We'll ask the larger Black organizations and ministers all over the country to talk about the plan so that everybody knows what we're focused on.

Then I found out that two of the major leaders didn't even have one another's telephone numbers. They said they were going to get together, and there was a meeting planned. The whole thing fell apart, and it went nowhere.

MAXINE WATERS: Leadership, young and old, should come together now in the way we used to do in the past. Millennials have learned a lot, especially now having compared, say, Trump and Bernie Sanders, who many of them started to lean toward about Wall Street, the 1 percent, et cetera.

KILLER MIKE: We have to ask ourselves: What are our demands? Who is qualified to offer up our demands, and what are we going to do if they are not met? The fact that we can't answer any of those things says to me that we don't have an agenda, and that is scary.

What are our demands?

WILLIAM BARBER: We need not so much a Black agenda but a moral agenda. A moral agenda that recognizes you cannot engage in any real moral transformation in this country without dealing with the issue of systemic racism. I don't mean the cultural stuff—who [can] call who the N-word—I'm talking about systemic, policy racism that has a disparate impact on Black people, i.e., mass incarceration, resegregation of public schools, coalitions for our immigrant brothers and sisters at the southern border, and the way in which we continue to hurt and harm the indigenous people who are still living under treaties that were written during wars where we committed genocide against those people. Reconstruction is my framework. When Reconstruction started, Blacks and Whites came together in the South to form fusion coalitions. Those fusion coalitions took several things seriously: racism, education, and economic development. What we've been doing in the Forward Together movement is building a moral agenda.

ED GORDON: So the agenda should really be more about commonality than color?

D. L. HUGHLEY: We have to understand that our plight is an "everybody who's an underdog" plight. Everybody who is less than, everybody who "they" counted out, those are our people. Not because they're truly our people but because they have the same interest. We're no different than the Native Americans, gays, women, or Latinos.

KILLER MIKE: I don't truly know who Black leadership is today. Who are our leaders? I don't know because we aren't being led to have the practical knowledge and logic that we need. Leadership? I know we have Black people and other people like Killer Mike and T.I., but our first job is singing and dancing for a living. Yes, we disseminate information, we mobilize people, but who are the organizers? We are disenfranchised from one another. What I can say about past Black leaders is at one point they had some very innovative answers that worked for us. Today, we are not even focusing on the right people. We're focusing on people from religious backgrounds, politics, and even sports and entertainment. If you look at it from a practical standpoint, a company should not be run by a preacher or politician because preachers and politicians are at the whim of other people.

MARC MORIAL: The civil rights movement became organic; while you had this national movement taking place, local movements and local activism festered, whether in Montgomery, [Alabama]; Baton Rouge, [Louisiana]; Nashville, [Tennessee]; Albany, Georgia; or Mobile, Alabama—people picked up the mantle on their own. Ministers did, lawyers did, activists did, and everyone got involved in the same kind of community issues that were being played out nationally. By the very same token, we have to be civically involved and not wait for a command from a supreme leader. There is no supreme leader; there are multiple inspirational figures nationally—people in politics, civil rights, media, business, and that's today's leadership. We need to be more involved in our own initiatives and not wait for [other] people. When people say things like, "When our leaders get together, they'll tell us what to do," that's just a romanticized view of the civil rights movement of the '50s and '60s.

MICHAEL ERIC DYSON: Whether it's the NAACP, or the National Urban League, or the National Action Network, or Jesse Jackson, those groups have been significantly altered, in some cases weakened, but they remain— along with the Black church—the best shot that Black people have to raise consciousness, raise awareness, and resist in the face of White supremacy. We've got to be conscious of our political efforts to resist the rising tide of White supremacy.

ED GORDON: Where do you think traditional Black leadership has gone wrong?

AL SHARPTON: We have not been able to translate commitment to a political level. So, we empower the wrong Blacks. I say that outright. They have no regard for the lineage of political empowerment that we sacrificed for. When I was a kid growing up in the movement, John Johnson, Earl Graves, George Johnson, and the likes were part of the movement. They came to everybody's meetings and conventions and supported [us]. These new people think that their success is totally predicated on how far away from us they can run, until they get in trouble.

BEN CRUMP: The only reason they're in those seats is because of the controversial actions of people in the '50s and '60s, who were getting water hoses turned on them, dogs unleashed on them, and some were killed— therefore, you were elected because of controversial actions. Politicians have to go back and really listen to what King said about our conscience: "Cowardice asks the question, 'Is it safe?' Expediency asks the question, 'Is it politic?' Vanity asks the question, 'Is it popular?' But conscience asks the question, 'Is it right?' And there comes a time when one may take a position that is neither safe, nor politic, nor popular, but one must take it because one's conscience tells one that it is right." That's a lesson many of today's politicians and leaders should learn.

DERRICK JOHNSON: I think we've failed to move away from the egocentric leadership model that relies on individual personalities and charismatic leaders rather than convincing people to see the power they have in themselves. The egocentric leadership style will fail us every time.

*   *   *

The perceived crisis in leadership is best exemplified by how many view the National Association for the Advancement of Colored People (NAACP) today. Founded in 1909, the group became the most powerful civil rights organization in the country. Formed as a biracial group that included W. E. B. Du Bois, the NAACP was on the front lines for the fight for civil rights. The organization would be involved in seminal protests and legal battles that changed the course of race relations in this country. Over the years, local branches played key roles in keeping African Americans safe and protected under the law. The NAACP became legendary. Today there are those who question the relevance of the organization, believing their leadership has not kept up with the times and that their methods of protest may be outdated and ineffective.

HOW CAN BLACK LEADERSHIP CHANGE THEIR STRATEGY TO BETTER ADAPT TO THE NEEDS OF THE PRESENT MOMENT?

ED GORDON: Van, I know you still believe that the NAACP has a role in the fight, but you also think these times call for everyone to look at methods that better fit the times we're in.

VAN JONES: We're in a post-MLK, post-Obama moment, where new strategies are going to have to be pursued, and some of those strategies are going to have to be very different than what we've done in the past. I don't think we can protest and vote our way out of this. We're the only community in the country that has had our primary strategy through government, politics, voting. There's no other group that says, "Well, we've got to protest or see if we can vote our way out of our problems." Most communities have focused more on economic empowerment and development first. We've tried that at different times; Black Wall Street was burned down, and financial centers have aggressively redlined our communities.

DERRICK JOHNSON: The relevancy question becomes one we all have to wrestle with, because we're all as relevant as we understand the importance of our existence. That importance cannot only be in times of controversy when we're fighting against something.

AL SHARPTON: You are absolutely right. You can't take shots at Black leadership and then just show up when something happens and be gone after that. People have to support for the long haul.

SYBRINA FULTON: There are issues that we all need to put our heads together and solve. Instead of looking at others, we should look within and say, "What can I do to help make this community, this world, a better place?"

DERRICK JOHNSON: We have to be ready to pivot and learn how to proactively fight for equality so we can move forward. The NAACP is a membership advocacy organization. We have twenty-two hundred units across the country; we exist in forty-seven of the fifty states, including Hawaii and Alaska. As long as individuals continue to join and carry out the mission of the association, we will always be relevant.

ALICIA GARZA: There are a lot of Black people around the country who want to get involved in political engagement, and they're going to some of the traditional places like the NAACP, the Urban League, and the institutions that they grew up with. What we see is that some of these groups need to be updated in order to match [the] politics of the moment.

This isn't to talk "mess" about NAACP or the Urban League. I think they'd even recognize that they are trying to be more relevant to the politics of today and the people who are shaping them.

* * *

National leadership has always been given too much credit for social victories and shoulders too much blame for the defeats. Most real change, in any movement, happens because of the soldiers—not the generals. Community leaders have long been the ones with far less rhetoric and far more action. Take Jitu Brown, a Chicago community activist who heads the education organizing group Journey 4 Justice, a multicity alliance that is working to provide all children access to world-class public education. He personifies the thousands of unsung heroes who remain in the trenches long after the big names have moved on to the next thing. Though the boots-on-the-ground leaders often have more intimate knowledge of the issues, they are often overlooked or taken for granted. We get enamored of the big name—the person who makes headlines, appears on television, and exudes charisma. The irresistible allure of celebrity and star power defined the public's perception of Black leadership during the civil rights movement, and it remains that way today. Frederick Douglass, W. E. B. Du Bois, Booker T. Washington, Marcus Garvey, Elijah Muhammad, and Martin Luther King Jr. were all considered leaders in their own time to varying degrees. We think of them as players on the same team, and they did share some common beliefs. But we often forget that most of their philosophies regarding the best ways to gain respect, dignity, and equality were substantially different.

In the mid-1990s, I attended a closed-door meeting of the most influential Black leaders of that time, including Jesse Jackson, Al Sharpton, Louis Farrakhan, and Dorothy Height. Everything was off the record. The idea was to forge synergy and come up with a plan on one issue facing the Black community and collectively fight to eradicate it. I sat in awe of the greatness assembled in the room but quickly realized how human these larger-than-life luminaries really were. The bickering over who would lead or speak and then over which agenda item was most important showed me that even the iconic among us can be felled by the green-eyed monster. The monster becomes fiercer once it's been magnified by social media, where public praise or condemnation of Black leadership reaches an audience of millions in mere minutes, and where the murmur of celebrity starts making the rounds before the job is even done. Adoration has always been a perk of leadership, which can otherwise be a thankless job. Rising to become a leader of the community used to take years of toil and diplomacy, but now, notoriety and widespread influence are just a viral post, tweet, or YouTube video away.

The critiques of traditional leadership keep getting more strident as the measures of Black advancement decline. Over the last couple of decades, many of the indexes of how we gauge Black advancement have been stagnant or falling; on the whole, we aren't closing the wealth gap, climbing the corporate ladder, improving public education in the inner cities, reducing poverty, or curtailing the staggering homicide rates in many urban areas. These areas show little to no improvement for people of color. Some members of the Black community blame the leadership for this lack of progress and say they deserve a failing grade.

HOW CAN WE EVALUATE THE EFFICACY OF BLACK LEADERS TODAY?

HARRY BELAFONTE: I don't think that grading Black leaders would be possible because nothing stands still. There are different levels of participation in the evolving of Black America. I don't know that there is any single answer or grade. I don't think the promises of yesterday are reflective of the behavior of today. I do believe that we have retrogressed in America. President Trump has stimulated a right-wing presence in this country that we have not heard from in a very long time. America is in a crisis. I have no faith that what we have achieved in the past will bear fruit in the present. The Black Caucus and a number of people who sit as the voice of Black America have their work to do.

JITU BROWN: What national leaders, the folks who are not in our neighborhoods, miss is that there's a wealth of strength, wisdom, and power in our communities. We have folks who have adopted this really dangerous perception, or narrative, that the 'hood is the 'hood because the people in the 'hood don't want no better. The leadership has to be rooted in the lived experience of people in our communities. They can't be fueled by the opinions of the dominant culture. Most Black leaders [of the past] have been males who rose

> *The leadership has to be rooted in the lived experience of people in our communities.*

from the church or have notably been viewed as intellectuals of some kind, but there is change on the horizon. Many African Americans today are not looking for a messiah on the mountain.

STACEY ABRAMS: One of the important facets of the twenty-first century has been a diffusion of leadership to different levels of community and of issues. With Black Lives Matter, there are a number of leaders who are transforming communities. Their names will never be in the headlines, but they elected DAs and helped change how policing is being done in our communities. And they've created more of a space for an actual articulation of the challenge. There continue to be obstacles, but we continue [to address] them on national platforms and not in whispered conversations among ourselves. I don't think that there's a negative in the fact that we may not have a roster of appointed leaders, but what we do have is a cross section of people who are forcing real change and who are accountable to their communities.

ANGELA RYE: There are more local and regional activists and leaders because of social media. People's platforms may differ in size on a national level, but there are people developing national profiles. Some people are leaders in media, others are leaders in activism or entertainment, but they're using their platforms to talk about our community. It would be a terrible thing if we don't learn how to harness our collective power.

MAXINE WATERS: Black leaders, elected officials, community advocates, and civil rights leaders have arrived at a time where our numbers, and the work we have done over the years, has put us in a place where we have the potential for a lot more influence. It has also shown that a lot more leadership could be produced and that we have yet to realize all of the possibilities of our newfound leadership potential.

ED GORDON: Charlamagne, how would you grade Black leadership?

CHARLAMAGNE THA GOD: Black leadership would get an F because Black leadership, as we want it to be, does not exist. Today's Black leaders are the people who shouldn't necessarily be the leaders. The Black leaders are the rappers. The Black leaders are the athletes. The Black leaders are the so-called influencers—all of those are the people who have influence on the kids. They have influence on a generation, and they really haven't taught them anything, except how to get money. Society has taught young people how to be capitalists, but they taught our kids how to be capitalists in the worst possible ways. In the last twenty years, you've seen a lot of Black people get rich, especially in entertainment, and they've celebrated all the wrong things. They celebrated the gang culture. They glorified the drug culture, the use, and the selling of drugs. A lot of kids gravitated toward that, and I think that ruined a generation.

AL SHARPTON: Yes, the music industry's "get mine," "my Benjamins," "my money" has contributed [to that]. But we also have to create a whole new environment and culture. Megachurches are talking prosperity and have gotten away from talking about the struggle. We have got to dematerialize our values. We have to say success is making your family comfortable. We have to think of success as empowering our community.

Let's be clear: in the last ten or fifteen years, Black leadership has helped to elect and reelect a Black president. If Barack Obama had not been there when the economy collapsed, those advancement measures for Blacks would have been four times worse. We're measuring by what yardstick? We are by any measure still unequal. But it could have been worse. I don't accept that most of Black leadership isn't doing its job. We were in the room and in the streets. The thing that gets me is that people act like we left the streets with Obama. Who did Trayvon? Who did Eric Garner? Who did Michael Brown? We did all of them; we were in the room and on the streets.

MICHAEL STEELE: I give our leadership a C+. In so many ways, Black leadership has been co-opted by the White system, to put it in stark terms. If I want to get that rec center and that program at the church, this is how you have to play the game. You want to be relevant in the state legislature or the city council, you want to have a voice in the US Congress. You want to be in the room, this is how you have to play the game. And when we stepped into those rooms, I dare say, a lot of times, we've left what makes up our agenda outside the door, and we have willingly given over our vote with no expectation of a return.

*   *   *

This is the conundrum Black America finds itself in. There is a desire to independently control the fight against intolerance and bigotry, but the economics of that fight don't allow for that to occur. Blacks have never battled hate without the assistance of others. That aid comes in many forms, including benevolent individuals who believe in the cause and corporate assistance that usually comes in the way of financial aid. The latter becomes a complicated alliance because at times it couples freedom fighters who become, to some degree, beholden and dependent to many of the same institutions that set the very rules, laws, and systems that keep the playing field uneven.

IS BLACK LEADERSHIP COMPROMISED BY ITS DEPENDENCE ON THE ASSISTANCE OF OTHERS?

RICHELIEU DENNIS: The one thing that is (unfortunately) consistent is the reliance of our communities on the wealth of others. When you think about our organizations, our institutions, all needing the wealth of others to just exist, we then have to start to recognize the influence that external, but necessary, wealth has on the decisions our institutions make.

TAMIKA MALLORY: A compromised leader can't help people who are considered to be at the bottom. The main issue is if you are really going to help the underclass, as society has named it, then you're going to have to stare White supremacy in its face, and you're not going to be able to back down based upon a few contracts or some benefits to certain organizations. You're going to really have to get to the root of the problem, and that takes a certain type of courage and staying power. The issue is funding. You find yourself as a leader having to balance the need to keep the lights on, to keep the staff paid, in order to be able to do the work, and the place where those checks are coming from is often in direct conflict with the healing that needs to take place in our community, because they are often the ones actually taking advantage of our people. So, if we take money from corporations, even though we may use that money to distribute resources to the community, there is still a certain level of compromise that takes place in that transaction.

MAXINE WATERS: Remember, in the nonprofit world, it is customary for a nonprofit group to go to corporate America for sponsorship, for support. African American organizations, civil rights organizations, nonprofit organizations do likewise. They go to corporate America, and they don't often consider that the very operations that they're seeking support from are some of the ones that are hurting our community. The financial services community falls into that category. So when you're going to the same people who are causing this kind of devastation and harm and putting their banners up at the church banquets, it does not really tell the whole story about where the money is coming from and what it costs. It's unfortunate that that is the way it works, but that is the truth.

MICHAEL STEELE: It's a catch-22; [civil rights groups] sought out White money because Black folks weren't supporting them, and Black folks weren't supportive because they don't see the results that they think they should. It's a perpetual cycle.

AL SHARPTON: Civil rights organizations have always taken money, and it hasn't stopped us from fighting companies if we had to. Those critics that complain about us being compromised would need to cite an example of where we didn't fight a corporation that was wrong. Because the corporations that we get donations from come to our conventions or buy a table at a dinner to expose themselves. We don't have a corporation foundation grant; we don't get federal or state money. So it's a matter of them coming to show their own wares. It's not like they funded the network. If candidates come to my convention, that doesn't mean that I am going to endorse them. Michael Bloomberg used to give us money when he was mayor of New York City, and I led the fight against him on stop-and-frisk. They're all clear on that!

Stop-and-frisk laws have often been challenged in the courts. The controversial initiative allowed police to temporarily detain, question, and at times search civilians on the street for weapons and other contraband. Forms of stop-and-frisk were used in various jurisdictions. Statistics showed that people of color were disproportionately subjected to these stops. Many of the stops were not reasonable and were simply a form of harassment.

DERRICK JOHNSON: It's a legitimate question. The reason the NAACP is 110 years old is that the base of our existence has been our membership dues, and everything from there is extra. So, if everything else falls apart, [at our core we have] members across the country, and that is the reason we've been able to last with an advocacy voice, not a service voice—even when it's not popular and even when corporate interests will be against our position.

ED GORDON: Could you sustain the organization without the corporate money?

DERRICK JOHNSON: Yes. Would it be the same level of interaction [without corporate funds]? Maybe not, but it's sustainable, and there's proof in that fact that we still exist after 110 years, after taking some unpopular positions, after filing some unpopular lawsuits, after taking on the government. We're still here!

JULIANNE MALVEAUX: Anand Giridharadas's book *Winner Take All* talks about how these corporations that are funding social justice movements actually often work against the interest of social justice. It looks good to be the lead sponsor of an NAACP Freedom Fund banquet…meanwhile, back at the ranch, you're discriminating. It means something to provide these scholarships while the people at the bottom of your corporation haven't seen raises since who knows when. It is a dilemma for these organizations because if you dance, you got to pay the band, and that works both ways. The organizations that are doing good work often can't do it on a not-for-profit basis; they need support. But at the same time, what is the cost of that support? I think that individual philanthropists probably offer at least some freedom from the corporate shackles, but I'm not really sure how much. Some of this money has to be turned away because you're basically endorsing the people who are exploiting you.

MAXINE WATERS: I agree—we should examine the organizations that are willing to give support to us and accept some and reject some. I do believe that there are organizations that we can accept money from and feel proud about it. We should learn to reject money from those that don't act in the best interest of our people. We should also make a better appeal to the richest African Americans in our society, ask[ing] them to understand the power of their resources and what they can cause to happen.

*   *   *

The responses to the police-involved deaths of Trayvon Martin and Eric Garner are good examples of movements that didn't need funding. It was the free platform of social media that proved itself most efficient at spreading the word. Social media has changed the game; it enables instant, emotion-driven critiques of leaders. It also allows for meteoric elevation to the nebulous position of spokesperson for "the people," but even so, it has been effective in launching women's movements and Black movements in recent years.

HOW CAN SOCIAL MEDIA HELP TO SUSTAIN AND RETAIN BLACK LEADERS TODAY?

VAN LATHAN: We're seeing a tendency to cannibalize Black leaders every time they say something that we don't 100 percent agree with. We have so many platforms to say more things. The Black leaders we have in this particular time are fantastic. When I look at some of the people who are doing great work; DeRay Mckesson and Phillip Agnew are two examples of intensely gifted young thought leaders who have real, concrete plans, explanations, and goals about how to get us moving forward. However, there is a tendency now for our leaders to lean on celebrity. That's always shaky ground to stand on. People of our community want to believe there's a oneness with our leadership, that we can relate to them. It's getting harder to relate to leaders you see hanging with Beyoncé.

TIFFANY CROSS: African Americans overinvest on usage across social media. So, with these social media platforms, people have built digital spaces and communities and made themselves leaders of those spaces. If you look at folks like Shaun King, Alicia Garza, Tarana Burke, they all built spaces. I appreciate that some of the social media development has democratized the process of who can be a leader. But with that power comes responsibility. All of those people are using their platforms in a great way. On the other side, there are some who chase celebrity and not necessarily leadership. It's very seductive to have people praise you. You can sometimes lose sight of the journey, and we do see some of that in the conversations of Black leadership. But, thankfully, [those] who are doing the work and who have been doing this work for a long time tend to outshine the others who are not necessarily in it for the cause or for the greater good of the people.

> *Social media development has democratized the process of who can be a leader.*

DERAY MCKESSON: I am reminded that when the rubber met the road in 2014 [after Michael Brown's death at the hands of the Ferguson, Missouri, police], I was one of many people who chose to be in the middle of the streets for the duration of the protest, when we didn't know if we would win. A lot of people gave good speeches and talked about the work they would do "when the moment arises," and when the moment arose, they didn't do it. I am proud to have been one of many people who did rise in that moment. I also know we haven't won. So, I am really mindful when people congratulate me.

I definitely helped get the narrative [out], like many other people, but we haven't won. I am able to put in perspective the work that all of us did with regard to the narrative versus the outcome. From the beginning, a lot of people criticized me for being on TV. They don't remember when nobody would go on TV criticizing the police. At the beginning of the protest, I was like a lone ranger out there saying the police did this, the police did that. This was before Angela Rye, Symone Sanders, and Bakari Sellers were on TV every night—that space didn't exist. I take it with a grain of salt. I also know that people have short memories. I ask people often how long we were in the streets—they say something like a month. We were in the streets for like four hundred days.

DeRay Mckesson has been lauded and condemned. Coming out of Ferguson, some praised him as a strong new voice against police brutality, while others said he was simply trying to grab the "celebrity-activist" spotlight for self-promotion. Critics said that he had not paid enough dues to be called a leader.

STACEY ABRAMS: The question of celebrity leadership has been true in every single generation. So, it's not a new critique, and it's not a new worry. The issue is to always make sure that those who are only seeking celebrity know that we're only supporting those who are doing the work. Today, we've got thinkers who have called the question on issues that for literally centuries have been verboten. I don't think there's a negative in the fact that we may not have a roster of appointed leaders, but what we do have is a cross section of people who are forcing real change and who are accountable to their communities and to our people for keeping that change moving [forward].

*　　*　　*

In order to maintain that forward progress, our community and leaders must start to find more ways to work in tandem. We are seeing a shift in style and personas at the top of the justice fight. New faces are emerging as the leaders of a more inclusive time, one that allows for a more organic form of leadership. One that is driven more by happenstance than anointment. Most of this generation's leaders won't come from behind a pulpit—their ascent will likely come from behind a keyboard. Like any group, there will be frauds and flameouts, but all the same, we'll have our share of brilliant thought leaders and inspirational speechmakers. Those who have grown long in the tooth in this fight for fairness should continue to push and do so with the memory of when they were cutting their teeth in the movement. We need patience from all generations of leadership to continue the battle. There will be those leaders who won't be able to find common ground to work together. So be it. But those who really believe in the greater good should stop working in silos and attack issues in a collegial manner.

Aside from protest and politics, one of the most memorable and beneficial approaches has been to form a consortium. Whether implementing a broad or a granular approach like the Black Covenant Convention or a smaller platform at a town hall meeting, or even using digital media, as Black Lives Matter did, a consortium selects one issue to tackle. Maybe the intention is to curb the violence that has ravaged many African American families in the city of Chicago by choosing a slate of candidates to build a groundswell of support and resources, and working with established groups like 100 Black Men or the National Council of Negro Women to give reinforcement to an in-place initiative. The goal for the group would be to deploy their expertise and resources in a way that makes it and the coalition stronger—by banding together.

Collaborative leadership is possible and can be done for us by us! Can the National Action Network, the NAACP, and Rainbow Push coexist with Black Lives Matter, #MeToo, and a new group of independent thought leaders? Yes. Can an Avengers-like super team of real justice fighters be built to take on mass incarceration in Black America? Yes. How great would these combined efforts be? Black solidarity is more than a symbol.

The climate of hate and the push to roll back the gains people of color have made are real, and so should the fight against them be. The definition of a leader for Black America has been ever-changing over the years. We are in the throes of redefining that term once again, but no matter what the era, the goal of good leadership for African Americans hasn't wavered. The objective has always been to continue being a catalyst for the advancement of our people.

HOW CAN WE EVALUATE BLACK ADVANCEMENT?

ED GORDON: Not all leaders are those who make headlines and history books. The truth is that for many of us, the most impactful leaders are the people that touch us every day.

JITU BROWN: I'm fifty-three years old, and I remember a Black community where the liquor store wasn't our grocery store. Our grocery store was owned by a Black man. It was called Whitehead Pantry, on the South Side of Chicago. The man [who] owned the gas station was Black. He was my father's friend. So I had this experience of actually thinking that we could lead, because I saw it.

D. L. HUGHLEY: I've never once, ever, considered myself a leader by any standard or by any stretch of the imagination. But what I refuse to do is not be Charles Hughley's son. I don't ask, "What would Jesus do?" I ask, "What would Charles do?" I ask if my father is going to understand or believe in what I'm doing. I ask that of my son too. And I think that leadership is much smaller than people imagine. If you can lead your home, you've done something. If you can lead your area, you've done something. It's not war; it's battles. Battles win wars.

ERICKA HUGGINS: People can be leaders without followers. That is the way that, for instance, Rosa Parks, Fannie Lou Hamer, all of these women— we've held them in amber for things they've done, but they started out just feeling like, "Something needs to be done, and I will be part of doing it." Actually, that's how I started. I started as a fifteen-year-old at the March on Washington for jobs and freedom. It isn't like one day you go to leadership school and take a remedial class.

*   *   *

A great leader will set aside egotism and even autonomy for the community's benefit. We are in a time of crisis that demands this kind of sacrifice. Prodigious leadership does what is needed to make a difference and so should those who say they are willing to get in line to fight the good fight.

Strength comes in numbers, and powerful leaders bring in those numbers. The best way to describe this is the African proverb "It's the general's war, but the soldier's blood." The soldiers always have more to lose, but with each battle soldiers believe they can win, the fight gets a little easier. There is a mighty storm brewing in Black America that will start to take down injustice in a way we've never seen. Not because of the generals but because of each and every one of us.

Leadership comes to both those who seek it and those who unexpectedly have it thrust on them. Some who seek it aren't equipped for leadership, while others who find it by happenstance can end up being the ones who achieve the greatest accomplishments. Those who are thrown into the fire, who have randomly taken charge, can often be those who motivate the masses most fervently. The one commonality among all effective leaders is that they have to be present—first and foremost. At some point, they must experience the fire for themselves. In truth, we must all be willing to feel a bit of the heat and be willing to back those who are in the front lines being scorched by the flames.

For those who are comfortable with the mantle of leadership, step forward and share your work and your ideas. Don't hold back! But you must also understand that there are differences between those who only have thoughts and opinions and those who can lead. Leadership is in actions and deeds—it's a continuum, and it takes many forms. Leadership isn't always standing on a soapbox or podium. It's not always championed by a great orator or a firebrand confronting detractors at a rally. We all have a responsibility to participate, to try to turn down the heat and extinguish the flames of racism and intolerance, but to do so means we'll all have to be uncomfortable.

STARTING YOUR OWN CONVERSATION

- With so many factions with diverse interests, do you think it's possible to establish a collective agenda for Black America? If so, how should we try?

- Which issue facing Black Americans is the most pressing in our current moment? Is it police brutality, education, employment, voting rights, or another issue?

- How are organizations in your community addressing this most pressing issue?

- As we've seen in this chapter, organizations often need to take corporate money to help fund their groups—but that can come at a cost. How can these organizations stay true to their original agenda?

- Are you more of a general or a soldier? What different roles do you play in different parts of your community, and how can you encourage others to participate?

6

"SOME THINGS MAKE CHANGE...OTHER THINGS JUST MAKE NOISE."

ACTIVISM TODAY

WILLIAM BARBER	Minister & Activist
HARRY BELAFONTE	Entertainer & Activist
TARANA BURKE	Founder of #MeToo
CHARLAMAGNE THA GOD	Radio Personality & Author
LAURA COATES	CNN Analyst & Radio Host
JAMES CRAIG	Police Chief of Detroit
BEN CRUMP	Civil Rights Attorney
MICHAEL ERIC DYSON	Academic & Author
SYBRINA FULTON	Mother of Trayvon Martin & Activist
ALICIA GARZA	Cofounder of Black Lives Matter
JEMELE HILL	Journalist & Broadcaster
ERIC HOLDER	Former US Attorney General
ERICKA HUGGINS	Activist & Educator
D. L. HUGHLEY	Comedian & Author
HAKEEM JEFFRIES	US Representative from New York
DERRICK JOHNSON	President & CEO of the NAACP
KILLER MIKE	Rapper & Activist
VAN LATHAN	Television Producer
MALCOLM D. LEE	Film Director & Screenwriter
TAMIKA MALLORY	Social Activist
DeRAY MCKESSON	Social Activist

MARC MORIAL	President & CEO of the National Urban League
BRITTANY PACKNETT	Vice President of Teach for America
APRIL REIGN	Founder of #OscarsSoWhite
BAKARI SELLERS	Attorney & Political Commentator
AL SHARPTON	President of the National Action Network
TOMMIE SMITH	Activist & Professor
MICHAEL STEELE	Former Chair of the Republican National Committee

Modern technology has made an immense difference in the way we gather and disseminate information. Because of this, it's now much easier to share information about our collective struggle. Activists today have a tremendous advantage over activists from the past; for instance, they have the opportunity to share videos of police brutality or parcel out information on events instantaneously. Social media has changed the game of activism. Today, the public is no longer solely reliant on wire services like the Associated Press and news networks to expose these iconic, and often horrific, moments; anyone with a smartphone and an internet connection can document these incidents and share them with the world. But some critics argue that posting photos of a protest or retweeting a hashtag is not "real activism."

CAN SOCIAL MEDIA ACTIVISM BE CONSIDERED "REAL ACTIVISM"?

BRITTANY PACKNETT: With the internet, there has been a democratization of voice in a really special way. There was no Black Facebook, there was no Black Myspace, but there is a "Black Twitter." I think the medium, in particular, allows for a level of storytelling, self-promotion, creativity, and community building in much more rapid and broad ways. That helped enable us to accomplish so many more things.

MALCOLM D. LEE: We have cell phones now, where we get to catch people doing stuff. Yes, there's a new consciousness about what's real. People had to look again. "Well, maybe Black people are being profiled. Maybe Black people are being unfairly treated." These videos have made those who are skeptical face certain truths, because there's an awareness now.

MICHAEL ERIC DYSON: We should never deny the value of hashtags or digital culture, but we should never exaggerate the means by which digital culture can achieve the extraordinary results we've seen. It's still shoe leather on the ground; it's still protesting and voices being raised. It's still strategic intelligence in defense of Black humanity that suffers and ways in which we can figure out how to leverage our authority. So, I don't beat up on those young people, though I do warn them that getting together and organizing [with others on social media will not substitute for political organization]. But studies suggest that people who use digital culture are also more likely to be involved in real-world protests and activism as well.

APRIL REIGN: Although #OscarsSoWhite was born on social media, it clearly hasn't stayed there. Not everyone is on social media, and I believe in meeting people where they are. I'm not sure that this movement would have been as successful had it just been Twitter-based. Had I not done interviews, had I not written articles and made my point clear.

TAMIKA MALLORY: Social media is a tool. If the interest is there, anybody can call for a gathering or meeting of the minds, and people will show up. Now, whether or not we are able to sustain that is a different issue. Those of us who have social media followings are actually shifting the needle because we have the ability to organize and we have the following. There are a number of networks that are able to move mass groups of people: #MeToo, Black Lives Matter, the Women's March, and the Black Youth Project are popping up.

ED GORDON: How do we know if these changes will stand the test of time? Will these movements have sustainability?

ERIC HOLDER: The Black Lives Matter movement is really a continuation of other movements that have existed in the African American community over the course of many years. It might not seem like it, but I can tie the Black Lives Matter movement to Walter White in the NAACP and flying the flag A MAN WAS LYNCHED TODAY! that used to fly outside NAACP headquarters every time that happened. There are direct connections between Garvey and King and the Black Lives Matter movement. Their aims for equal treatment, for dignity, for justice are consistent with what other Black protest movements have been about.

TAMIKA MALLORY: That's the constant question we get. I can look back at things that I worked on for years in the social justice space. Some things we changed and with other things, we just made noise. As an example, there's a connection between what the Women's March started and the diversity of women who were elected to public office recently. To see that Black women, Muslim women—a diverse group of women with progressive platforms—were elected, that is directly connected to the work that the Women's March did and specifically the diversity of the organizers at the helm of the women's club.

TARANA BURKE: I believe in organizing. It's my answer to almost everything. It's part of the reason why I'm really comfortable in the fact that it's taken a year to build our organization. I don't want to put out something that's just a flash in the pan, and I don't want to use this opportunity to build on more nonsense. We have an opportunity to really do something different and start making a real shift, and that takes time. But society doesn't operate in that paradigm anymore. Things have to be right away, right away, right away. We're not seeing a lot of feet to the streets. What happened in Ferguson was an anomaly. You might see a march or a rally, and that's it. Recently, I was on a college campus that has a serious racial injustice and sexual violence problem, and I asked the students, "What does organizing look like on this campus? What's the organizing culture?" They started talking about meetings: "We sometimes meet with the so-and-so group, and then we get together." I was like, "Baby, that's a meeting. What are you doing to push back against the administration?" The administration had set up spaces where students could protest, and if you did anything outside of those zones, you'd get kicked out of school. It has been so watered down that people don't even know what it means to knock on doors and to have a community meeting. It's a lost art. I think hashtag activism is useful, but what I keep trying to tell these young people is that it's a galvanizing tool. Hashtags should be used to galvanize and get them excited, and then give them something to do.

*   *   *

Some seek to be activists. Some see it as their calling; others are thrust into that role, becoming a force for change or a disrupter more by circumstance than by intention. Social media has made that occurrence more and more frequent.

ARE ACTIVISTS BORN OR MADE?

JEMELE HILL: It's something that has been a little overwhelming because, as a journalist, you don't want to use the word *activist* in conjunction with your work. Because that implies that you're taking a side. Though absolute objectivity is usually impossible, it is the goal in journalism. Prior to this [incident], I viewed myself as more somebody who was there to chronicle, document, and contextualize. Now that people are looking for me to be a voice, it's shifted my position a little bit. It's not a responsibility that I've wanted or one that I feel burdened by. I'm just trying to redefine it within the context of what I was trying to do. Journalism is my activism. It's not me creating petitions; it's not me organizing unions or organizing groups of people or doing some of the on-the-ground work that we see full-fledged activists do. My role as a journalist is to disrupt and to have conversations about issues that people are really uncomfortable with. And lean into the discomfort and to tell the truth, whether it be a truth that people want to accept or not. We're there to call people in positions of power accountable and to disrupt systems that need to be challenged. If that is considered to be activism, then I'll accept that role as being an activist.

Jemele Hill was a longtime staple of the ESPN network, where she hosted and reported on sports. In 2017, during a Twitter conversation, she tweeted about Trump and his reaction to the racially fueled violence in Charlottesville, Virginia. She commented that she believed Trump was a White supremacist. The White House called for her firing. Trump himself took a jab at her on Twitter, suggesting that she was part of the reason for the network's sagging ratings. Later, she had another Twitter "moment" on NFL players not standing for the national anthem. It all led to Jemele and ESPN parting company and Jemele becoming a voice for change.

APRIL REIGN: I'm forty-nine years old, so I am not by any means Generation Z or a millennial. I made my bones as an attorney for nearly twenty years, but not in the entertainment industry. I am new to this [social media]; less than five years. I haven't received any interaction with the stalwart leaders of the civil rights movement or the struggle, but I also recognize where I am on this continuum in the fight for liberation. I don't like to call myself an activist because there are people who are putting their bodies on the front lines every single day to fight for basic needs and rights of our people. People who are still protecting and serving. That's not me. I am an advocate for diversity and inclusion issues, but there are so many more people who deserve that title. Even within the entertainment industry, right? Those folks who have been around for decades and have been fighting for the same things. I make no bones about the fact that I stand on the shoulders of Harry Belafonte and Spike Lee and all the way back to Hattie McDaniel. There was a convergence of the right message, at the right time, on the right platform, meaning social media, but I wasn't saying anything new. We all make choices to help to further the culture as much as we can. And I absolutely agree with the elders that this is a full-time job, but we shouldn't discount those who aren't able to show up full time. As long as your intentions are earnest, you do what you can. And if you're a weekend warrior, then I will take that over people not doing anything at all.

In 2015, April Reign watched the nominations for the Academy Awards, noticed that no person of color was nominated for an Oscar in any of the leading or supporting acting categories, and then tweeted #OscarsSoWhite. The hashtag went viral and reenergized a long-standing debate about inclusion—or lack thereof—in Hollywood. It also brought worldwide attention to the lawyer. Reign quickly became a media favorite when it came to discussions of diversity and inclusion in this powerful industry.

VAN LATHAN: We shouldn't confuse the term *voice* with someone who is an activist. They are two completely different things, and I think we do that a lot. Community activist Phillip Agnew, [who is the] cofounder of the Dream Defenders, is a guy I really respect. He doesn't have as much social currency right now as I do, but he is a person I believe in. [Also], Jason Wilson, from the Cave of Adullam in Detroit, a transitional academy that teaches young boys how to deal with all sorts of things that are going on in their communities. Those people are activists! Because they were doing it way before it was profitable for them. They didn't have to go viral to wake up every single day and do the work on behalf of their people. They're doing it because it's their calling to do it. What I told Kanye was, some of what you're saying is disrespectful to the people who are doing this work in communities every single day. They need you; they need voices like yours, like mine, to make sure that they're funded, to make sure that people know who they are, to make sure that awareness is up on them, and to make sure that all of their efforts aren't in vain. That we need to get behind the right people. What we have to do is help people follow the ones who are really dedicated to activism because those are the people who are going to be in this fight whether it's popular or not. They're going to be the most genuine to the actual problems on a day-in-and-day-out basis. I'm going to do as much as I can for any community wherever I am, but I'm a writer slash media personality. That's my calling. My calling is to always use my art and my talents to lift my people up. There are people who are actually physically lifting Black people up, and part of my platform is to make sure they have a platform; people need to be clear on those distinctions.

Van Lathan was a producer at TMZ and a content creator in Hollywood with a strong social media following. In 2018, when Kanye West appeared on TMZ, Lathan questioned West about implying that slavery had been a choice for Blacks. Within hours, he went from "Yeah, that's my man from TMZ" to a respected Black spokesperson.

---

*   *   *

Every generation faces a shifting of power in activism. In the San Francisco 49ers' final preseason football game on September 1, 2016, Colin Kaepernick opted to kneel during the national anthem to bring attention to the growing injustice toward people of color by some in law enforcement. The move was controversial, and some tried to paint his stance as an unpatriotic slight to the military, the flag, the country, even Mom and apple pie—although his protest was against none of those things. And he paid a heavy price for it. The controversy around his protest was so strong he opted out of his contract and ultimately was blackballed from the league in what was clearly a concerted effort to punish him for his actions. No NFL team owner or general manager has been brave enough to give him a job. The NFL would eventually pay Kaepernick and fellow player Eric Reid, who also protested, a settlement. At the end of the day, Kaepernick lost millions of dollars in contract and endorsement money and was banished from a game he loved—but he was willing to take a personal loss to stand by his principles. It is harder to decide to take a stand when you have a lot to lose as opposed to nothing at all. Kaepernick followed in the footsteps of other high-profile athletes who have risked their careers by taking a political or social stand against injustice, including Billie Jean King, Muhammad Ali, Bill Russell, Jim Brown, Curt Flood, John Carlos, and Tommie Smith. In the 1968 Olympics, after Carlos won the bronze medal and Smith captured the gold in the 200-meter race, they each wore a black glove, removed their shoes, and bowed their heads in prayer when they were presented with their medals. While "The Star-Spangled Banner" played, both men raised their fisted, gloved hands to the sky in one of the most iconic silent protests of our time. Like Kaepernick, Carlos and Smith were painted as Black militants and malcontents, and there was an attempt to destroy their careers.

WHAT ARE SOME OF THE CHALLENGES BLACK ACTIVISTS SHOULD EXPECT TODAY?

TOMMIE SMITH: There will possibly be a backlash if you go against the status quo. You need to be able to explain what you are doing, [because] whatever position you take, there's going to be [a need] to explain yourself. You're not doing it just because it's cool. It is a sacrifice. If you believe in it deeply enough, you're going to do it and there's someone who is going to agree with you.

ERICKA HUGGINS: Activists think we can keep going. I know that we did in the Black Panther Party and all the movements that we worked with. We did not take care of ourselves. There were so many of us jailed and killed that we just moved through the day without processing what was happening to us emotionally. Today, young activists are wondering, "Is it okay to take care of myself?" Yes, it is—that's part of sustainability. I can't tell you how many people who were activists have fallen by the wayside. They've become prey to both physical and emotional diseases. The Black Panther Party members' median age was nineteen. We didn't even know if we were going to live to the next morning. I've talked with the cofounders of Black Lives Matter and to Alicia Garza privately. Her struggles were just like the ones I was having when I was in the party, being a woman. Also, she's queer. All these things were so familiar. "How [can I] take care of myself?" "Should I have children or not?" "How would I raise my children?" We didn't know how to do that. So she, Opal [Tometi], and Patrisse [Cullors], are paying dues big-time. And all they did originally was develop what became a hashtag, which became a movement. There's no such thing as the FBI counterintelligence program now, but there is something like that, and they're also facing that kind of stalking.

Ericka Huggins understands the trials of being an activist as a leading member of the Black Panther Party in Los Angeles and then head of the New Haven, Connecticut, chapter. In 1969, her husband was gunned down by a member of a Black nationalist group. Investigations later showed the confrontation between the two groups may have been fueled by interference by the FBI.

ALICIA GARZA: Yes, we had activists and organizers who were visited at their homes by the FBI. They have been surveilled and continued to be surveilled, and [there are] those who've received death threats daily. Especially in places that are not robust and liberal urban centers, like New York, the [San Francisco] Bay Area, or Los Angeles, even though these things are happening there too. So many of our activists are in places where there isn't [a] robust infrastructure, so for them to step out and protest or be active in their community means that they have come under a level of scrutiny that is really dangerous and makes them very vulnerable.

ED GORDON: Should like-minded groups work in tandem?

ERICKA HUGGINS: We [the Black Panther Party] worked with an organization called the Young Patriots in the Appalachian Mountains— White and poor—because of the goodness and the vision of a person like Fred Hampton in Chicago, who said, "Let's go see what poor White folks are doing." And they did, and we worked in coalition. I remember when I found out that ten out of a thousand babies in Oakland were dying in their first year of life. This was in the late 1960s, early '70s. I [also] knew about an organization called the Third World Women's Alliance. It was created because the women's movement at the time was not speaking to the needs of women of color. The Third World Women's Alliance was originally started by Asian American women. I called and asked them, "Will you join me? Let's form a coalition to fight infant mortality." And we did. And then we brought in Latinos and other Black organizations. We went to the County Board of Supervisors to speak about the county hospital and what occurred there. And it worked.

KILLER MIKE: Two or three years ago, a group of us joined together. T.I., Usher, Jermaine Dupri, and I had a Black banking day and told Black people, "You don't have to close down your big bank account; just take your small bank account and give it to a Black bank." Those Black banks were flooded with new customers. From that, Wells Fargo developed a Black mortgage program. Not a diversity program, not a people of color program, a *Black* mortgage program in which they allocated $60 million. That's the power we have as a collective. They didn't want to lose our accounts. And we can use our power and broker it everywhere. We can do that, but will we be organized enough to do that? Are we going to get off this person–versus–this person, or this religion–versus–this religion? We must work together!

ED GORDON: Are young activists and older activists working together effectively?

WILLIAM BARBER: I was on a panel the other day with the leader of Black Lives Matter—Alicia [Garza]—and we're building unity together and working together, because it's rooted in this moral agenda. I argue that, for the first time in history, we have the money, power, and the population to actually solve these problems.

It was the religious community, the moral community, a coalition of Whites and Blacks in the 1800s that spoke out against slavery and the denial of women's right to vote. In the 1900s they fought for labor and fought for social security. We now have this regurgitation of the slave-master religion or the moral majority religion that basically has hijacked the moral debate in the public square.

ED GORDON: So we have to join forces to combat this?

WILLIAM BARBER: I did four lectures about social justice at St. John's University, each with literally a packed room full of young and older people. The audience packed the room because people are hungering. This is the kind of moral fusion coalition I believe in. They understand this moment we're in right now is not worse than things we've faced before, but every so often America comes to a moment where the question is not whether or not a particular party is going to survive but whether the democracy itself can survive, whether the Constitution can survive. I really believe we're in that moment right now. People are starting to see that.

ALICIA GARZA: Yes, nobody on the ground listened to Obama saying, "Go back home." And can you imagine if we had? Nobody on the ground listened to Al Sharpton or Jesse Jackson telling people to go back home. Can you imagine if there wasn't a [Black Lives Matter] movement, seven thousand people would still be in jail—because criminal justice reform was not at the top of Obama's list, even though he came from Chicago. If this movement hadn't erupted, we wouldn't have seen the Department of Justice do as many inquiries into local police departments as we did.

DERAY MCKESSON: It feels like, as people get older, they get less willing to actually challenge the power structure because they are protecting some sort of normalcy or comfort, and it's a reminder that the status quo often reinvents itself over and over; it doesn't change as often as we think. I've met a lot of people from the previous generation with great vision, [but] I have not seen that generation be as willing to take risks.

ERIC HOLDER: We saw this as the civil rights movement started to fracture a bit toward the end. My hope would be that you'd see the Black Lives Matter movement expand into more areas than it presently identifies with. Also, to expand and be receptive to the inclusion of other people. Given what we've dealt with in the Trump administration, there's a need now for a new civil rights movement. We've gotta come up with a new Voting Rights Act. There's a whole bunch of things we have to reverse that this administration has done, and there's a need for an effective movement, an effective countervoice to that which we've had to experience the last couple years.

DERRICK JOHNSON: Social justice is not a competition—Black Lives Matter versus NAACP, or Black Lives Matter versus the Urban League, whatever the case is. Anytime we have young people who emerge on the scene and add their voice and energy to the conversation, it is the role of groups like the NAACP to embrace and support [them]. When they come under attack, it should not be by us—it should be us *protecting* them, because their energy today is the building block for leadership tomorrow, and their leadership for tomorrow is actually what's going to sustain us.

> *Social justice is not a competition—Black Lives Matter versus NAACP, or Black Lives Matter versus the Urban League, whatever the case is.*

The average age of Black folks right now is around thirty-four years old. And if that's the average age, we need to cater to them—not cast them aside, not run from them, not chastise them—because that's the new reality.

MARC MORIAL: We need the next generation to participate and to be involved. I also think that they've got to be educated and not fall into the trap of believing in generational divisions. I was once told, "Young men for war, old men for counsel." Historically they've both played a role for Black

Americans in the fight for freedom. Millennials and the Gen Zs are now the largest voting bloc; it's a chance to participate. They bring an energy to the table, and the community has more clout and more influence with them.

ERICKA HUGGINS: It's important for us to affirm younger activists in the good work that they're doing rather than blaming them for not doing what we did. So, let's affirm them as much as we can and have intergenerational conversations publicly about how we can work together. I work with young activists intentionally, and I remember being in three different public conversations with Alicia [Garza], as well as private discussions. She is eloquent, intelligent, brilliant, and courageous.

ALICIA GARZA: My personal relationship to elders has become complicated. I've been embraced by many of the elders from the political left and the radical activist left. Elders like Angela Davis or elders like my sister Ericka Huggins—I love her. I don't think we would be here having this conversation if they hadn't shown up for us the way that they have. Reverend Jackson expressed support for us, and for me particularly once after an interview. But we've never actually been in conversation. Reverend Sharpton at first was very dismissive of our work and of our movement. That has changed over time. Elders like Hollis Watkins or Margaret Burnham, those folks have been really supportive. I think that there may be some differences around strategies or tactics [between us and our elders], but in general, [they] have been very open and offering support.

AL SHARPTON: Alicia and I have talked about doing some political things. I've seen Brittany Packnett do well. I think that everybody [needs to] understand that the movement has always been a multilane highway. It's those who come like "It's my lane" or "You ain't going nowhere" who become dangerous. A lot of them want to be anointed, and they don't want to take no hits. I mean, if people understand what we all went through…I was stabbed. I look at a scar on my chest every morning when I shave. It indicates all I went through. Some people don't want to pay those prices. Some of them just walk in and have a half million likes on Facebook and get on a cable show. It ain't like that. It's not that easy. Show me, don't tell me. Show me. The generation ahead of me, I had to show them. It wasn't like everybody was embracing me. Show me. Some say, "I can do this, Al. I speak for the people now." Fine. Come on with it. They're just showing me social media likes. Half your likes on social media are critics. Activism is not reacting; it's "pro-acting." A lot of people get known too quick; then they can't handle the spotlight. There is a reason that people like Jesse Jackson, mentored by Dr. King, or Ben Chavis, mentored by Ben Hooks, or Al Sharpton, mentored by Jesse Jackson—there's a reason we lasted decades. Because we were trained by people who were lasting. Didn't mean we didn't have differences. Didn't mean we didn't get our feelings bruised. Didn't mean we didn't think they should be more aggressive. But you had a context.

> *Activism is not reacting; it's "pro-acting."*

ED GORDON: What should we hope for the rising generation of activists?

BEN CRUMP: I'm hopeful that because of their positions—regardless of political correctness, regardless of people telling them that they don't know what they're doing—this generation of young people [will] keep standing up for what's right.

HARRY BELAFONTE: I think young people are doing quite a bit; I think elders have capitulated. There are a lot of young people around this country, some of whom I've met with, that I think are absolutely admirable in the fact that they have not committed to becoming part of the problem but are more slanted to revealing in a deeper way what the problem is. And they, as young people, are taking an active position. Added to that are people like Bryan Stevenson and his work in the field of criminal justice. I think there are a lot of examples of people, especially young Black people, and White people, in Ferguson. I think that the problem is still being viciously pursued and attended to by a lot of these young people.

ERIC HOLDER: It's always young people who are the ones who tend to drive change in this nation. People tend to forget that the founding fathers were all young people; except for Ben Franklin, they were all pretty young, and they took on the mightiest empire in the world to create this revolutionary society that we call the United States. The young people in Birmingham—King was a baby in the '50s during [that] boycott. Their aims for equal treatment, for dignity, for justice are consistent with what other Black protest movements have been about, including today's.

BAKARI SELLERS: Generation Z is leading the reform on guns. They've been the generation that has called upon state legislatures and the United States Congress to take action on gun laws, and it's the first time in the history of our country that we've seen progressive legislation take hold, especially in southern states.

Numerous surveys, including those done by Gallup and Rasmussen, show that a record number of voters believe that our nation needs stricter gun control laws. Generation Z (born between 1995 and 2015) are the largest voting bloc to hold this view.

SYBRINA FULTON: I put my faith and I put my all into the young people. I actually believe that they are the key and they're going to make changes because they're not afraid. They're energized, and they are ready!

*   *   *

Given the transition in leadership, the question becomes whether the agenda for change should be set through a combined effort from those with experience and those with zeal and new methods. While this new generation wants to do things differently, they should be smarter than previous emerging activist groups by accepting in a more open way the guidance of those who have long been in the fight. There are lessons to be learned and adopted that still apply today, lessons that can only be taught by those who've walked through the fire before. At the same time, the elder activists must accept that the world can and often does outgrow solutions that worked previously and that not every nugget of hard-won wisdom dispensed is relevant to today's conditions. New ideas do not signal the "mothballing" of those who came before.

Successful activism is based on the ability of those leading and following not to let the past, present, or future get in the way of the cause. The question of boots on the ground or in cyberspace should be looked at situationally rather than universally. Activism for today's fight must be waged with today's weapons, but we should never discard maneuvers and people who are vital and relevant, despite their age. At no time should any of us forget the most powerful artillery in the arsenal of any generation fighting for justice—having righteousness on your side. No generation has a monopoly on that.

Black Lives Matter is the most important social justice organization since those formed during the height of the civil rights period. Born out of that same frustration with injustice, Black Lives Matter has become a galvanizer for this generation's youth, as was the civil rights movement for young people in the '50s and '60s. Key flashpoints marked important turns in both movements. The infamous Bloody Sunday in Selma, Alabama, showed the world what peaceful protesters were up against. The footage of marchers, men and women, being beaten and bloodied helped persuade a nation that something had to be done to bring voting rights to Blacks. Forty-nine years later and almost six hundred miles away in Ferguson, Missouri, the unrest after the police killing of Michael Brown exploded on national television, and this time, social media ignited a movement. Uneasy interaction and combative actions between law enforcement and protesters led to rioting and a military-like takeover of Ferguson. Initial cell phone footage played out in real time, making it hard for even doubters to turn away from the questions about the growing number of suspicious deaths of Black people at the hands of police officers. The coverage brought greater national attention to a matter that the African American community had been complaining about for years.

But Brown was hardly the first example of a Black man's murder eliciting such a vocal public outcry. The killing of Emmett Till was one of the monumental watershed moments in the fight for civil rights in the 1950s. Till was a fourteen-year-old boy from Chicago who was lynched while visiting Mississippi; his murderers claimed he was flirting with and whistling at a twenty-one-year-old White woman. Till's body would later be retrieved from the Tallahatchie River. When his body was returned to his hometown of Chicago, his mother, Mamie Till-Mobley, decided to have an open-casket funeral, showing his decomposed, bloated body to the world. Till-Mobley also decided to allow a picture of Till in the casket, displaying the grotesque aftermath of his killing, to be published in *Jet* magazine. Her decision demonstrated to the world the hate, bigotry, and racism that killed a boy whose life was just beginning, whose promise was stolen. Mamie Till-Mobley channeled her grief into the fight for civil rights by becoming an activist. Her brave decision to publish the picture and not to lie down and wallow in sorrow served as a catalyst for others to take up the fight.

Fifty-seven years later, the killing of another teenager and his mother's unrelenting advocacy born out of tragedy moved a new generation to fight back against rampant prejudice. Like Emmett Till, Trayvon Martin would become the face of the fight for change. Like Till's mother, Trayvon's mother, Sybrina Fulton, would not allow grief to end the fight for her son's legacy. She has become a champion for those who lost their lives to gun violence; for those who've lost loved ones; for mothers who cry themselves to sleep after another day of living without their child. Fulton has become an activist by default, driven by devotion to a son she never saw become a man.

Like the photo of Till, Martin and his hoodie became a symbol, a clarion call, signaling that the fight for Black lives is real. So many people of color identified with Trayvon. He's our son, our brother, ourselves. President Obama proclaimed during a statement about the killing, "If I had a son, he'd look like Trayvon," and declared Martin's killing a national tragedy. A seventeen-year-old with only an iced tea, a cell phone, and Skittles candy in his hands, a hoodie on his back, was killed for no reason other than his skin color. Trayvon's murder showed the world that for Black men in America, you need nothing more than harmless items in your hands, the "wrong" attire, and your pigment to be marked for death.

Trayvon's killer, George Zimmerman, a self-appointed neighborhood security guard, a man with a wannabe-cop mentality, would show the ugly racist tendencies that can bubble under the surface for some. The "I felt threatened" defense, used by Zimmerman, echoes the often-flippant justification for the killing of a Black person by Whites. Just tell the world you feared for your life, and America will acquit you for murdering a person of color. The "I was afraid" phrase is seen by many as a get-out-of-jail-free card for Whites and law enforcers who find themselves embroiled in the legal system for killing a Black person.

WHAT CAN BLACK AMERICA DO TO PREVENT THE DEATHS OF INNOCENTS LIKE TRAYVON MARTIN?

SYBRINA FULTON: I don't know if there's something that we could've done as a community, because the people that are shooting and killing have a mind-set, and until their mind-set changes, this will continue to happen. People have to remember that Trayvon was not killed by police. It's not just officers—it's the people who are shooting and killing and then are not being held accountable. I simply don't think America values our lives.

A 2018 *Washington Post* analysis of homicide arrest data showed that police arrest someone in 63 percent of the killings of White victims and only 47 percent of the time when the victims are Black, the least likely of any racial group to have arrests in connection with their killings. The *American Journal of Public Health* reported that Black men are nearly three times as likely to be killed by law enforcement officers of any race than White men are.

BEN CRUMP: Laws have legitimized the killing of Black lives and the criminalization of people of color. That makes people lose their faith in the criminal justice system, because we, as people of color, always get the least justice and the most injustice throughout history.

MICHAEL STEELE: It feels like we're struggling with a lot of old demons that have haunted us for four hundred years. It's manifested in the modern era through the deaths of Tamir Rice, Freddie Gray, and others. Young Black men are still, regardless of time or place or generation, having to confront the [harmful] consequences in their encounters with law enforcement, and their encounters with the justice system, and their encounters with the education system, and their encounters with the economic system! That is a narrative that continues to play out in devastating ways.

Ben Crump: In America, all you have is a chance at justice, but there is no guarantee that you will *get* justice. All the Constitution provides is that twelve people will sit in a jury box, and they will decide what justice looks like. There's no guarantee that those twelve people will conclude that justice looks like what our community believes justice should look like. A lot of that is by design.

*   *   *

The 1988 song "F*ck tha Police," by the rap group N.W.A, warned listeners that the Los Angeles police were misusing their power and harassing young Black men. In spite of this country's history of police misconduct, directed against Blacks, many Americans still believed it was an exaggeration. Three years later, a videotape showing the malicious beating of Rodney King by Los Angeles police officers would shake the nation awake to this realization.

Police brutality, particularly against Black Americans, has been a constant in our nation's history. Known Klansmen were employed on some southern police forces as late as the 1950s and '60s. And this brutality was not confined to the South, either. For example, in 1985, the Philadelphia police were responsible for an aerial bombing of row houses where members of MOVE, a Black liberation group, resided; this devastating act resulted in the death of eleven people, including five children. And that legacy of racist injustice goes all the way to the top. Birmingham's public safety commissioner, Bull Connor; Los Angeles police chief Daryl Gates; and FBI director J. Edgar Hoover are all men in leadership roles that were infamous for supposedly allowing people of color to be terrorized.

Today, technology has been able to showcase what has been denied, whispered about, covered up, tacitly accepted, and in a few corners proudly displayed for decades: police brutality is real. And there's tons of footage that proves it, much of it taken by happenstance, like the footage taken of the Rodney King beating in 1991. George Holliday just happened to be on his apartment balcony with a video camera that night. Technology offers us a lens that puts America's ugly biases and violent acts on full view. Strained interactions between the community and the cops are now front and center, daily, in the news, the national media, and online.

Eric Garner's last words, as he struggled for his life as an NYPD police officer applied a deadly choke hold—"I can't breathe"—became a rallying cry for BLM protesters. A ghastly picture of Michael Brown's lifeless body, covered by a sheet and lying in the street after he was shot by a police officer in Ferguson, Missouri, was another flame that ignited us, rousing us to keep fighting back. The Facebook Live broadcast of Philando Castile being shot to death by police officers in front of Castile's girlfriend and her young daughter horrified us. And the dashcam footage of Sandra Bland being pulled over for a minor traffic infraction by a state trooper in Texas and then engaging in a heated verbal exchange that resulted in her arrest infuriated and deeply concerned us—and not without reason. Just seventy-two hours after the recorded incident, Sandra was mysteriously found dead in a jail cell.

These and many other incidents have left Black America more skeptical, afraid, angry, and concerned than ever that any encounter with law enforcement could be tantamount to a death sentence.

HOW CAN WE REPAIR BLACK AMERICA'S RELATIONSHIP WITH THE POLICE?

HAKEEM JEFFRIES: We have to find common ground between police and the community. In order to move from problem to promise, we should identify areas where real accountability can be brought to the system. One possible ray of hope is the growing agreement that [we need to] understand what's taking place in these police-civilian encounters,

We have to find common ground between police and the community.

and now the presence of body cameras [on police officers] is the rule and not the exception. This provides one pathway to altering behavior that is abhorrent on the one hand and providing accountability when a bad actor does something wrong on the other hand. It's interesting to me that both activists, as well as, increasingly, law enforcement professionals, have agreed that the presence of body cameras as a regular thing is one part of the solution to improving the dynamics that occur in [these] street encounters.

JAMES CRAIG: Diversity is important; training and retraining are too. The internet and social media have changed policing dramatically. We see more attacks that end up in fatalities against police officers today than we've seen at any time in history. However, it goes two ways. These shootings have eroded Black America's trust in police, and, yes, Black lives matter, but let's remember all lives—[including] blue lives, police officers' lives—matter.

ERIC HOLDER: I would have said Black Lives Matter Too—that way, you just do away with this whole notion of all lives matter. Black Lives Matter Too!

JAMES CRAIG: We must reestablish that relationship between police and [the] community. Police leaders today absolutely must be transparent. We also need to establish programs where police and the community have communication. What we've done very effectively in Detroit is form programs where police have discourse with young people about making better decisions.

KILLER MIKE: Back in the day, the Police Athletic League (PAL) was something that I was involved in. Not only did it teach you how to defend yourself or get exercise, it taught you the normalcy of dealing with police officers. Community policing has proven to be an effective way to ease tension between police and the people they serve. Law enforcement agencies that have improved relationships with constituents say it all starts with finding common ground and getting to know one another in times when the tension level is low.

AL SHARPTON: You've also got to change the legislation. You've got to be able to work with those who can organize around the situation [and] change the politics, which changes the legislation.

LAURA COATES: We have to test the laws. The laws are not written in stone. It's not like the Ten Commandments. We treat them as if they can never be changed, improved upon, or thrown away. We have relegated ourselves to a world where we think if there is a law in place, it can never be challenged. But that actually is the role that prosecutors and the executive branch have to be willing to test and willing to call to the attention of Congress to help [them] approve. Specifically in the area of police brutality cases. It infuriates me that very few prosecutors have been willing to test Supreme Court precedent about giving the benefit of the doubt to officers in their decisions and the determinations of what levels of force to use, including lethal force. We're allowing the officers to be judged by what a reasonable officer believes as opposed to what a reasonable *person* would believe. And just that idea, that nuance of reasonable standards, has led so many prosecutors to say, "Well, it's set in stone. [There's] nothing I can do about it." Well, that's absolutely false. There could be a legislative remedy put in place because the judiciary only interprets the laws that are actually out there. There is a need for legislative action to equalize the treatment of all people, especially at the hands of police officers, and to ensure that there is accountability—not only for the community but for the great police officers who are out there [and] are being judged by the worst among them.

HAS THE BLACK LIVES MATTER MOVEMENT HELPED CURB SYSTEMIC POLICE VIOLENCE AGAINST PEOPLE OF COLOR?

ALICIA GARZA: This movement is still very much alive. People ask, "Why aren't you protesting anymore?" What I try to explain is that movements don't exist for people's entertainment. While they may begin organically, they also need to be adaptable to the conditions [in which] we're fighting. Many people who've been involved in this movement over the last five or six years have started thinking about power really differently. Some of them may have thought that protest would solve things, but it doesn't solve things. Protest is a pressure tactic, but it is not a solution. This iteration of the movement is really focused on changing the political condition, and that doesn't always involve marching in the street.

Alicia Garza is a cofounder of the Black Lives Matter movement. She quickly realized that it would take more than rallies and social media buzz to make a real difference. She understood that real change follows legal and political change. Garza hopes through Black Lives Matter and another initiative she helped conceive, Black Futures Lab (BLF), that is working to build political and social power for minority communities, she can build bigger political and social influence for minorities. But many, especially those who feel besieged by law enforcement, want to see BLM move faster; for them the change is too slow.

BEN CRUMP: My hero, Thurgood Marshall, understood that this battle is the long game. It won't be won overnight. When you consider that we were in slavery for hundreds of years, and then we suffered under Jim Crow for another hundred years, you can see this battle is going to be long. We can win it if we stay focused and keep fighting. Always keep fighting. In the case of *Brown v. Board of Education*, Thurgood lost nine cases, if not more, before they got to *Brown*. The fight took place over the course of years, and people doubted and attacked Thurgood, saying that he didn't know what he was doing, that they should change lawyers—and all different types of criticism came from his own people! What Thurgood Marshall understood is that you keep fighting the fight because even though the law may get it wrong, we're on the right side of history. [As] Martin Luther King said, "Just because they say it's legal, that don't make it right."

> *We can win it if we stay focused and keep fighting. Always keep fighting.*

ALICIA GARZA: Our communities are getting organized and ready to change how politics happen in the country, which is essential to being able to win any of the things that we've been fighting for. Just because you don't see us in the streets does not mean we're not working. What's really important for people to understand is that the more visible you are, the more vulnerable you are.

ED GORDON: There is some disagreement among African Americans that people are more complacent when Blacks kill Blacks than when police kill Blacks. Does the Black Lives Matter movement apply to Black folks too?

CHARLAMAGNE THA GOD: I know people are going to get upset about this, because I see what the Black Lives Matter people are protesting against, but I also understand when people ask, "Do Black lives matter to Black people?" That's a great question to be asked. You expect certain things from your enemy, right? You expect certain things from your oppressor, but when it really hits home is when you see your own people doing destructive things to you. Like the situation with Nipsey Hussle, where a Black man from his community killed him—which is something we see all the time. Now, that in itself is troubling, and often collectively traumatic, but it reflects a deeper and more persistently entrenched resistance to Blackness. A hate of Blackness, a fear of Blackness, a skepticism about what Blackness means. And whether that means calling the first Black president of the United States of America out of his name, as was done, or the spike in police shootings of Black people that continues apace.

KILLER MIKE: Nipsey was saying, "Enough is enough," and he made some real change in his community. He grew other businesspeople around him. Before he died, Nipsey had a friend who was killed, and that damn near killed Nipsey. And Nipsey's death damn near killed me. Knowing he had a wife and kids should break us as a community. Like my man Charlamagne said, there's a lot of people running around with trauma, undealt-with issues, and stuff like that. Because it's no way we should be able to kill each other this easily. There is no way I can kill someone with the ease that we kill in this country. Black people are acting like the people who owned them, and it's important to take note of that.

ERIC HOLDER: If you're gonna talk about Black Lives Matter, Black lives must matter not only in [terms of how] Black people are treated by law enforcement but also in how Black people are treated by other Black people. That examination is absolutely necessary if we're going to make true progress. We've gotta deal with this illness within our own community. That has to be treated, while at the same time, we must still focus on the forces from outside our community that are having a negative impact on us. We all have the responsibility to do that.

TAMIKA MALLORY: Black folks must get out in our own communities and start doing the work to heal or to straighten the crooked areas. I am definitely dedicated to what it looks like for us to invest in antiviolence groups, small mom-and-pop organizations on our street corners and in our 'hoods.

ALICIA GARZA: What I appreciate about the Black Lives Matter movement is that we have not allowed that conversation to be derailed by talking about anything Black-on-Black because that's an inadequate statement. We start talking about gangs and gang violence, for example. We have to have an unwavering belief in our own capacity to transform and do bigger and better than the worst thing we've ever done. If it's gangs now, it was something else thirty years ago. We have to make some decisions as Black people. What are our standards for who we'll be together? We should be involved with the question of violence if we're going to develop our own standards for what kinds of transformation are possible and who's going to lead them. A big barrier to dealing with intracommunity violence, violence that happens at our own hands, is our inability to set those standards.

> *We have to have an unwavering belief in our own capacity to transform and do bigger and better than the worst thing we've ever done.*

*　　*　　*

Chicago has become ground zero for urban homicide and the media's latest example of rampant "Black" killings. In 2018, seventy-two people were shot and thirteen killed over a single weekend, and the majority of the victims and perpetrators were people of color. This kind of violence is not reflective of most Black people, nor should anyone flippantly try to explain the reasons why these kinds of abhorrent actions occur. The reasons are many and varied. Poverty, lack of education, and a sense of hopelessness are just a few of the factors that underlie the violence we see in these urban areas. It's not being Black that brings the rage—it's the conditions that often accompany being Black.

IS THIS INTRACOMMUNITY VIOLENCE UNIQUE TO BLACK AMERICA? AND HOW DOES IT AFFECT OUR DAILY LIVES?

ERIC HOLDER: We can't fall into this false narrative that there's this wave of Black-on-Black crime. That it is somehow different than what you see in other ethnic groups. It is true that over 90 percent of the Black people who are killed in this country are killed by other Black people, but if you look at Whites who die by murder, they're killed by other White people and the rate is about 86–87 percent. We never hear about White-on-White crimes; we've gotta keep some perspective. Having said that, we see in raw numbers, disproportionate numbers of the murder victims in this country are people of color, and that's an issue.

HAKEEM JEFFRIES: It is incredibly important to make sure that we don't allow for the sanctity of life to become important when that life is taken by a police officer but an accepted occurrence when the killing is done by another Black person and happens in one of the "rough neighborhoods." We have to do everything possible to make sure that every single Black life matters. Dream and have the opportunity to fulfill their potential.

SYBRINA FULTON: People always say that time heals all wounds, but it's not true. We're not recovering addicts or recovering alcoholics or recovering from some type of disease. It's just something that we have to deal with on a daily basis. I'm recovering from depression. I'm recovering from sadness. I'm recovering from my loss on a daily basis.

*   *   *

Tupac said, "[If] there ain't no hope for the youth, the truth is, there ain't no hope for the future." Black life doesn't yet have the value it deserves. Black lives will matter when Black futures matter. The need for activist leaders has never diminished, but over time the enthusiasm for different manifestations of that activism does. Activism is often ignited by tragedy, calamity, or extremes. After segregation ended, protest and action became splintered. Civil rights activists no longer seemed to have a singular focus. The movement appeared to be adrift, even as further barriers were broken by some Black Americans and economic conditions improved for many. Still, blanket issues that affected all Blacks were harder to find. The rise of social media—and the rising visibility and apparent inevitability of police brutality—changed all that. When it became clear that any Black American—no matter your income, gender, age, education—could become a possible target for police harassment, violence, even murder, a singular pressing issue emerged, and Black Lives Matter took hold. The Black Lives Matter movement has galvanized a generation, and Black Americans from all walks of life continue to be impacted by this issue. If we want things to change, we must continue to speak truth to power and raise the level of defiance against injustice in every generation and in every way possible until it's completely extinguished.

START YOUR OWN CONVERSATION

- In what ways can young activists learn from elder activists? What could elder activists stand to learn from their younger counterparts?

- How can we heal the broken relationship between law enforcement and the Black community?

- Does Black-on-Black crime differ from other types of intraracial crime? If so, how and why?

- In this chapter, Laura Coates says, "We have to test the laws. The laws are not written in stone." Can you think of some laws that we could create or amend to better help Black people in America today?

- What do you think will be the lasting impact of the Black Lives Matter movement? How has it changed life for you, your family, your friends, and your colleagues in your community?

STAND UP, BLACK MEN, STAND UP!

BLACK MEN STRUGGLING IN AMERICA—AND HOW TO HELP THEM

JITU BROWN	National Director of Journey for Justice Alliance
CHARLAMAGNE THA GOD	Radio Host & Author
BRITTNEY COOPER	Academic & Author
JAMES CRAIG	Police Chief of Detroit
BEN CRUMP	Civil Rights Attorney
RICHELIEU DENNIS	Founder & Chair of Essence Ventures
ERIC HOLDER	Former US Attorney General
D. L. HUGHLEY	Comedian & Author
DERRICK JOHNSON	President & CEO of the NAACP
KILLER MIKE	Rapper & Activist
VAN LATHAN	Television Producer
TOMMIE SMITH	Activist & Professor
T.I.	Rapper & Activist
IYANLA VANZANT	Inspirational Speaker & Life Coach

Throughout history, Black men have overcome all types of odds and reached the top of their fields. Most Black men are law-abiding members of society who go to work every day, love their families and communities, and strive to live the American dream despite a system that has depicted them as the face of evil. Too many Black boys and men feel devalued, overlooked, undermined. They feel left behind, without hope. They are, more often than not, a product of their environment. The trajectory of their lives is determined by the zip code they are born in. As clichéd as it sounds, many of these boys grow up with little or no positive influence from an older male. Society tells them that their kind "ain't sh*t." There are few incentives to go to school or get a job. The whispered suggestion is that the only ways out of their circumstances are by selling drugs, playing ball, or rapping. The odds against becoming a drug kingpin, NBA or NFL superstar, or successful music star are astronomical. It's extremely difficult to escape the conditions you were born into. In many cases, underachieving has become a self-fulfilling prophecy for these men. They believe their futures are so limited that there is no reason to put any real effort into becoming successful. Their minds are underfed; their creativity dies on the vine because no one took the time to harvest it. Many could achieve their dreams if they received attention and encouragement to share their gifts.

For years, I have witnessed the hopelessness many young Black men feel. I worked on a community project with a group of young people and one young man, "Kenny," talked with me a lot during our downtime. He said he wanted to do something more with his life than most of the men in his family. He said his brothers sold drugs and his uncles struggled because they were laid off from their jobs every few years. He wanted to provide for his mother and sisters and saw too few options other than following his brother into the pharmaceutical street trade. We talked about his options, including schools. He felt those options provided little or no help in bettering his chances for a brighter future. I talked to him about careers and other work opportunities. We discussed not living the same life his brothers had to, always looking over their shoulders, concerned about retaliation from rival drug dealers. After the program ended, we talked for a few months. Sadly, I lost touch with him, and I don't know what path he walked.

Years later, I did a story on gang members in Los Angeles. Former NFL great Jim Brown convened a summit and brought a number of these young men together in LA. Many of them shared with me their belief that no one was really concerned about their dreams and the only thing they saw with structure was the gang they grew up in.

More recently, a young man in Cincinnati told me he did "whatever I want to do, because I don't care if I die. I got nothing to live for." Another young brother in his sophomore year in college told me that I was the first man he had talked to about his career aspirations. He said he appreciated our conversation because he now believed that he could be successful because now he'd actually met a man who had "made a real career." Before meeting me, he said that he wondered if it was even possible.

Life for young Black men can be overwhelming, and without guidance, it can be paralyzing. They need positive role models. Without that, their anger turns into violence as a misguided way of coping.

HOW DO WE HELP STRUGGLING BLACK MEN AND BOYS?

CHARLAMAGNE THA GOD: We got a lot of trauma and a lot of pain and hurt that we don't deal with. When we don't deal with it, it manifests itself in other ways, and we end up redistributing that pain, and that's how you get the violence. That's how you get the anger. That's how you get the shootings, the stabbings. You mad at me because I bumped you in the club? You mad at me because I stepped on your sneaker? You mad at me just because I came through in a fly car, and your girl said hi to me? Your ego is that fragile? No, not only is your ego fragile, it's because you've got so much pain and so much hurt that you're willing to do something bad to someone just because they're not living the life that you live.

JAMES CRAIG: Unfortunately, young African Americans in these urban centers are quick to go to a gun and use that type of violence to settle a dispute. That part of it is the evidence of mental illness or PTSD among some of these young people who have been left untreated. We really need to put significant focus on treating not just our children but the adults.

Anybody who is managing a jail will tell you a lot of the people of color are suffering from some sort of mental illness and they're not being treated.

KILLER MIKE: Part of the violence comes from our boys having been mistreated, misused and abused, given power or authority when they should not have them, and wanting some type of paternal friendships, and they don't have them. If you want someone to throw a ball with you and you don't play football, basketball, or baseball, where are you getting that from? That's when they turn to street violence and gangs.

JITU BROWN: Young people don't grow up wanting to kill people or wanting to be killed. Every shooter was once in third grade. Every shooter had this time when he was an innocent little boy and anything was possible. What was their experience? Well, a lot is clear that they've grown up through massive school closings. They've grown up through zero-tolerance policies in schools. Being pushed out of school. All of this stuff is relevant.

CHARLAMAGNE THA GOD: You know how many potential Black architects and doctors and lawyers and engineers we lost because they were doing things in the streets? They heard these guys [in the streets] talk, and they actually wanted to be like these guys? That's why you have so many of these street guys who turned rappers. When they look around in their community, the people that are getting the money, the people that are getting the girls, that are driving the big cars, wearing the fly clothes and jewelry are probably the drug dealers and then those drug dealers turned into rappers. And some of those rappers weren't even selling drugs, but they were rapping about the lifestyle of the drug dealer, so all of these kids were like, "Oh, that's what I need to be doing. I need to be selling drugs. I need to be using drugs. I need to be carrying my gun. That's how I become successful."

Charlamagne knows from experience what it's like to grow up in this sort of environment. Born Lenard McKelvey, he grew up in Moncks Corner, South Carolina; fell into the drug trade; and was locked up multiple times. After he was jailed for a third time, his father refused to pay his bail, believing his son needed to learn a lesson; he remained in jail for over a month. Charlamagne finally asked his mother for help, and she raised the bail, but this wake-up call led to a huge turnaround in his life. He furthered his education, and eventually he worked his way up the ladder to a tremendous career in media. Through his show business persona, Charlamagne tha God, the boy born as Lenard has now become one of the most powerful people in media today.

WHAT CAN BLACK MEN DO TO OVERCOME SOME OF THESE DESTRUCTIVE PATTERNS?

CHARLAMAGNE THA GOD: One of my homegirls said to me a few years ago, "Black men do not want to admit they're damaged." If you don't admit that you're damaged, then you'll never go out there and do the work. I agree with her. A lot of us are damaged. When you're damaged, you have pain that you don't know you're dealing with. For years, you've been suppressing that pain through other means: drugs, alcohol, being a player with a bunch of different women—things to boost the ego that we all have. But when you're doing all that stuff, you're not paying attention to what's really going on in your life. Then you get older, and you start to feel really empty. You start to feel really hollow because you haven't filled yourself up with anything good. Now you're a hurt person, and hurt people hurt people. I think that's the problem with a lot of Black men. That's the thing we're doing wrong.

For the past four or five years, I've been doing more unlearning than I have learning. It's not like I didn't know. That's the crazy thing. It's not like we don't know the difference between right and wrong. We knew what was right, we just were choosing to do wrong and then wondering, "Why [do] we feel no sense of fulfillment? Why [do] we feel no sense of happiness? Why [do] we have this depression? Why [do] we still have this anxiety?" You've got to let all of the wrong go and just focus on what's right.

*   *   *

Many of the issues and pain that Black men suffer from stem from systems that were designed to hold back men of color, but some of these challenges are brought about by the man in the mirror. This growing pain causes them to simply check out and step away from many of the responsibilities that men once viewed as a badge of honor. When I was young, you strove to be the breadwinner and protector of your family, no matter how hard that was. No matter what it took, you would find a way! Racism made it hard to provide for your family when you were the last hired, first fired, or constantly passed over for promotions. It became difficult to feel like a man when the world called you "boy" and often humiliated you in front of your family. For some Black men, it all became too much, and they found it easier to walk away than to stay. That absenteeism became the learned behavior of the struggling young men we see before us today, passed down from generation to generation.

Not enough conversations are taking place between Black men about the expectation of manhood. Black men need to encourage and uplift one another. We need to make sure we don't isolate ourselves and our problems. We need to be collectively strong. We need to affirm our greatness and pass that on to the next generation of young men who need to see accomplishment and achievement coming from men who look like them. They need to hear positive affirmation from other brothers who know what their lives are like.

DO WE NEED NEW ROLE MODELS FOR YOUNG BLACK MEN IN OUR COMMUNITIES?

JITU BROWN: Yes. Many of the men in the neighborhood are gone for nonviolent drug offenses. You're locked up because you sold weed. You got ten years for twenty dollars' worth of crack. You had drug dealing going on back in the day, you had violence, but there were rules; nothing can happen around schools. Now, with all these cats gone, the leadership is fifteen to eighteen years old. And now you have all these little cliques. So now there is no order.

JAMES CRAIG: The impact the war on drugs had on people of color was real. Remember when rock cocaine was the drug of choice and the violence associated with that? Mass incarcerations, people would be placed in prisons for long periods of time, where people of other persuasions who were dealing with powder cocaine weren't given the same prison time, [but] much shorter. It certainly destroyed the Black family.

I believe we have to quickly integrate them back into a community. Again, first and foremost, we've got to make sure that if they are suffering from mental illness, they are getting the type of treatment needed so that they can get to be effective citizens. We have to make job opportunities, more opportunities, available so that they can live the kind of life that would prevent them from returning to crime.

WHERE CAN WE FIND BLACK MALE ROLE MODELS? WHERE DO WE NEED THEM MOST?

D. L. HUGHLEY: Black leaders are fathers and husbands and mentors, to a great degree. Unfortunately, Black men have disappeared [from our neighborhoods]. We haven't been as prominent as we should be, and you're seeing what happens to people who don't have a head.

BEN CRUMP: What we have to do is not allow the legal system in American society to define our young Black men. We have to define our children. We must let those who have been convicted of felonies in America know that they have some redeeming qualities, *especially* after they have been defined as having no redeeming qualities. We have to encourage them—we gotta tell our young men that if nobody else is gonna believe in [them], we still believe in [them]. We just gotta quit letting society define their character.

TOMMIE SMITH: We have to tell our Black men that "you are blessed with a gift, and with that gift you're gonna have to sacrifice to make that gift a part of everyone you love. It's not always because you're a gifted athlete, because you're out on the field working your tail off. You have that gift through other means, a divine means that is moving forward. Of course, you're gonna have to work. Everything you work for is going to pay you later. Not necessarily in dollar bills; it might even be greater than dollar bills. It's called a healthy life."

According to the Centers for Disease Control and Prevention, the average life expectancy at birth for Black men is 71.5 years. That trails the expectancy for White men by nearly five years and for Black women by more than six years.

T.I.: We gotta tap into our greatness and learn to love ourselves—see what I'm saying? The true source of peace comes from understanding and loving yourself. Most motherf*ckers been raised up in an environment where they weren't expected to be sh*t. They were never loved properly or nurtured or taught much. They [place] very little value on their own existence. It is chillingly impossible to give someone else more value for their existence than you have for your own. That's where the senseless killings and all that sh*t comes from.

VAN LATHAN: Right, we need to learn how to love ourselves a little bit more. To prioritize ourselves a little bit more. And hold ourselves to a standard where we keep our communities clean. Where we punish people who are victimizing other people in our community. Black men have to engage in collective fatherhood. I know everybody has their own families; I know everybody [has] their own kids. But it's just not enough. What's missing in the African American community are Black men who know how to teach other men how to be men. I am not talking about teaching them the virtues of masculinity and how to dominate, how to be tough, how not to cry. I'm talking about a male example and someone who you know as a man loves you, cares about you, and will put your life first. My father is an incredibly flawed man, but there was only one lesson that my dad had to teach me, and he did it very well. He taught me that my life has worth. That it matters whether or not I live or die. That it matters what I do with my life. It matters to me because it matters to him. He sacrificed for me; he didn't always teach me the right thing to do, but he taught me. He took an interest in what happened to me. I knew that what I did had a consequence or a benefit.

RICHELIEU DENNIS: What we haven't done as Black men is unite in our brotherhood. We have an obligation to create the framework and the pathway to start actually actively uniting in our brotherhood. Getting together and building businesses together, investing in each other, breaking down barriers and doors for each other. Not one leader doing it here and one leader doing it there, but one kid in the 'hood connecting with another kid in the 'hood and doing it right in the community. We all need to be involved.

CHARLAMAGNE THA GOD: Black men have to start telling each other, "I love you. I value you. I appreciate you." When is the last time a brother came up to you and said those words? If you're a person who's full of love, you can pour from your cup. Maybe him knowing that somebody else thinks he matters will make him start valuing himself a whole lot more. Your first love and best love is self-love.

T.I.: If you love yourself, there is no way that you can just go out there and just f*ck over people. I feel like that's more science than it is anything else. When we begin to love and value ourselves, that starts healing. When we don't, we project our flaws onto other people, and so a person will senselessly kill someone else who looks just like him when he would not do that to someone who looks like his oppressor.

KILLER MIKE: We have to start to honor Black masculinity in a different way. We need to encourage boys to take refuge in their fathers and not feel as though they have to pick a side and to somehow defend their mothers. I talked to a couple of boys at a manhood program, and I said, "The same father you think you hate, because of what he did, he and your mother didn't work out— you're doing the same thing to her he did. You're doggin' her out, you're misusing her,

> *We have to start to honor Black masculinity in a different way.*

you're abusing her heart, because if that wasn't true, you wouldn't be in this program at eight in the morning. She doesn't want to be here, but as a son, you never think in those terms. You've never been taught to respect Black masculinity."

ED GORDON: That's an interesting thought because, when men check out, when they leave, they force the woman's voice—the matriarchal word—to become the dominant one. How can we empower these young Black men as they grow older?

Iyanla Vanzant: It's very clear to me as a spiritual technician that African American men have arrested development. Psychologically, emotionally, and, in my line of work, spiritually. That they are underdeveloped in their sense of esteem, value, worth, and respect. And because that's missing within them, they don't get it from the world, and as a result, they're devalued, they're diminished, they are dishonored, disrespected, and dehumanized. I call it the Bee and the Butterfly Effect. When people see a butterfly, they swoon; the butterfly can land on them, and they think it's so beautiful and nice. They go, "Oh, look, there's a butterfly!" And when they see a bee, the first thing they do is start swatting, running, and screaming. I think in our society today, Black men are bees. As soon as we see them, we start swatting. We run; we scream. When I say *we*, I mean the general society.

Brittney Cooper: Black men are underemployed and discriminated against, and White folk have a very deep investment in not allowing Black people to have access. I care deeply about the challenges that Black men face. But I also think that part of the challenge for Black men is that what they want is the level of power that White people have, and sometimes the way they treat Black women in that quest for power is they will step on them—they will agree with the most racist assessment of who Black women are. Black men culturally traffic in a lot of ideas about Black women as gold diggers, untrustworthy, disloyal. You don't just see those narratives coming from hip-hop, [even though that's] usually what everybody likes to get up on. You see those narratives coming from church pulpits; you see those narratives coming from social media, from some of our most famous and well-known Black male authors, [from] talk show hosts who are talking about all the ways that Black women need to fix themselves in order to be worthy of love. Black men actually owe us. They owe us more care, more loyalty. They owe us an investment in doing their emotional work. What does it mean to stay wed to the most traditional, conservative ideas about manhood in a White-driven world that never wanted Black men to be able to be those kind of men in the first place?

IYANLA VANZANT: Believe it or not (and I may be the only one), it has a lot to do with Black women because we are the mothers, and we're teaching [our sons]. The more we lose touch with ourselves and who we are, the less able we are to teach, raise, and nurture our sons. That's not a blame; it's not fault-finding. It's an identification of [an] imbalance that has had such a devastating impact on our community.

ED GORDON: Some will certainly say you're blaming the victim; the mothers are the ones who are there with their sons.

IYANLA VANZANT: If we look at it as a blame as opposed to an experience that needs to be corrected, then we're not going to handle it. Our culture, as descendants of Africans, says a man is who his mother makes him. That's what our culture says. Do we know that? Do we understand it? Do we teach it? It's not about blame. It's about accountability. It's about responsibility. It's about owning who we are as a people. Understanding from a spiritual and a cultural perspective what our roles are. Not blame at all. Yes, we're there, but the fathers who abdicate their throne can leave the queen alone to raise the prince. What did his mother teach him? If we hold it as blame, then we're not going to be able to find the ways to address the devastation that we are experiencing.

*   *   *

Rapper Nipsey Hussle was an example of the power of one Black man to make a difference. Born Ermias Joseph Asghedom, Hussle initially joined an LA gang, but at nineteen, his father took him and his brother to East Africa for three months. That trip changed his life—for the first time, he saw people of color in charge of their own lives, controlling their commerce and future, and that inspired him to become a community activist and entrepreneur. After he gained fame and wealth, the Grammy-nominated musician used his newfound resources to give back to underserved areas. He was the very personification of what so many hope young men in urban areas will become: a positive change maker. He overcame the odds and became a successful rapper, but he was also a family man and, by all accounts, a doting father. In addition to using his good fortune to make things better for all around him, he was set to meet with members of the Los Angeles Police Department. Unfortunately, Hussle was shot and killed the day before that meeting—by a Black man, someone he knew. Had he not been a celebrity, the murder most likely would have gone down as another statistic, another Black man killed by a Black man. Just another "Black-on-Black" crime, as some call it. His story is pivotal as we discuss the plight of Black men in America because although his murder was shocking, his life was inspiring. His service would be held at the Staples Center, and a great part of a city, community, and nation grieved the loss of this man who was a shining example of what can be.

HOW CAN WE USE NIPSEY HUSSLE'S LEGACY TO INSPIRE MORE BLACK MEN TO SUCCEED AND GIVE BACK TO THEIR COMMUNITIES?

ERIC HOLDER: Nipsey Hussle seemed like a guy who was in the process of not only turning his life around but turning lives around within his community. The individual journey was great, but what he was doing with his fame and influence was to have a positive impact on his community.

CHARLAMAGNE THA GOD: When it really hits home is when you see your own people doing destructive things to you. Like Nipsey's situation, another Black man from his community, which is something we see all the time. That's why when everybody was like, "Oh, it's a conspiracy theory." Well, how about the eleven brothers that got killed last weekend? What about the brothers that got killed in Philly and Chicago? What about all of those brothers that get killed by other brothers every single day?

When you see somebody like Nipsey get gunned down, you collectively see Black people get depressed because of that situation. Because he was a brother who represented the best of everything that we're supposed to be.

[He] came from the worst circumstances and made the best circumstances out of his life, and was making the best out of the worst parts of his community.

D. L. HUGHLEY: Nipsey Hussle has given young Black men and young men of color something aspirational besides being an athlete or a rapper or entertainer. Now they can just be. If you're human, you can still be remarkable.

EARL "BUTCH" GRAVES: I'm beginning to think that young Black men are starting to ask, "Why are we engaged in violence against one another when we can draw strength from working with one another to move forward?" Everybody is kind of tired of the same narrative that Black people don't care about each other's lives, which I hear White people say: "Well, if Black people don't care about each other's lives, why should we be upset that cops don't?" As if it's some moral equivalency to the two. It's really not.

It basically comes down to examples. Do you see enough people who are Black males who are successful in whatever measurement you want to look at success being? Why can't I become an engineer? Can I become a broadcaster? Can I become whatever? Maybe they didn't think it was possible before, and now perhaps their eyes are opening to what is possible. I'm a person who always looks at the glass as half full, not half empty. My hope is that young Black males and young Black females look at their future as having boundless opportunities, not limitations, not someone telling them, "Oh, you can't do that," as our own parents and grandparents have told us.

According to a report conducted by the *Washington Post*, Kaiser Family Foundation, and Harvard University, the share of Black men in poverty has fallen from 41 percent in 1960 to 18 percent in 2018.

VAN LATHAN: We have a generation of young Black men right now who care. Look at LeBron, Charlamagne—you look at all these guys, [and you] can see they care about what's going on in their community, with the kids who don't share their last name. It's becoming cool to care. This is not a shot at Michael Jordan, but Mike said, "Well, Republicans buy shoes too"—he really didn't have any type of presence in the community. That's now become important; it's becoming part of the success tool kit to understand how you'll represent yourself to the people who need you the most.

KILLER MIKE: We're not embracing [the fact] that boys do need some type of organized warrior culture; that could be a basketball or football team, a hunting or fishing club—something that allows them to exercise their masculinity in a positive way. They don't need to wait to go to college to join a fraternity because they may end up in a street fraternity—a gang. We should have something that is comparable to a boys' and girls' club that is exclusively ours, and I am not talking about Jack and Jill where you got to dress up. I mean something that gets us out in the woods and gets this stuff out of us. There are some programs in Jacksonville and Atlanta like that. I believe problems get solved when we start addressing the trauma that our children have and give our boys some place to talk, some place to be honest. Allow boys to get out and clean up their own communities. We should look at things we have done successfully. Sometimes, it's finding out things like what's preventing our boys from being police officers; sometimes it's a low credit score that is keeping young Black men off police forces, and if it's a low credit score, [we need to figure out] how do we get our young men to get their credit scores up and get more of us on the police force? So that we get used to seeing people who look like us, so we don't have the hostile relationship with policing that we have [now].

JAMES CRAIG: We do a Ceasefire program where we bring young men who are most likely to engage in violence, either as suspects or victims of violent crimes, and we present them with opportunities. Imagine if we could use that as the template in preventing or reducing recidivism. It could impact this whole issue of mass incarceration. If a Black man kills another Black man, two lives are lost, and there's no way to adjudicate that type of crime other than incarceration. The real key is preventing it, addressing the symptom of mental illness as one part, but also making sure that we have opportunities for those who have made mistakes in the past so that they are not continually wed to this vicious cycle.

RICHELIEU DENNIS: As unfortunate as Nipsey Hussle's death is, he had a plan for his community and for his neighborhood, and he was working to execute that plan. Take a look at Nipsey's model that he was building and create your own neighborhood model, create your own economic movement and your own cultural movement. But do it collectively so that you collectively have impact and influence. That's one example. I hope that we as a community flip the model that he's created or that he set for us. Let's maximize it.

* * *

Nipsey Hussle's life showed that being a famous person pales in comparison to being a person of consequence. It also showed the possibility of change and growth. Jesse Jackson once said, "I was born in the slum, but the slum was not born in me. And it wasn't born in you, and you can make it." It's never been easy to be a Black man in America. We must continue to work to ensure a better future for young Black men, even if—especially if—they are struggling because they find themselves on the bottom rung of society's ladder. Groups including 100 Black Men and My Brother's Keeper, which started in the Obama administration, are taking the reins to make sure these vulnerable Black boys and men survive in spite of the odds. Many Black men are thriving, contributing members of society—we are scholars, businesspeople, philanthropists, artists, athletes, politicians, social justice fighters, spiritual leaders, doctors, lawyers, police officers, office workers, chefs, and IT managers, and one of us was even president of the United States. We are the personification of beating the odds. And our young Black men need to see and hear that. It's time for us to show them that they will make it, just as we did.

STARTING YOUR OWN CONVERSATION

- How do you define *Black masculinity*? How does it differ from how you define *masculinity* more generally?

- What tools and resources do young Black men need to help them build confidence and succeed in life?

- What incentives could motivate young, vulnerable Black men to stay away from gangs and look toward a life of education, community service, and success?

- What programs are available in your community that cater to and provide opportunities for young Black men?

- How can older Black men be better mentors to young men in their communities?

BLACK GIRL MAGIC

EMPOWERING BLACK WOMEN TODAY

8

STACEY ABRAMS	Politician & Author
TARANA BURKE	Founder of #MeToo
LAURA COATES	CNN Analyst & Radio Host
TIFFANY CROSS	Managing Editor of *The Beat DC*
SYBRINA FULTON	Mother of Trayvon Martin & Activist
ALICIA GARZA	Cofounder of Black Lives Matter
JEMELE HILL	Journalist & Broadcaster
TAMIKA MALLORY	Social Activist
APRIL REIGN	Founder of #OscarsSoWhite
ANGELA RYE	Attorney & Political Analyst
SUSAN TAYLOR	Former Publisher of *Essence* & Founder of the National Cares Mentoring Movement
IYANLA VANZANT	Inspirational Speaker & Life Coach

Risking their own lives for the sake of their cause, Sojourner Truth and Harriet Tubman overcame unimaginable obstacles and helped countless other African Americans find freedom. Fannie Lou Hamer and Shirley Chisholm blazed trails in politics that would plant the seeds for the Black political clout that has since become a major cog in today's political machinery. Today is no different; Black women are at the forefront of all areas and issues, shaping and influencing the world at their feet. Michelle Obama was critical to Barack Obama's historic victory. Serena Williams changed the face of tennis and the way we view women in sports—no longer can "playing like a girl" be considered an insult. Beyoncé is an entertainment phenomenon; with cultural sway and power, she asks us, "Who runs the world? *Girls!*" And then there is Oprah! A supernova in a world of stars, rising from a local journalist to a national talk show host to an international mogul. She is a zeitgeist shaper of her own making. Not to mention the countless Black mothers, grandmothers, and others who have kept Black people afloat—including me—without ever asking for anything in return. They are the ones who nurture and sustain us.

When I was eleven years old, my father's sudden death turned my mother into a single parent overnight. She always gave me love and support and anything else I needed to feel important and vital. She certainly sacrificed her wants to make sure I had whatever I needed. With my father's death, my mother, like many Black women, became the financial pillar of our family. Statistics show that Black women are the primary breadwinners in the majority of Black families today, even though—like all women—they lag behind the pay afforded to men. And according to the National Women's Law Center, Black women are 2.5 times more likely to be single mothers than White women. Oftentimes, the absence of a man in these houses is not a result of abandonment by a Black man; it's usually rooted in systemic issues rather than stereotypical assumptions. No matter what the reason, this leaves these women with less money to take care of their families—there is rent or a mortgage to be paid, lights to be kept on, car payments, child care, and somehow…abracadabra! Black girl magic! They get it done.

"BLACK GIRL MAGIC" HAS BECOME A CATCHPHRASE FOR THE GROWING EMPOWERMENT OF BLACK WOMEN. WHAT DOES "BLACK GIRL MAGIC" MEAN TO YOU?

TARANA BURKE: Look, I believe in Black girl magic, but I also think that it's Black girl work that is really making stuff happen. Ain't nothing magical about what we're getting up and doing. We're putting our bodies on the line every day.

> The Center for American Progress found that, in 2017, nearly 85 percent of Black mothers were primary, sole, or co-breadwinners in their households.

IYANLA VANZANT: I think it is the celebration of the fact that we've been able to do so much with so little—that's our genius, our resourcefulness, our perseverance, our presence. It's now being acknowledged.

APRIL REIGN: I think that the phrase itself is incredibly important because it elevates our status closer to where it should be. It indicates that there is truly something special about Black girls and Black women that should be appreciated and honored and celebrated at every opportunity.

TIFFANY CROSS: I don't know that this is a new phenomenon. I think the only thing new is that we claimed the phrase "Black girl magic." But when you look at our history, from the day that we stepped foot in this country, Black women have always been the backbone and conscience of our community.

ANGELA RYE: I talk all the time about Zora Neale Hurston saying, "Black women are the mules of the world." I think at some point the mule [morphed] into "I can do the work; I can be the workhorse *and* the show horse." I also think there is a realization and understanding that for the work we've always done in the back, we now can maintain and handle a platform in the front as well.

TAMIKA MALLORY: What I'm seeing right now is that it's a new day for Black girls, and that's the special part of this moment for me—that Black girls are having an opportunity to see Black women not as the support system for men, not as those in the background, but actually in the forefront.

ED GORDON: What resources do Black women have now that they have not historically always had access to?

STACEY ABRAMS: I'm deeply gratified to see Black women given not [only] opportunity but given space to fully realize who they are and what they're capable of. You've got Black women running for office at every level of government, but you also have Black women taking a range of power across our economy. And as those changes happen, as those opportunities unfold, my mission is to be a part of always helping fill the pipeline, whether it's filling it with me as a candidate, training Black women, creating platforms for Black women, or supporting Black women who are doing the work.

Stacey Abrams has become one of the brightest stars for the Democratic Party. After a controversial loss in the 2018 Georgia governor's race, where many suspected voter suppression, she became an aspirational figure for so many women who see her as compelling, intelligent, and uncompromising.

ANGELA RYE: I remember during a budget negotiation process where women in the Senate and women in the House were coming together to say, "Let's come together and figure this out." There's something to be said for the ability to lay your ego aside and just get the work done. We've always done that and probably disproportionately performed in spaces that way. So, yeah, we're happy to be here, but we won't take the seats at the table for granted.

SYBRINA FULTON: Well, you know, Black women are resilient, and I believe that women heal differently from men. I think together we stand, united we stand, together we heal. We can empower each other. I see all of those things in strong Black women.

IYANLA VANZANT: I would say that we need to define *magic*. I don't think there's a common definition for *magic*. Some people think it's what we look like; others think it's the strides that we're making in the worlds of business and entertainment, that kind of thing. We're not really defining it as how we hold ourselves within ourselves. We need that [knowledge in order] to approach the world; without that being taught, our young girls are just looking for the external magic or the worldly magic and not growing the magic within.

*   *   *

Black women don't always deal in fairy dust and magic. In fact, being the "magician" can prove to be draining or even traumatic. Carrying that kind of responsibility is burdensome. In 2019, *Sex Roles*, a research journal focusing on social and behavioral science from a feminist perspective, released findings that suggest that the need to identify as a "strong Black woman" and the significant obligations that are associated with that designation often lead to depression.

HOW HAS BLACK WOMANHOOD CHANGED OVER THE PAST FEW DECADES?

TIFFANY CROSS: For decades, Black women have felt like we are carrying all this weight on our own. We are carrying the weight of the world on our backs. We have stopped a child molester from getting into the US Senate. We helped elect the first Black man to the presidency.

JEMELE HILL: What basically happened is, Black women started feeling empowered to speak. We've always been comfortable speaking up for our community, speaking up for our men, but now we have decided we're going to speak up for ourselves. We're exposing a level of vulnerability along the way as well. People need to understand the psychological toll of feeling like you have to be the backbone of an entire community. That comes at a significant cost. We are strong, but there's a price that comes with that. Because of our strength, people tend not to treat us delicately and tend not to protect us, because they think we're so strong and we can handle it.

We've developed this sisterhood among ourselves. We instinctively call each other "queen." We instinctively celebrate each other. We instinctively uplift each other.

TIFFANY CROSS: We've developed this sisterhood among ourselves. We instinctively call each other "queen." We instinctively celebrate each other. We instinctively uplift each other. That's beautiful, and that's a wonderful thing. However, I think it sometimes comes at a cost of some relationships with our counterparts. There is still a lot of sexism in society, and somehow, the fault is ours, the blame is ours. The fact that we persisted and made these great achievements, and [yet] some Black men see it like it came at a cost to them.

TAMIKA MALLORY: The movement that we see happening around sexual assault from the Black woman's perspective is more about protecting Black girls and changing the narrative and the ways in which we have retrained our girls. We all know that Black girls have been told not to tell their stories, to protect "Uncle So-and-So," to protect the neighbor, not to bring up workplace incidents because they could lose their job. It's so complicated in the Black community and in other communities of color too.

The #MeToo movement has become another crucial tool for women. It has forced sexual abuse out of the shadows and at times complicated the interaction between men and women. According to the National Organization for Women, Black women are disproportionately impacted by sexual abuse. The organization's numbers suggest over 18 percent of African American women will be sexually assaulted in their lifetime. What's more, for every fifteen Black women who are raped, only one reports her assault to authorities.

TARANA BURKE: It's so complicated in the Black community and in other communities of color too. Black women have been super, super supportive. Black men have been really resistant. And it's an interesting resistance because in the last year when they see me on the street, they're like, "Oh, the MeToo lady, that's cool." But it still felt very contrary. I keep trying to impress upon folks that there's no special depravity in our community, and yet we're dealing with sexual violence at alarming numbers. We know specifically that sexual violence is intracommunal, so it's happening at the hands of other Black people.

Some people try to make this an anti–Black man thing or suggest that people are trying to make Black men the face of sexual violence. These are all excuses. All of these are deflections used to not deal with the actual issue. I had a conversation with a brother the other day who was like, "Oh, I think you're doing really good work. That R. Kelly thing [docu-series] was great. But why do you think R. Kelly got more attention than Harvey Weinstein?"

I said, "You know that's not true, right?"

He said, "What do you mean? They did a whole documentary on R. Kelly. They didn't have that on Harvey Weinstein."

I said, "No, [there are] three."

Tarana Burke started the #MeToo movement and is a tremendous force in giving women an affirmative voice in the fight against sexual harassment and abuse. For years, this has been a touchy subject in society; women have faced abuse and often have to decide to endure the treatment to keep peace in families or to remain financially solvent. She has been working for years to bring attention to this taboo subject.

TAMIKA MALLORY: Sexual assault is one of the most devastating issues for Black women, and it destroys your self-esteem in ways that make you less successful in other areas of your life. It's hard for you to function when you've dealt with sexual abuse that has not been challenged. That's why

When Black girls have the confidence to stand up to a family member or a teacher, they can then walk into the workplace and take on a challenging issue there just as well.

this particular moment is so important, because when Black girls have the confidence to stand up to a family member or a teacher, they can then walk into the workplace and take on a challenging issue there just as well.

TARANA BURKE: Part of what I'm trying to do is help more people to understand what sexual violence looks like in the real world, help them understand how this affects us and what the ripple effects are. Our work is about hearts and minds. We also need to change policy; there's not really federal oversight for sexual violence. We need to change a culture that says Black girls are "fast" and that's why these men are attracted to them.

According to their website, the National Organization of Women found that over 18 percent of African American women will be sexually assaulted in their lifetime; this only accounts for the number of women who reported their abuse.

* * *

In our culture, when Black women are viewed as "ravishing" by the mainstream, they are usually of a lighter hue. Think Halle Berry. It's only been recently that darker women like Lupita Nyong'o have been given credit for their stunning beauty, and yet, even then, they are called "exotic." Or, even worse, it's done with a backhanded compliment, like when actress Viola Davis was described in the *New York Times* as "less classically beautiful" than some other actresses. Colorism is still a huge issue, even within the Black community; comedian Kevin Hart's joke about light-skinned women having better credit or rapper Kodak Black's vocalization about his preference for light women did not fall on deaf ears. Laura Coates told me that she had to address this with her four-year-old when her daughter said that she didn't like the way she looked because kids had said she couldn't play in a princess tent because she was Black.

HOW DOES THE WORLD LOOK AT BLACK WOMEN? HOW DOES IT AFFECT HOW THEY VIEW THEMSELVES?

LAURA COATES: I was traumatized that there was even a moment that [my daughter] didn't like any aspect of herself. I assumed that [she liked herself] because she was raised by two Black parents with tremendous amounts of pride, [and] because she sees her father obsessively in love with me, the look of the Black woman he's married to. That since she saw her own mother on television, I assumed that would be enough pride to somehow occur through osmosis. I needed to have an awakening, that heart-stopping conversation, and [the] realization that you have to teach your children not only about the world doing something to them but also about the pride and joy they should feel [for themselves] because of the color of their skin. We can't take for granted that the overwhelming majority of their self-awareness and self-love will come through proactive conversations that point out why their skin is so beautiful.

TIFFANY CROSS: We are frequently viewed as unattractive. We are frequently judged by our hair or our marital status. You know, the single woman is somehow lesser than the married woman. Or the race-ambiguous Black woman with the wavy hair is somehow greater than the darker sister with the short natural.

SUSAN TAYLOR: Not enough men see the beauty in their own race. They don't. It's a European lens they continue to look through. What I would say to our sisters [having a hard time seeing their beauty] is, "You are so beautiful"—from those of us with ivory skin, blue eyes, and blonde hair to the sistas who are black as night with Nubian features. We have to own all of that.

Arguably, more than any other person, Susan Taylor has given Black women a sense of pride in their beauty. She helmed Essence *magazine from 1981 to 2000. The magazine championed all aspects of Black women—their intelligence, their talent, and their beauty.* Essence *has always highlighted the diversity of their beauty.*

*   *   *

Black women making it happen are everywhere. Look around and you'll see women of color, including Congresswoman Maxine Waters, senator and presidential candidate Kamala Harris, and Atlanta mayor Keisha Lance Bottoms, who are changing politics. Starbucks COO Rosalind Brewer, VEON CEO Ursula Burns, and Endeavor CMO Bozoma Saint John are all power players in business—and proud Black women. Director Ava DuVernay, singer Rihanna, and executive producer Shonda Rhimes are unapologetically Black bosses in the entertainment industry. Kimberly Bryant, founder of Black Girls CODE, is helping to usher a new generation of young women of color into the world of STEM. Misty Copeland has danced her way onto the biggest ballet stages in the world. These are all examples of the talented, powerful, and influential Black women who are taking their places at the top of many fields and disciplines.

And yet, with all of these female practitioners changing the world, not all African American women are thriving. The number of Black women in the criminal justice system, much like the number of Black men, is larger than most people realize. A 2017 report by the World Prison Brief states that the highest female prison population rates (in the world) are in the United States, and Black women are disproportionately represented in that number. The NAACP's Criminal Justice Fact Sheet notes that the imprisonment rate of African American women is twice that of White women. According to the Sentencing Project, a Washington, DC–based research and advocacy center, created in part to address racial disparities in the criminal justice system, there are eight times as many Black women incarcerated today as there were in

1980. Girls of color are much more likely to be incarcerated than White girls. On the plus side, the Sentencing Project's numbers show that the rate of imprisonment for African American women has been declining since 2000. Between 2000 and 2016, the rate of imprisonment in state and federal prisons declined by 53 percent for Black women.

Still, African American girls are three and a half times as likely to be incarcerated as White girls. The ripple effect on the families of these incarcerated women can be devastating. The Vera Institute of Justice, an independent nonprofit national research and policy organization, reports that nearly 80 percent of women in jail are mothers, and most of them are single mothers or the primary breadwinners for their families. Kids with parents behind bars are six times more likely to enter the criminal justice system themselves, and the numbers are worse for children of incarcerated mothers. There are three *P*s—prison, pregnancy, and poverty—that often keep these women from fulfilling another *P*: promise.

The spiral they find themselves in often afflicts them for years and their families for generations. Iyanla Vanzant told me, "We keep losing those young girls because no one is telling them to look inside. They are trying to find their magic on the outside and not turning within. They are ending up being disciplined in school, discharged from school. They are in these gangs; they are turning to all levels of violence. Because they think their magic is external, not internal." Therefore, we must continue to loudly applaud those Black women who are making history and breaking down barriers.

I am someone who was raised by a strong, independent, fierce Black mother; someone who is married to an intelligent, beautiful, fly brown-skinned Black woman; and someone who raised a daughter who has now taken on the world with a Beyoncé-type confidence that generations of women before her didn't or couldn't have. And while I understand the lack of appreciation or acknowledgment that Black women on the whole may feel from Black men, I've seen up close the magic of my Black sisters.

STARTING YOUR OWN CONVERSATION

- What does "Black girl magic" mean to you?

- How have the Black women in your community empowered themselves in recent decades?

- What unique burdens do Black women face that other women and Black men don't?

- How can Black men better support and empower Black women?

- How can older Black women provide effective mentorship for the next generation? What resources do these young girls need to succeed?

9

"A MIND IS A TERRIBLE THING TO WASTE"

CORRECTING OUR MISEDUCATION

STACEY ABRAMS Politician & Author

MARILYN BOOKER Corporate Executive at Morgan Stanley

JITU BROWN National Director of the Journey for Justice Alliance

TARANA BURKE Founder of #MeToo

BRITTNEY COOPER Academic & Author

JAMES CRAIG Police Chief of Detroit

D. L. HUGHLEY Comedian & Author

VAN JONES Commentator & Author

KILLER MIKE Rapper & Activist

MALCOLM D. LEE Film Director & Screenwriter

TRACY MAITLAND President & CEO of Advent Capital Management

JULIANNE MALVEAUX Economist & Author

DeRAY MCKESSON Social Activist

BRITTANY PACKNETT Vice President of Teach for America

STEVE PERRY Founder of Capital Preparatory Schools

BAKARI SELLERS Attorney & Political Commentator

MICHAEL STEELE Former Chair of the Republican National Committee

SUSAN TAYLOR Former Publisher of *Essence* Magazine & Founder of the National Cares Mentoring Movement

T.I. Rapper & Activist

MAXINE WATERS US Representative from California

Nelson Mandela said, "Education is the most powerful weapon which you can use to change the world." Colonizers understood that knowledge was—is—power and that if they could keep the enslaved ignorant and illiterate, it was easier to keep them in bondage. Postslavery, barring newly freed Blacks from education made it easier to pass laws that hoodwinked African Americans back into servitude and kept generations undereducated. In 1954, the landmark Supreme Court case *Brown v. Board of Education* declared that an unequal education was unjust and mandated that equal opportunity and equal caliber educational facilities be available to all Americans. Generations of African Americans told each other to "get your education" because "they can't take that away from you." But the ability to access a good education is still critically uneven nationwide and tremendously difficult for many people of color. Those who have the most resources are given the advantage. And in spite of the Supreme Court's order to desegregate "with all deliberate speed," we are still far from reaching educational equality.

The economics of education is a way of dividing the haves and the have-nots, and it is often a de facto way of keeping the races educationally separated. White flight and redlining caused shrinking tax bases for many areas that left once-thriving school systems strapped for money and floundering. Other regions that had been neglected prior to *Brown v. Board of Education* never even received the resources that they were promised and are still missing them to this day. Misguided spending of allocated funds has been another long-standing problem. All of these and more have created a substandard educational system for generations of African American students. Many believe that our schools have become little more than day care centers for children of color.

HOW HAVE BLACK AMERICANS BEEN AFFECTED BY A LACK OF EDUCATIONAL ACCESS AND OPPORTUNITY?

D. L. Hughley: Never in America's history have Black people been afforded a decent education. Everything we got was what they gave us. We got the schools they weren't using, the books they weren't using anymore. If you want to be fair, let my children have a decent and fair education, with qualified teachers and resources.

MARILYN BOOKER: Education is the ultimate equalizer. It doesn't matter what your socioeconomic status is. If you've got education, you have power. Struggling households, you've got the single parent trying to support their children on their own—how can they use the educational system to better their lives? It may be too late for the parents, but what about their kids? They can help their kids become better educated and then, [those kids] can reach back and help their mom, and help the single dad for that matter, who can reach back and help other family members.

> *Education is the ultimate equalizer. It doesn't matter what your socioeconomic status is. If you've got education, you have power.*

MAXINE WATERS: I really don't want to sound trite, but education has to be a number one priority. We've got to pay attention to what's happening in elementary and preschool, up to high school, through college. We've got to take responsibility for our children being educated, and the whole community has to take responsibility for the school boards—how they operate—and we have to elect people to the school boards who make the right decisions. We have to set aside monies in our own families to ensure that we can help support our children through school. Education has to be *the* number one priority. You've got to go to the school board meetings; you can't be anonymous in this fight.

KILLER MIKE: We know public schools turned into day care centers [are] not working. We are not teaching our children what we should be. When I was in the tenth grade, Dr. Asa Hillard of Clark University was able to put as a part of our syllabus the study of Egypt—the cradle of civilization, the cradle of the world—and those people looked like us. That knowledge radically changed my life, for the rest of my life. Why is that not a part of not just Black schools but White schools? If we keep letting government just be government, we're going to get products of what government gives. And government gives us dumb White and Black people. It's not just abusing us; it's abusing everyone. We can't keep letting local politics be the least of our focus and the romance and lure of national politics be our big focus; if we do, we're going to keep losing.

JULIANNE MALVEAUX: The fact is schools have become community centers; when schools are feeding your child, providing after-school care, and doing all that, that's sometimes a burden on the teachers. We have to talk about what is our responsibility to young people, from kindergarten to college and beyond—with prison not being an option, with detention not being an option, with police interference not being an option. We need to begin to talk to some of the folks who are on the ground delivering services. It's really easy to talk about educational theory. It's simple to say this is what ought to happen. It's far more difficult to talk about educational delivery. A lot of people, including myself, who are talking about theory have not been engaged in the K–12 delivery. I say K–12 delivery because if you didn't do K–12 successfully, college is going to be a huge obstacle.

DERAY MCKESSON: I get people's philosophical stances, but I don't think that will be the fulcrum by which we decide what the best educational outcome is. I am worried that the achievement outcome for kids remains so low; when you look at standardized test scores in Baltimore, it's around less than 20 percent achievement in math and reading. Either you believe that kids are dumb, or you accept that there are a whole lot of things that adults did that failed these young people. One of the superintendents in Baltimore used to always say, "No superintendent ever lost their job because kids don't learn." That's the truest statement I can think of about the state of public education. Superintendents get fired because of cheating scandals, because people didn't get paid, or because someone stole textbooks. They don't get fired because one in five students can read.

DeRay Mckesson is a former educator who worked in administration in both public and alternative systems in a number of cities, including Baltimore and Minneapolis.

JULIANNE MALVEAUX: The education system is so broken. If I were a mayor for a day, I would just burn all the schools down and start over because literally you're replicating segregation patterns. Often you're replicating racial patterns; you're replicating the worst of what the public school system is. My cynical self says, "The Blacker and browner our country gets, the less the 1 percent care about the rest of us." And poor White people are taking it on the chin as well. And when we look at education, the browner and Blacker it gets, the more folks are like, "I don't care about them."

T.I.: In the public school system, there are substandard curriculums and the people who come up with the curriculum, the people who make the standard for what is and is not to be taught, are the same people who look to hold us back and who look to sabotage any significant progress that would allow us to become a self-sustaining ecosystem within our own community. If their agenda is to discredit or dismantle anything that could bring about the best-case scenario for us and our people, why would we allow them to teach our children? Why would we expect them to offer our children the necessary tools and the proper information that would position them to do exactly what they're working tirelessly to make sure that we can't do? And our response to that, more times than not, is to stand up in groups and say, "Hey, that's not fair! Stop doing us like that! Stop holding us down!"

BRITTANY PACKNETT: Yeah, look at the kind of work that various organizations and underhanded entities are doing to try to dismantle affirmative action in higher education and in particular the way they are trying to make affirmative action a wedge issue between various groups of color. That said, I think it's an opportunity to decolonize education. I have seen so many creative educators in public school settings and [other settings] decide to create the kind of curriculums that work for our students and pedagogy to make that happen. I am worried about what is happening to us, but I am hopeful about what we are doing inside of our own spaces. There are so many ways in which Black academics found new faith. A lot of Black women are leading the charge in that space and creating space for others. When we look at the work of Professor Melissa Harris-Perry, she's creating opportunities for young Black undergrads with her position, and Brittney Cooper is doing similar work. If we don't continue to fight to have access to the spaces to which we belonged for quite some time, then we won't always have them. The access is not guaranteed. We have to maintain, and we need to expand that base over each generation.

VAN JONES: What's our strategy for getting the top fifty or one hundred Black students into MIT, where they can be on the ground for the next round of innovation and technology and entrepreneurship? I don't know if anybody has that strategy. That's not to say we shouldn't try to save all of our historically Black colleges and universities, but it is to say, we fight to get our kids into these schools. Once they get accepted, you got the video. Everybody is jumping up and down. Well, two years later, what is the kid doing? Is there some strategy to continue to support that kid's development? I hear people say, "Well, Black kids don't know anything about coding computers. Black kids don't know anything about CRISPR technology or gene editing." Well, 90 percent of White kids don't, either. So that means that there's an opportunity for us as a community to focus on trying not to get in the back of the line for the last century's jobs. There's an opportunity for us to get in the front of the line for the new century's cutting-edge jobs. It will probably pay off greater for us to focus on that.

What's our strategy for getting the top fifty or one hundred Black students into MIT, where they can be on the ground for the next round of innovation and technology and entrepreneurship?

*   *   *

I am a product of the Detroit public school system; both of my parents taught in that system. That system, and others like it, gave many children of color a solid academic foundation. The dedication of the teachers in those classrooms was unquestionable. Many of that generation's teachers instilled in us a sense of pride and determination. But those days are gone in most large public school systems. I don't say that with nostalgia; I say that with biting anger. All children deserve a fair chance at life, a real shot at gaining the tools that will allow them to live comfortably.

The altruism of teaching the next generation has often been challenged by greed. Education has become a big business, and the cost of that business is being paid by students trapped in a broken system. Ill-equipped students regularly end up being funneled into the prison system. Like education, prisons are fighting for dollars or profits. State and federally run institutions want to hold on to every dollar in their budgets because more and more of these institutions are privatized and run for profit. However, the more schools become social promotion factories, the greater chance many of these students will fall behind and even end up in jail. America has the largest prison population in the world, housing 1.5 million people in 2016. From 2000 to 2016, people housed in private prisons increased five times faster than the total prison population. The easiest—and fastest—way to get this number down is to improve our community's access to education, for the young and the old.

IS THERE A FINANCIAL INCENTIVE TO KEEP BLACK SCHOOLS, OR SCHOOLS WITH A PREDOMINANTLY BLACK STUDENT BODY, SUBSTANDARD?

JITU BROWN: Let's use Detroit as an example. In the late 1990s and the early 2000s, Detroit had created an African-centered curriculum called the Four Corners Initiative that was actually improving education in Detroit. The school board ran with a surplus. Privatizers invented an education crisis, and they took over the school district. Betsy DeVos, our current federal education secretary, was behind much of that. Detroit was moving to the middle of the pack. Now, I'm not satisfied with middle of the pack, but I can see my way to the top [from there]. Eighteen years after the state takeover, Detroit is [now] at the bottom of public education.

STEVE PERRY: Kids are not learning, man. I swear to God, they're not learning. It's making them act out really badly. When you don't think you have any hope for a future, you don't ever try.

On a macro level, we have to get out of the long-term abusive relationship that we have with the apartheid school system that we call public education. It has destroyed us. It has robbed us of our culture. It has robbed us of our sense of self. It has made [us] bad at subjects such as math, reading, and writing. We have to break up with it. It ain't never going to do right [by us]. Many millions and millions of parents will awaken their children to another Monday in which they know that, at the end of the day, they're going to ask the child, "What did you learn?" and their child will say, "Nothing," and [their child] will be right. We are in trouble. There are millions of Black children who are languishing in failed schools, who cannot read at all. Ninety-nine percent of the sixth graders that [our school, Capital Preparatory] took in can't do math at grade level. Ninety-four percent can't read at grade level. We have crossed over into a place of darkness.

Susan Taylor: They can't read, Ed. They can't read! We can teach our kids how to read. We can teach our kids how to write. We can help them with college applications. That's what the Divine Nine should be doing, you know. We're not gonna be changing public education. There's no way they are gonna allow that. We need to convince ministers to open the sanctuary after school so our children can come and learn from the elders. I believe that we should have Saturday schools, like other races do, so we can learn our history, learn our culture, learn what sustained our people. We don't know our history. We don't know what we've been through or what our arrival cost. That's why Saturday schools are important. That's why those retired teachers have to come into those schools and help our kids with math and reading.

Steve Perry: If just 50 percent of the Black churches in any Black community would decide to do one thing for one calendar year, just to address that as an issue, I believe the issue would go away. By year's end, it would not be known in the same frame.

There are people who are in fraternities and sororities who would argue that they do quite a bit. They pay their $400 to be a Que or a Delta or a Sigma or whatever it is. Then they do a scholarship dinner. But I'm optimistic. The people that I travel among who are Black, who are in positions, we want our kids to do better.

JITU BROWN: America knows how to educate children. It's not about a broken system; the system is doing exactly what it's intended to do. We have to change the direction of the ship. It ain't about abandoning the ship. If you take my property tax to fund schools, then I'm going to benefit from it. So I believe as long as we pay taxes, it makes good sense to organize ourselves to make sure the institutions function a certain way.

Financial hardships are often the biggest hindrance for minority students earning a degree. The United Negro College Fund reports among students enrolled in four-year public institutions, 45.9 percent of Black students complete their degrees in six years—the lowest rate compared to other races and ethnicities.

---

*   *   *

Another issue with Black student achievement is the extra stress carried by people of color. External social factors are rarely accounted for when evaluating the academic performance of young people of color. Poverty, violence, lack of resources—these and other burdens can be the difference between success and failure for many students.

HOW MANY CHILDREN IN OUR COMMUNITY ARE AFFECTED BY THIS LACK OF RESOURCES?

JAMES CRAIG: I went to an event where the assistant superintendent of Detroit public schools was speaking to a group of three hundred young women, all high school age, from five different high schools across the city of Detroit. She did something that was remarkable. She said, "How many of you are living in a one-parent household?" I would say 80 percent of the room stood. "How many of you have a parent who is an alcoholic?" More people stood. "How many of you have a parent who is incarcerated?" More stood up. Before you knew it, the entire room was standing. That's why we have to look at [the lack of] opportunities and poverty as reasons [for our young people's poor academic performance].

*   *   *

A 2019 *New York Times* article explored the shrinking number of Black and brown students who enter the city's elite schools by passing admissions tests. There are numerous reasons for the decline, but one of the largest is the inability of some to pay for preparation testing. For years, the goal of many low-income and gifted students was to try to enter academically elite schools. But many of those students of color at the top of the educational food chain find their academic pursuits more difficult than most. Prep for these standardized tests is a big business and is costly for the families. In some cases, the most basic prep testing session can cost $1,000 or more. This gives a decided advantage to the student whose family can afford to pay for the test-prep tools. Other issues for many students of color in elite academic surroundings are alienation and prejudice. These pressures, coupled with the inherent stress of heavy workloads and highly competitive school environments, add to the anxiety and angst following a student's matriculation.

WHAT DO YOU THINK IS HOLDING BLACK STUDENTS BACK?

VAN JONES: Yeah, I went to Yale. I didn't make good use of that campus. I was so busy just trying to figure out who I was and defend myself from what felt like an overwhelming amount of racism. I was just happy to walk off campus with a degree.

MALCOLM D. LEE: It's especially difficult if you're a kid that goes to these prep schools where they talk the king's English, so to speak. Then there's your peers in the neighborhood: "Oh, you a White boy, you trying to be White, you Oreo!"

BRITTNEY COOPER: I didn't go to prep school. I was just a gifted and talented kid in a predominantly White school, and Black kids said I was acting White. I think parents and other adults who are close to those [gifted

Black] children have to remind them there are many ways to be Black, and that's what our ancestors fought for—the right to show up in your Blackness however you choose. There is an old standing idea that when Black folk become educated, they all of a sudden think they are better than everyone or they are qualified to lead. For those who stake their identity on getting their degrees, they should be mindful of an inflated sense of ego.

VAN JONES: It is a symptom of a deeper problem of helplessness— economically and politically. I have a law degree, and a lot of African Americans I know have law degrees and, frankly, multiple degrees. We're made to feel insecure, and that's why we will sometimes "overcredentialize" and go get multiple degrees.

BRITTNEY COOPER: Most of our history, getting an education hasn't meant you were inherently more worthy or intelligent—it simply meant you were the beneficiary of opportunities that many of our folks didn't get. We also have to think of what the jealousy and insecurity are all about.

MICHAEL STEELE: When I was reviewing our education system as lieutenant governor in Ohio, I had conversations with Black parents who were actually jealous of their own child and resentful that their child was getting the education that they didn't get. We've got all these systemic issues inside our own homes that we need to begin to get our hands and our hearts around and be woke about before we go out into the world.

BRITTNEY COOPER: We are giving kids a contradictory message. We tell them their whole life, "Go to school. Get your education. Make something of yourself." As soon as they do that, we say, "Don't think you're better than anybody! Just because you're educated doesn't mean that you know more than us." I had a relative say to me, "I am so happy you turned out *so Black* because you seemed to really want to be White when you were a kid." I told her that wasn't the case and the Black kids made my childhood really hard because I had dreams bigger than the small town that we were from. But I don't blame [those other kids] for that. I blame the social structure that pitted us against each other and told us that one of us got to be great and everyone else got to be mediocre. It's all because of the fundamental lie of Black exceptionalism, which [says that] because you have managed great achievement, you are somebody special. If we're honest, we know a lot of our folks are talented, but few of our folks have access. I was one of the few who was lucky and/or blessed to make it this far; my responsibility is to bring my folks along and to always deal with them with dignity and care, even when, in many cases, they didn't deal with me in that way.

*   *   *

America spends more money on education than any nation in the world. According to the Organisation for Economic Cooperation and Development, in 2014, the United States spent an average of $16,268 a year to educate a student. The global average is $10,759. The annual US federal budget for education is over a hundred billion dollars.

WHERE DOES ALL THE MONEY GO?

JITU BROWN: Tons of money has been poured into the system, but if we don't control it, then that money can be allocated toward things that are not good for our people. For example, millions of dollars have been plugged into safety in schools. But not to get more school counselors, not to see that every child has early childhood education, [instead] to create a police state in many Black and private schools. So schools have more police than they do counselors. More money spent for metal detectors than supervised home visits.

STEVE PERRY: Ninety-one cents of every dollar in some school systems are going to salaries and benefits! Do the math on that. From the budget, there still are buildings to pay for, furniture to buy, and books to purchase. So if these schools don't come up with upwards of $35 million by the end of the year, they'll go belly-up. Taxpayers gave them money—you gave them the money—and your kids still can't read!

JITU BROWN: You can pump $10 million into a school, but you're pumping $10 million into a school within a framework that sees us as "less than." We can create our independent institutions, but they can't starve public schools because most of our children go to public schools. If we don't control the institutions, then the schools are run based on the value systems of White supremacy.

In 2019, Oprah Winfrey donated $13 million to Morehouse College. This became the single largest endowment in the school's history and continues a scholarship program started in 1989. The scholarships have assisted in funding almost six hundred scholars. In total Winfrey has given $25 million to the school.

*   *   *

Historically Black colleges and universities (HBCUs) were established when the law prohibited Blacks from attending the vast majority of White higher education institutions. Most HBCUs were established in the South after the Civil War, largely because almost all southern schools of higher learning prohibited Blacks from attending. In 1862, the federal government passed the Morrill Land-Grant Acts, which provided states with grants of land in order to finance the establishment of colleges specializing in agriculture and the mechanical arts; however, Black students were excluded from many of them. Congress would then pass the Agricultural College Act of 1890, requiring states to establish separate land-grant colleges for Blacks if Blacks were being excluded from the existing ones. These land-grant schools continue to receive annual federal funding, and there is no denying the momentous impact these institutions have had on educating and training Black Americans and nurturing Black talent and creativity. In fact, according to the United Negro College Fund, 70 percent of Black doctors and dentists, half of all Black engineers, and 35 percent of Black attorneys are HBCU graduates.

However, as segregation faded and other institutions opened their doors to Black students, many began to choose White schools. Slightly more than 100 HBCUs still exist today, down from 121 in the 1930s, and most have struggled to remain fiscally viable—particularly over the last quarter century.

In 2009, President Obama did not move to renew the $85 million earmarked for HBCUs by the previous Republican administration. The Obama administration chose instead to put more money into general grant programs, allocating more federal money to more schools across the board, including HBCUs. According to the Thurgood Marshall College Fund, which lobbies for Black colleges and supports students with scholarships, HBCUs received, on average, 3.5 percent of federal money going to institutions from 2000 to 2008; however, by 2013, HBCUs' percentage was down to 2.8 percent. A year later, the Obama administration restored the $85 million for HBCUs, and the money for HBCUs continued to go up. During Obama's eight years in office, overall federal funding for the nation's HBCUs rose to more than $4 billion.

Naysayers claim that these funds did not compensate for the damage done by other federal policy changes, including those that made getting certain loans more difficult, causing many students to default. The Obama administration would later move to ease these restrictions so that most of the students affected would be able to regain the money; however, some were still unable to retrieve their funds, and others remained unaware that the restrictions had been eased at all. The Obama years were fraught with these educational back-and-forths with HBCUs. After announcing his plan to make community colleges free to qualifying students, Obama received complaints from many HBCU leaders who understood that it would impact their schools' enrollments greatly, and he was forced to scale that proposal back.

Certainly no one believed that Trump's administration would prove itself to be more beneficial to HBCUs than Obama's had been. Even so, HBCUs have tried to establish bridges with the current administration since Trump entered office. The United Negro College Fund sent Trump a memo titled "Ten Ways to Invest in Historically Black Colleges and Universities." Among many other suggestions and ideas, the memo included a request to both protect and increase the amount of funding for Pell grants—federal aid that a majority of HBCU students rely on to be able to pay for their higher education. Unsurprisingly, most of UNCF's requests have gone unaddressed by

Trump. Still, there has been some debate as to whether Trump has appropriated more money for HBCUs than any other president. Trump signed a $1.1 trillion government spending bill that included funding for a twenty-five-year-old federal program for HBCUs, which would finance construction projects on their campuses. However, after signing the bill into law, he immediately backtracked and questioned the funding for such schools, saying it might be unconstitutional to allocate money to schools that cater to a specific race. Though HBCUs are historically Black, they serve a much more diverse student body today and look to provide education to all races and ethnicities. Following Trump's public retreat, the federal education secretary announced that Howard University was going to receive "heightened cash monitoring" and would no longer be given millions of dollars in advance to award to students in need of financial aid. Instead, the school will have to first give its scholarships to the students and then seek reimbursement from the federal government. Many voiced concerns that this was just a way to dismantle pillars that keep HBCUs solvent and economically feasible. Moreover, there is growing concern that this move might signal the beginning of the end for HBCUs altogether.

WHAT ARE THE UPHILL CHALLENGES THAT HBCUS FACE? AND HOW CAN WE HELP SUPPORT THEM?

MICHAEL STEELE: Look at the fight to get the funding and resources for HBCUs under the Obama administration. A lot of people scream about what Republicans didn't do. Well, George Bush put a hell of a lot of money into HBCUs and brought a number of them to the table that weren't at that table before. The expectation, of course, when Obama got elected was that you would see a greater sense of support and response to the needs of these institutions. That was not necessarily the case. Certainly not at all times.

BAKARI SELLERS: I had a big concern with Obama's lack of understanding of the necessity and the prominence of HBCUs in our community.

JULIANNE MALVEAUX: There are a handful of HBCUs that are financially secure and have robust endowments. The smaller ones are in financially precarious positions because their endowments are small, and that's from a legacy of historical racism. Their endowments are small, and their challenges are large. The higher education tableau is so very different now than it was fifty years ago. The best Black students have the opportunity to go anywhere, and if they don't have the financial aid award they could get at a predominantly White institution (PWI), unless they are completely Afrocentric focused, why would they go to an HBCU? The students who don't get the best awards from PWIs come needing scholarships. And that means we need endowments and Black people to invest in HBCUs. That doesn't always happen, so we end[ed] up with a situation where, [when I was president of Bennett College], I found myself often pushed to the corner where, do I ask this young person who is very promising to leave because she has a bill, or do we invest in carrying her debt? You can't do that because the creditors look at the debt you're carrying as a ding on you. A lot of our students come in need of financial aid. We give them what we can. They take out loans and owe the college. It's an untenable long-term situation.

We need endowments and Black people to invest in HBCUs.

Julianne Malveaux was the president of Bennett College from 2007 to 2012. She understands better than most the financially precarious space many of these schools find themselves in. In her years at Bennett, she experienced the ups and downs during the Obama administration. In a 2009 newspaper editorial, she asked, "Why is it that a recalcitrant Bush would do more for HBCUs than an ostensibly sympathetic Obama would?" As she was leaving her position at the college, she wrote praising the president's efforts: "External forces work against HBCUs. President Obama has been great in managing to keep the Pell grant level, but it needs to be larger."

---

*   *   *

Billionaire businessman Robert Smith's generous gift of paying the debt of Morehouse College's class of 2019 raised national awareness of the rising student debt issues faced by many students of color. Too many of these students struggle just to find money to finish a single semester, let alone the funds it takes to graduate. Smith's magnanimous gesture took a load off the shoulders of this group of graduates; some members of the class—nearly four hundred students—would have been individually burdened with hundreds of thousands of dollars of debt upon leaving the graduation stage. The only requirement Smith had of the recipients is that they pay his kindness forward.

WHAT DO WE OWE BLACK STUDENTS? HOW CAN WE GIVE BACK?

MAXINE WATERS: Look at the impact Robert Smith had. All [of us] in the African American community must get in the habit of giving. It doesn't mean you have to be rich, but it does mean that you've got to care about your alma mater. You have to care about your church. You have to care about your civil rights organization. [Even] if you do nothing but donate ten dollars a month.

ED GORDON: Tracy, like Robert Smith, you're one of the wealthiest people in America, and as the Bible says, "To whom much is given, much is required."

TRACY MAITLAND: It's tough, because when we give, then we get bombarded with a thousand different requests. I can't tell you how many [requests] I get almost every week. It's tough; you can't help everyone. You want to help, but there are so few Robert Smiths who are Black. There are so few of us—we get inundated. We don't have enough people who have [financially] knocked the ball out of the park. There are other ways to assist. You don't have to be a millionaire. Think about parents or maybe a single-[parent] household barely making ends meet, having no time to talk to their kids about careers, or even knowing much about other careers. That's where to fill a void. People should go by their local public school and talk about their jobs; you might change a couple of kids' minds there. Just having those conversations is helpful. If you don't have that much money, just do that.

ED GORDON: Because of the long history of good these schools have provided to the Black community, many find it hard to be critical of these institutions. Some schools have to work with "wing and a prayer" budgets. Others have faced accreditation issues, and some colleges are charged with lack of administrative competency and professionalism. In addition to financial concerns, what other challenges do Black schools face today?

STEVE PERRY: Listen, there are HBCUs right now that have a graduation rate that's under 12 percent! That's not okay. We can talk about the fact that they were dealt a bad hand by getting students from some of the lowest-performing schools on the continent. We can talk about [how these schools] have alums who may not necessarily make as much money as alums at other schools because of pay disparities between African Americans and Whites. We can talk about the fact that these schools, too often, are run like churches, straight up. I went to a school, [and] there was a brother who was there. I asked him what he did. He said, "I'm the president's driver." The president of what? Where do y'all go? The school ain't but ten acres.

ED GORDON: Some people will say Steve is being too hard on these schools. They will argue that these schools should be able to have the perks that White universities have and that we shouldn't chastise them publicly.

TARANA BURKE: We should hold HBCUs accountable for the quality of education that they're giving our young people, for the type of analysis that they graduate with. That's something that we should be talking about and not just the quality of education but the quality of service. There shouldn't be just a running joke that "Oh, HBCUs ain't doing this, that, and the third." This is about resources and a way of thinking that we've settled into. We have to have more conversations about accountability.

STACEY ABRAMS: I came into political awareness by critiquing my college at Spelman [laughs], so I'm very comfortable with the critique of the HBCU. I think that part of the obligation of critique is not simply to identify flaws but to offer change, opportunity, and solution. Critiques shouldn't be done only to diminish. Some institutions are so essential to how we see ourselves, how we understand our progress—it may be very hard to hear. I don't believe it means you don't do it. We just have to learn how to do it in a way that lets people hear it.

BRITTNEY COOPER: I am an HBCU alum; I went to Howard. I like to tell people, "You can't come to my house and talk shit about Howard. I will put you out." [laughs] But that doesn't mean that I don't have some critiques about my own institution and other HBCUs. The challenge is that I want the critique to be valid. My challenge with folks is when they critique Black colleges because they automatically think White institutions are superior. But if you understand that these institutions can train and produce excellence in the exact same way as their White counterparts can, then the critique comes from a place of "You're not living up to your capacity," and that, I support.

*   *   *

Former secretary of state and Stanford professor Condoleezza Rice once told me that you can often predict the academic success of students based on their zip code. Too many of our children are predisposed to academic failure through no fault of their own. Some of our young people must deal with the conditions of poverty and underserved neighborhoods; their schools are using outdated books and materials. Underachieving peers exert pressure on other students not to study. In some environments, the stigma of being educated is real. As an example, a national sports columnist shared a story with me of an NBA superstar who would hide the books he was reading to avoid ribbing from his peers. This was a multimillionaire! Imagine what a teenager in the 'hood striving for education must be feeling at times.

Education has been one of the greatest tools for African Americans' climb to success. Our greatest advancements as a people have always been grounded in education and faith. During the early days of Reconstruction, the Freedmen's Bureau, a government agency established after the Civil War, was tasked with issuing provisions for freed slaves in the South. The bureau opened one thousand schools for Black children in the South, and that changed the game. Education for the masses allowed us to have more control over our circumstances without relying on others to dictate the direction of our lives.

We've pretended that education is important and money has been poured into educational programs, but the reality is many of those programs were ill-suited to solve the problems. The best and the brightest people of color often moved away from Black neighborhoods to ones that had better educational resources. Cries to improve conditions in schools they left were muted.

Moreover, we've turned a blind eye to these students trapped in dysfunctional schools. During our conversation, Julianne Malveaux called for a total overhaul: "We have to completely retool the education model. We have some Black people who are superintendents who are leading charter schools, who are doing other things that are amazing, fantastic, and innovative." We can do a lot more good once we're in the right places. And, by *all* means, let's support Black colleges, Black scholarships, and students however we can. The more that we can lift up the generation that follows us, the better off we all become.

STARTING YOUR OWN CONVERSATION

- What obstacles do Black schools face that other schools don't?

- What policies could we implement on a local, state, or national level that would help Black schools tackle some of these obstacles?

- What are HBCUs able to provide for students of color that other institutions may be unwilling or unable to offer? What are the advantages and disadvantages of attending a historically Black college or university?

- Is it fair to criticize underperforming Black schools for their shortcomings? Why or why not?

- What are some ways you can help mentor and guide the next generation in their quest for education?

"MO' MONEY, MO' PROBLEMS?"

10

THE ECONOMICS OF BEING BLACK AND BUYING BLACK

WILLIAM BARBER	Minister & Activist
MARILYN BOOKER	Corporate Executive at Morgan Stanley
CHARLAMAGNE THA GOD	Radio Personality & Author
RICHELIEU DENNIS	Founder & Chair of Essence Ventures
BUTCH GRAVES	President & CEO of Earl Graves Publishing
DERRICK JOHNSON	President & CEO of the NAACP
VAN JONES	Commentator & Author
KILLER MIKE	Rapper & Activist
TRACY MAITLAND	President & CEO of Advent Capital Management
JULIANNE MALVEAUX	Economist & Author
MARC MORIAL	President & CEO of the National Urban League
SUSAN TAYLOR	Former Publisher of *Essence* Magazine & Founder of the National Cares Mentoring Movement
T.I.	Rapper & Activist
MAXINE WATERS	US Representative from California

In 2019, rapper and businessman Jay-Z joined the list of Black billionaires. This elite club also includes media mogul Oprah Winfrey; former basketball great turned businessman Michael Jordan; and David Steward, majority owner of World Wide Technology. Nigerian business magnate Aliko Dangote is the richest Black person in the world. His estimated fortune of nearly $11 billion was built with businesses in the sugar, cement, and flour industries. Nigerian billionaire Mike Adenuga is close behind him with an estimated fortune of $9 billion, largely from telecom and oil production.

By comparison, the richest person—of any color—in the world is Amazon's Jeff Bezos. His wealth is estimated at $110 billion, followed by Microsoft founder Bill Gates ($96.5 billion) and Berkshire Hathaway chair and CEO Warren Buffett ($82.5 billion). Even at this level, the huge financial gulf between Blacks and Whites is astonishing. This gap continues down every rung of the socioeconomic ladder, as Blacks lag behind Whites in every single category of wealth. And it's not just between billionaires. According to the Institute for Policy Study, the median wealth of White families is forty-one times the median wealth of Black families. In 2016 (the latest numbers as of this writing), the percentage of White families with zero wealth, where debts exceed assets, was 15.5 percent compared to 37 percent of Black families. Unemployment overall in America is down, according to the federal Bureau of Labor Statistics, yet Black unemployment is still double that of their White neighbors. As we discussed in an earlier chapter, Black women have made great strides in higher education, but they must pay an exorbitant price. The American Association of University Women notes that Black women graduate with the most debt of any group of grads—$30,400 on average—compared to $22,000 for White women and $19,500 for White men. Although people of color have made significant advancements since the 1960s, the road to wealth remains elusive.

HAVE BLACK AMERICANS MADE ECONOMIC PROGRESS OVER THE PAST FEW DECADES?

JULIANNE MALVEAUX: Black folks who graduate with the same degree are within 85 percent of earnings of what their White counterparts earn.

We have made some progress for Black people at the top of the income [ladder]—significant progress, [but] not necessarily equivalent progress. For Black folks at the bottom, it's as hard as it's ever been. We have a significant portion of our population earning the minimum wage or just a little bit more than that. You even have Black women with BA degrees earning below $30,000 a year. There are amazing disparities all over. These gaps are supposed to be narrowing. They are better than they were ten years ago, but we really see almost a plateauing in terms of the income ratio. There's still clear race discrimination.

RICHELIEU DENNIS: Our communities are still not economically better off—not better today socially or structurally. And that has led to a regression in our economic standing as a broader community. Are more individuals doing better? Absolutely. In absolute numbers, are the numbers better? Yes. But, when you think about it, we're regressing from a period where there were actual laws in place to prevent us from moving forward.

Home ownership is where the bulk of Americans' wealth began. We were redlined deliberately through the laws and practices and kept out. There's a lot of work that's been done to make those things illegal and to limit their impact, but we're still lagging. In fact, we're falling behind. The common denominator must become wealth. Wealth is the thing that has built communities. It is the thing that has sustained communities. The lack of it is also the thing that leads to the decaying of those communities and the eventual subjugation of those communities.

MARC MORIAL: This is the analogy that I like to use: African Americans are the caboose on the American train. When the train speeds up, we may speed up a little bit, but we're still behind. We're still the last call on the train. When the train slows down, we are the last on the train that gets stuck in the tunnel or stuck in the worst weather. We look at a lot of numbers at the Urban League. One story is that while we have more African Americans who are middle class, perhaps more than ever before, there are also more White middle-class Americans than before. So relatively speaking, the differentials between Black and White Americans, from an economic standpoint, have not changed markedly in the last forty years. So the income gap doesn't close, the wealth gap doesn't close, the home ownership gap doesn't close, the college graduation gap doesn't close. Even if you have more African Americans with college degrees, our relative standing in the country has not markedly changed.

MARILYN BOOKER: That wealth gap can be directly tied to income and job disparities. Black males earn sixty-nine cents to every dollar of their White male counterparts. Black women earn sixty-one cents to every dollar of our White male counterparts. Relatively speaking, there are still very few Blacks in influential positions in corporate America. There are still very few Blacks on corporate boards. There are still very few Blacks who are CEOs of Fortune 500 companies. Building wealth is still a bit challenging because the same opportunities for economic security, economic prosperity, economic advancement, and paychecks are not there yet. The wealth gap cannot be closed until that economic disparity is addressed. The civil rights battle is real, and it remains real. But the most pressing battle now is that of dealing with economic inequality. I love to say, "What difference does it make if you have the right to live in any neighborhood that you choose and you can't afford the mortgage?"

> *The civil rights battle is real, and it remains real. But the most pressing battle now is that of dealing with economic inequality.*

ED GORDON: Here's what's interesting: These companies still don't see that diversity can help the be-all and end-all for their company, the bottom line.

MARILYN BOOKER: You're going to have that challenge until you have people who have an appreciation for the impact that diversity brings to the workforce. Just look at the challenges that some of these companies, like Gucci, for example, are having. People are saying, "Well, if there were people sitting around the table who all didn't look the same, who thought differently and could say, 'Well, I'm not sure this is a good idea,'" maybe the companies wouldn't be in the situations they find themselves in. You've got to have folks who have different perspectives.

*   *   *

Starting in the 1970s, there has been a slow progression of Blacks into corporate America, where the higher-end salaried jobs exist. One of the first stories I produced in the mid-'80s was about Blacks in corporate America and the obstacles they faced coming into an environment that, up until then, had been very exclusionary. Expectations were that, within a few years, Blacks would be readily accepted and have the full range of career possibilities afforded to them. Almost fifty years since that first group of African Americans joined corporate America, many Blacks still feel isolated and left behind. A small number of African Americans have made forays to the top of the corporate food chain at some of the nation's most powerful companies, including Ken Chenault, who was CEO of American Express for seventeen years. Yet the advancement of these Blacks in corporate America has mostly been an anomaly and proportionately smaller and slower than many had hoped for. More recently, there has been a decrease in the number of African Americans hired in white-collar jobs. In the tech industry, the numbers are abysmal. And for those who do find their way to jobs, it continues to be difficult. A study published in 2017 by the *Harvard Business Review* still found that "hiring discrimination against Black Americans hasn't declined in twenty-five years."

In 2018, according to the *Harvard Business Review*, the US Equal Employment Opportunity Commission's study of white-collar employment data revealed serious gaps in income, promotional opportunities, and advancement for minorities and women of all races. Similarly, analysis by the Ascend Foundation shows that White men are the most represented group in (executive) management. They are followed by Hispanic men, White women, Black men, Asian men, Hispanic women, Black women, and Asian women.

HOW HAS BLACK LEADERSHIP CHANGED IN CORPORATE AMERICA?

Butch Graves: We have fewer senior executives within corporate America today than we had decades ago; with senior management, we are at all-time low levels. While we have a few more African Americans sitting on corporate boards, corporate America itself is more diverse on its boards than senior management teams. So, from just that perspective alone, African Americans are not doing well at all. You can find the Ken Chenaults of the world, but, overall, we are well behind in corporate America, and [we] do not hold positions of authority and responsibility to be able to make inroads to change things.

Earl "Butch" Graves Jr. is CEO of Earl G. Graves Publishing Company. His father, Earl G. Graves Sr., founded Black Enterprise *magazine in 1970. The groundbreaking magazine has highlighted Blacks in business for almost fifty years. The African American Graves family has been able to pass a business and wealth on intergenerationally.*

ED GORDON: Corporations will tell you that they have made great advancements in diversity. Almost all companies have diversity and inclusion departments that were created to ensure fairness and equity in the workplace.

MAXINE WATERS: If you start a diversity office and you have no resources and you don't report to anybody who really makes a decision, then you've been used. I've seen a lot of examples of that, so I created a new congressional subcommittee on diversity and inclusion. Now we engage with corporate America, both public and private sectors, on what it means to have diversity, and what it means to have an office with resources for diversity and inclusion. We have also said we want to see measurables a year later to show a difference.

> *Part of an elevated strategy is to make sure African Americans get on the front lines of burgeoning career opportunities and growth areas of employment.*

RICHELIEU DENNIS: We are now entering a different time, and it's time for elevated strategies. Part of an elevated strategy is to make sure African Americans get on the front lines of burgeoning career opportunities and growth areas of employment. For years, people of color have been on the tail end of entering fields because of segregation or prejudice. Minorities have systematically been kept out of or discouraged from entering schools, unions, even entire fields and disciplines. By the time those fields opened to minorities, those jobs were becoming obsolete or overcrowded.

VAN JONES: I see a whole bunch of young people who consider themselves to be woke coming to college and studying the humanities or criminal justice. They want to study Black literature. I'm beginning to aggressively discourage that. A lot of African Americans I know have law degrees and, frankly, multiple degrees. But I don't see a lot of us with MBAs or PhDs in upper sciences. We've been told that education is the answer, and that's true, but honestly, entrepreneurship is really the answer. I tell people all the time, "If you want your kid to be successful, make sure they understand finance, technology, and Mandarin, because if they know those things, they'll be successful anywhere on planet Earth."

TRACY MAITLAND: People need to have exposure because if they don't, they don't know that certain opportunities exist. The only exposure many [of us] have is [to] professional athletes, entertainers, and actors. That's what they see. They don't see guys on Wall Street; they don't see the scientists who create things that could be worth a lot of money because they get the patent.

I'm a firm believer in affirmative action, because White people in general have invisible affirmative action. When it comes time for internships, people hire their brother, cousin, niece, neighbor, et cetera. Those kids have an opportunity to see a business working, [and] it gets their mind going. But, if you're a minority kid in an urban neighborhood, if you don't live in a "right" neighborhood, you're never going to have the opportunity to see what is possible.

Tracy Maitland ventured into rarefied air for African Americans as the president and CEO of Advent Capital, an investment management company that handles $10 billion in assets. He started his career at Merrill Lynch, where he saw the benefits of exposure and mentorship.

---

*   *   *

As corporate America looks less viable now for African Americans than it has in past years, entrepreneurship is becoming a more appealing option for some. Prior to Reconstruction, even through years of segregation, Blacks generally had a greater entrepreneurial spirit than Whites. Historically, generations of Blacks weren't allowed to patronize White establishments, so they started their own. Today, millennials and Gen Zs seem to be resurrecting this spirit of proprietorship. Many younger workers now see corporate jobs as fragile and unstable; unlike the baby boomer generation, their sensibilities are not to "find a good job with benefits," especially since many of these jobs no longer come with benefits. Instead, they are charting their own paths through entrepreneurship.

However, according to a 2018 issue of *Black Enterprise* magazine, 62 percent of African Americans said their desire to pursue their passion motivated them to start a business. Another 53 percent said they were ready to be their own boss. Meanwhile, 30 percent said they launched a start-up when the "opportunity presented itself," and 22 percent said they were dissatisfied with working in corporate America. Twelve percent said they launched a business after being laid off or outsourced. Whatever the reason, an overwhelming 80 percent of Black entrepreneurs surveyed said lack of capital was the most challenging aspect of running a business. In spite of strong growth in the small business sector, minority businesspeople still find it challenging to get loans. They are less likely to secure small business loans than their White counterparts, and if they do, it is usually at a higher interest rate. Loans are denied for a number of reasons, including lower net worth, poor or little credit history, poor or not optimal locations, and preconceived (and prejudicial) notions of some lenders that minorities are bad risks. The good news is, even with a minefield of deterrents in front of them, Blacks continue to forge ahead in starting their own businesses. A survey from Guidant Financial, a small business financing company, showed that, in 2018 alone, African American small business ownership rose 400 percent in a single year. The US Black Chamber of Commerce concurred, declaring, "African American business has grown at an exponential rate in the twenty-first century."

Richelieu Dennis is a key example. Born in Africa, Dennis came to America from Liberia to attend college, but due to war in his homeland, he and his mother never returned home. Dennis, his college roommate, and his mother created handmade soap from his grandmother's recipe, which included shea butter. Dennis expanded his company to produce other bath and beauty products, and Sundial Brands was born. As the creator of products like SheaMoisture and Nubian Heritage, the business became a major player in the women's personal care market. In 2015, Bain Capital purchased a majority stake in the company for an estimated $700 million. The business would later be purchased by industry giant Unilever, a consumer goods company. Dennis remains the CEO and executive chair of Sundial Brands. In 2018, *Forbes* estimated his and his mother's shares of the company to be worth $850 million. Later that year, Dennis purchased Essence Ventures, which includes the magazine and event properties.

WHAT ARE THE BIGGEST CHALLENGES FACED BY BLACK ENTREPRENEURS?

BUTCH GRAVES: Black-owned businesses have suffered by not having as great an access to capital as their White counterparts; however, the biggest hindrance to business is scale. Here's the issue: you can only get scale to the degree that a corporation will do business with you.

TRACY MAITLAND: If you're not involved with the people who are making those types of [capital] investments, [and] you don't know who they are, how do you get that access? We're a management business; we develop relationships with people, and then they invest with us. So access to capital is indirect, and direct relationships make all the difference in the world. We [people of color] are very limited in that regard. We don't have access to capital, and that is a stumbling block. You have to be trained in something that you're passionate about, do it well, demonstrate a track record of success, and then go out and raise the capital for it.

ED GORDON: There are those who believe there should be government intervention to correct the inequities. Butch, do you think that should be done, especially considering the current inhabitant of the White House?

BUTCH GRAVES: The only thing that has been consistent from [presidential] administration to administration over the years is that the opportunity for African Americans has not been as robust as it has been for everybody else. *Let me make this clear:* I'm not a supporter of the Trump administration— I'm just being candid and honest—but to suggest that Black business is worse under the Trump administration than it was when Clinton or Bush were in office would be wrong. Can you point to someone else's administration where Black-owned business boomed? My father would tell you that the best administration [of] all was the Nixon administration.

RICHELIEU DENNIS: Our mission is [to promote] economic inclusion, which leads to wealth creation. We run a community commerce model, using our business to invest back into the community that we serve. We take 10 percent, like you tithe in church. We invest in businesses so that they can build and develop in our communities, and that takes capital. When you build a business where all of the wealth goes back into the business, it's difficult to both scale that business and to have the community impact that we need to have. And that is at the core of what we do.

We've created a tremendous amount of value in this business, so we asked ourselves: How do we unlock it so that we can create wealth and scale other businesses? How can we share our abilities as entrepreneurs coming out of these communities? How do we empower those who are coming behind us?

Richelieu Dennis understands full well the pains of growing a business, and so he oversees the $100 million New Voices Fund, which invests in businesses owned by women of color.

ED GORDON: That support has to be reciprocal. Black businesses need support from the community, but that will take a dedicated commitment.

KILLER MIKE: I go to Koreatown when I am in Los Angeles, and they keep other people's dollars and their dollars in their community. We have to be comfortable being "Browntown." We have an opportunity like other communities to insulate our community through economics.

MARILYN BOOKER: I was [giving] a speech in Chicago a couple years ago, talking to primarily small business owners. I did a little research and found that *Black Enterprise* did a forty-year study about companies that were on their first BE 100 list in 1973 and how many companies still exist today. The answer: three. Of all those companies that started, only three still exist today. It's the plight of the minority business. We don't support our small Black businesses, [and] we must start [doing that]. One of the important things about the study was it showed all of these companies over the years that have tried to do the right thing, but it's a struggle for them. To transfer intergenerational wealth, to create jobs and income for people, and a road to wealth—[all that] is challenging.

BUTCH GRAVES: It is simply self-preservation. Every other culture does it. Name the ethnic group—they all do it. Indians spend with Indians. Hispanics spend with Hispanics. Jews are spending with Jews. This is not picking on any group; it's just self-preservation.

RICHELIEU DENNIS: Let me give an example. Today, you have very, very few Black-owned beauty supply stores. They are now predominantly owned and run by Koreans. You have to give [the Koreans] credit; they come into our communities, and they service our communities with staple products that we use and need. When this happens and we don't own [the services we use] in our community, then we're not generating the wealth to invest back into our churches, our schools, and our kids. [Others] come in, they do business, and they take those profits and invest it into their communities and their institutions. We need to start working toward doing the same in our neighborhoods.

Now, let's think about the costs (and what it takes) for a Korean [to do] business in our community: They need access to capital; [low] interest rates; years of entrepreneurship; a network of other family members across the cities, towns, states, and nation that [also] have beauty supply stores. The distribution models, the supply chain. Those are all things that they have built over time, that they can rely on, that makes it cheaper for them to deliver products into our communities. They can actually provide those services at a cheaper rate than those of us who live in our communities. It's just the pure economics of it.

So when a product is five bucks at the Korean store, but down the street, the Black beauty supply store is selling it for eight or ten bucks, you don't necessarily always make the calculus for what that difference is. More often than not, we will pick the same item for five dollars than we would for ten dollars. That extra five dollars is the cost of buying Black. And if we don't invest those five dollars in buying Black and helping our entrepreneurs build the same network and the same infrastructures that Korean banks in Little Korea are investing in the beauty supply industry, if we don't do the same for us, we'll lose those industries. That's how we lost ground in the beauty supply industry. We need to examine the cost of buying Black and how we go about lowering that cost.

We need to examine the cost of buying Black and how we go about lowering that cost.

A 2019 report on the state of small business commissioned by Guidant Financial and LendingClub showed African American small business owners are younger, happier, and more female led than the average of small business owners surveyed. The survey indicated a desire to "pursue my own passion" was the primary reason African American respondents went into business for themselves.

*   *   *

In Spike Lee's 1989 film, *Do the Right Thing*, he explored the complexity of culturally controlling commerce in the domain of another group and Black ownership, period. Economic self-reliance is not a novel concept. Booker

T. Washington, Marcus Garvey, and Elijah Muhammad all espoused some form of economic autonomy for African Americans. George Fraser and Tony Brown have pushed "buy Black" concepts for decades. Shopping with Black merchants, staying in Black-owned hotels, hiring Blacks would all make a significant difference if they were done en masse. We all should make a more concerted effort to keep our dollars and economic power circulating in our community longer.

In 2015, the Nielsen Company released a report that estimated the buying power of African Americans at $1.1 trillion (that figure includes credit spending), equal to that of the GDP of the sixteenth-largest country in the world. That same year, an NAACP economic specialist said that a dollar circulates in the Asian community for a month, in the Jewish community approximately twenty days, in White communities seventeen days, and in the Black community for six hours. They also suggested that for every dollar an African American spends, only two cents goes to a Black business.

This, in part, occurs because the—thankfully fading—notion of the "White man's ice being colder" leads many people of color to see any product produced by Blacks as inferior by comparison. It is time for Black America to make sure we become a more cohesive community when it comes to economic unity. It is simply doing what most other communities do: supporting their own. And the best way to do that is to practice what you preach and become more expert at the game of business—and money.

The history of Black-owned business is convoluted by the many racist obstacles designed to keep people of color from fully participating in our capitalistic system. Clearly, history shows that equal opportunity has only been theoretical. Wealth is as much of a struggle for individuals as it is for a community of business owners.

The doors of wealth are often impenetrable to those who don't have it, no matter what their ethnicity or race. The rich stay that way by keeping as much wealth as they can to themselves—redistributing their riches is not particularly high on their priority list. But staying wealthy, by any means necessary, is the American way. In this country, wealth is the closest thing to a great equalizer, so the door that leads to wealth is guarded more fiercely than any other portal. And even rich people of color understand that wealth does not necessarily erase prejudice.

I recall being in a hotel lobby with BET founder Bob Johnson, who at the time was worth over a billion dollars. One look at him would have told most people that he was not a hotel employee; however, a White couple still approached him about their luggage. As recently as 2018, Johnson was denied check-in at a luxury hotel because he refused to take off his sunglasses. Racial impediments and stereotypes are real, even for the wealthiest people of color.

And wealth is not particularly easy for people of color to attain. When you're working with a median household income of around $40,000, you'll find it difficult to grow wealth—and many Black households face exactly that problem. Wealth is often a misnomer that conjures up thoughts of beachside mansions and Bugattis. And though there are Black Americans in positions of great financial status, we have to remember that they are the exception rather than the norm.

According to a 2017 report on the website CareerBuilder, 78 percent of American workers live paycheck to paycheck. For most of them, putting aside 10 percent or 20 percent of their income is not an option, because their survival is based on every dime. However, some of them do have the wherewithal to grow a nest egg and are living paycheck to paycheck because they are choosing, as many Americans do, to live above their means.

HOW CAN BLACKS IMPROVE THEIR FINANCIAL STATUS?

Marilyn Booker: I travel all across the country and teach financial education. One of the things I say is this: "You want to work past retirement because you want to, not because you have to." Most people are working later years in life because they have no choice. Because they've been living paycheck to paycheck. The overwhelming majority of Black folks have nothing saved for retirement, and they have insufficient money saved in general. If an emergency were to happen, they [would] have to struggle to get $500 or $1,000 just to address that emergency. I tell people, "You've got to make smart decisions about your money; start planning. Take it off the top because you can't miss something you never see." Take savings and retirement off the top, before you start spending, before the cash register starts ringing up. That's the only way to get people to start getting that mind-set of saving.

We have to shift that dialogue from one of consumption to the one that's saying, "Let's get serious." We spend untold amounts of money on things like clothes and cars. The depreciating value [comes] after the sale is rung up. We need to start investing and putting our money in things that appreciate in value; then we can pass [it] along to our next generation.

> *We need to start investing and putting our money in things that appreciate in value; then we can pass [it] along to our next generation.*

Marilyn Booker is a veteran of the banking world and an executive for financial giant Morgan Stanley. She has dedicated much of her career to teaching people of color the ins and outs of wealth building.

BUTCH GRAVES: We're still underinvesting and undersaving compared to our White counterparts, regardless of income. We need to understand that the ninth wonder of the world is time and how money compounds over time. That will only happen by making a commitment and doing it. I've done it with my own kids! I had to talk with my daughter, who was making good money and who said, "Well, I can't really afford a 401(k)." "What do you mean you can't afford a 401(k)?" I asked her. "It's your money! Take your money and put it away for something, so you'll have something when the time comes."

ED GORDON: Some say that this mind-set of not being able to save was created by the fact that, for so long, we didn't have disposable income, and therefore, we haven't been able to shake the idea of forgoing consumption.

BUTCH GRAVES: I remember my father telling me that when he grew up he didn't have any clothes, literally. He said, "I had one jacket." So when he was able to, he was going to make sure he had more. I can accept that premise to a point, but that does not mean [that] now you have to have two hundred suits. We are consuming things that we don't need, and that consumption, by the way, also includes the time that is spent on television, entertainment, and movies rather than more cerebral activities that would enhance us further.

Marilyn Booker: Don't get me wrong—this is not a blanket condemnation. There are many, many, many Blacks who are doing exactly the right thing— I'm just saying, in general, you can't begin to address a challenge until you identify what it is. There's far more money in our community being spent than being saved and invested. More being spent than that's being put toward trying to build intergenerational wealth. That's the challenge that we have.

*   *   *

Black America's economic well-being is a tricky conversation. There is always the risk of offending people. Some feel it paternal that anyone would instruct them on handling money. There are those who believe that money is a taboo subject. Still others believe that these talks are usually started by "bougie" Black middle-class people trying to pass judgment on "real" Black folks.

The latter is ironic, because the truth is there are a fair number of "middle-class" Black families who are only a paycheck or two away from economic distress themselves.

Multiplying money is not easy, and for most it is not innate, even for those who have it from the start. Look at Donald Trump and the money he has lost. According to tax information first obtained by the *New York Times*, the man who often touts himself as a business "genius" lost more money than anyone in America between 1985 and 1994. Staying afloat monetarily is infinitely harder without means. The bulk of Black America has only been allowed to "share in America's wealth" fewer years than Trump has been alive. It should be no wonder that the many Black families that find themselves in the red continue to stumble in poverty, straddling the line between plus and minus. This uneasy fiscal dance is caused by systematic racism that keeps the playing field slanted against Blacks. Also, some wounds are self-inflicted.

WHAT ARE OUR BIGGEST OBSTACLES TO ACHIEVING WEALTH AS A COMMUNITY?

T.I.: Wealth is difficult for us because real wealth has never been exemplified to us. People usually learn best from experience, and our experiences have never been consistent with the experiences that are necessary to generate wealth. Therefore, it's somewhat foreign to us. What we must understand is that what we've been learning is insufficient. What we've experienced is what we have to unlearn, and [then we have to] relearn [something different]. Some of us are taught to stack money, but really most of us are taught to go to school, get a job, work, work, work until you can just get a little house, get a promotion, get a family, and so on and so forth, until you get too old to work. And then stock [is supposed] to pay you monthly, a monthly stipend that they call a 401(k) or a retirement.

MAXINE WATERS: It is not simply about going to work every day and saving 10 percent of your earnings. Everybody should have some savings, no matter what your income is, but that's never going to make you wealthy. What wealth building is all about is getting educated and learning how these systems work. We need to learn how Wall Street works and things like what mergers mean between big companies and how do you get the initial dollars to buy up housing and rehab that housing to put [those houses] back on the market at better prices, et cetera. And once we get wealthy, how do we not let the wealth stop with us when we die? How do we pass it on in ways that are designed to continue to support our families who inherit what we leave behind? That's how we can continue to build wealth and broaden opportunities.

MARC MORIAL: Leaders need to be more involved in economic public policy decisions and discussions. The recession kicked our ass, and some of the limited progress we have made from the 1960s and '70s to the mid-2000s was lost. In the postrecession economy, the wealth has been vacuumed up to the top.

> *Leaders need to be more involved in economic public policy decisions and discussions.*

KILLER MIKE: I am not highly critical of us because we're only fifty-five years into freedom. At some point, we have to look and decide what worked prior to those fifty-five years, because we had private communities in Harlem, Virginia, Maryland, DC, Atlanta, Detroit, Tulsa. There were dozens of Black Wall Streets, thriving areas of Black business all over the country. What happened pre- and post-desegregation? What happened economically to us? How were we better? Are we prepared to have that real conversation or do we just want to see lively debate?

ED GORDON: That debate cannot happen without talking about poverty. Dr. King was exploring the issue of poverty at the time of his death. In 1966, after a visit to Mississippi where he saw the abject poverty some families were living in, King decided something had to be done. From a moral perspective, he knew those conditions were unacceptable, and from a political perspective, he knew that in order for Blacks to move up the social ladder, this kind of poverty had to be eradicated.

The burdens of deep, generational poverty render all aspects of life more difficult and make it nearly impossible to shake the shackles that chain you to poverty, even when there are no legal or latent barriers to equal opportunity. King began to structure a poor people's campaign, a concerted effort to end the scourge of poverty. The movement would effectively die with him. Recently, Bishop William Barber, a national board member of the NAACP and one of the most influential clergymen in the nation, took up the mantle and has resurrected the Poor People's Campaign in hopes of completing what King attempted to do more than five decades ago.

WILLIAM BARBER: There are 15 million more people in poverty [today] than there were in 1968. We launched the [Poor People's Campaign] in 2018, and we're still building. We have forty-one coordinating communities in forty-one states and the District of Columbia. We had 25,000 to 30,000 people show up on the day we launched the movement. There are 140 million poor and low-wealth persons in this country. That's 43.5 percent of the population. We've got 37 million people without health care, even with the Affordable Care Act. Four million families get up every morning and can't buy unleaded gas and can't get unleaded water. Sixty-two million people work every day for less than fifteen dollars an hour, and many have to get subsidies and live in their cars or live in shelters.

We have to change the narrative by telling the truth and have a movement that's willing to put both body and brainpower behind building this coalition. We have to build coalitions where impacted people are leading, not following. Where it's not just people speaking out for the poor but the impacted people speaking for themselves, telling their stories and demanding a solution.

Susan Taylor: When we look at poverty, we have to understand that the Census Bureau calculates poverty [as a] family income of $12,195 for a family of four with two related children.

Julianne Malveaux: So many of our children live in a household headed by [a woman], [which] is problematic from the perspective of inequality of resources. With two parents, there is more wealth in the household and more opportunity. We need to look at [the following issues]: What is the living wage for women who have children? What are the social supports and structures for women who have children? Where's the child care? Where is the affordable health care? Where are all those things that, even given the lack of a second income, will make this woman's life better? You find too many women possibly cobbling together two part-time jobs because of child-care constraints or other kinds of constraints. So that becomes a challenge.

Marilyn Booker: We've got to figure out what is the best way to get folks who are in that situation to where they can be more economically viable, where they can earn more money. If not, then you have this vicious cycle of making below minimum wage, staying below the level of poverty—it's a cycle that's never going to change.

WILLIAM BARBER: [Look] at these numbers: 43.5 percent of your population is poor and low wealth…in the richest nation in the world. One to 2 percent of the population controls 80 or 90 percent of the wealth. No nation can survive this. Fifty-three percent of every discretionary dollar goes to the military, while combat soldiers make barely $30,000 a year, but military contract CEOs make $19 million a year, on average. What we have now is a poverty draft.

MARC MORIAL: We have to elevate the issue of economics. For example, take the discussion taking place among politicians, when they address Black voters. They talk about criminal justice: important; voting rights: important; education: important. But no one has really advanced an economic agenda. Now you hear several of them talking about reparations, but none of them talk about what it meant and what it is and how to operationalize it. They say, "I'll support a study of reparations." But does anyone say, "I'm going to make reversing the Black home ownership decline a key part"? Or "I'm going to make sure that African American businesses participate in government contracts, to the maximum [extent] possible"?

Where poverty ends, prosperity begins, and crime just starts to fade away.

KILLER MIKE: Where poverty ends, prosperity begins, and crime just starts to fade away. We are caught in the familiarity of crime, murder, of taking, robbing, and hurting each other. If we can start to rid ourselves of that through economics, we can start to stabilize and start to see how truly wonderful life can be.

BUTCH GRAVES: We do need to take some responsibility for saving and investing or putting some money into a 401(k). It's not as simple as assuming that if we just had better jobs, we would be doing that much better. We have to also train the people to grow money—it's a mind-set. Some of us would rather drive around in a leased BMW and live at home with our momma than buy a home. You're not gonna become Beyoncé overnight. If that's your aspiration and goal, most likely you're gonna be broke.

Ed Gordon: How do millennials differ from their elders in terms of how they think about money?

Marilyn Booker: Millennials have a very different relationship with money. I am actually pleasantly surprised by the number of millennials who come to me and they want to talk about their money. They're not afraid to talk about money. They're very thirsty for information—how to save their money and make it work for them. I've been moved by their interest in trying to make a difference in their financial lives. Yes, they don't care if they have small amounts of money. They just want to get started, and they're talking about getting started like yesterday. Get their money working. They're very aggressive, and that's a great thing. Some of the concerns about not trusting money and not trusting financial institutions is more historical, and it's not necessarily being passed along to that next generation because they want this immediate gratification. They want to focus on "How do I make things work for me right now?" I hate to say the word *baggage*, but they don't have that baggage necessarily that the previous generations have.

Julianne Malveaux: What I enjoy about this millennial generation and younger [generations] is that many believe they don't have to ask for permission. Whereas in our generation, we wondered, "Is it possible for me to start this business?" Their generation is, "Hey, I'm going to start this business." They're not asking for permission; they're just doing it. Baby boomers were taught [to] go get that education, get the brass ring, and very little about entrepreneurship. Our forefathers made a decision at some point to go after education as opposed to setting up small businesses and set aside business opportunities. [It] took from *Brown* [the Supreme Court decision] until the late '60s to really push for participation, stomping with the big dogs in terms of entrepreneurship.

Ed Gordon: We also have to widen the aperture for people to broaden their career choices or economic opportunities. It's what Nipsey Hussle had begun to do.

CHARLAMAGNE THA GOD: Black ownership, Black independence, the financial freedom that we talk about having as Black people. Nipsey had that, and he was cool. He was a cool rap dude. Man, do you know how many people he'd influenced? Think about that. He wasn't somebody that people would look at and say, "Oh, he's a square." They know him, they know where he came from, they know what he was about, and this dude had a whole shopping plaza that he owned in his community. Hamburger spots, barbecue joints, barbershops, hair salons!

DERRICK JOHNSON: It's like driving through a blighted neighborhood. Too many of us drive through them, lock our doors, and say, "Oh, this is a bad neighborhood." Others drive through that same neighborhood, and they see opportunity. We have to begin to drive through areas and recognize that something is there, seeing there's an opportunity to make something happen.

KILLER MIKE: I would argue the hottest thing right now is intellectual property—music, entertainment. It's worth more to the world than many of the brick-and-mortar things that we have come to associate with wealth, yet as a community, we don't respect that as a position of power. We don't say to these young men and women who are gaining tons of money and capital and opportunity, "Save 30 percent of what you're making. If you're going to make $100 million gross before [taxes], pay yourself $30 million, so when you retire, you'll have enough money to then start to invest and build."

Why aren't we targeting this class of people to financially get them literate and get them prepared for the bigger world?

TRACY MAITLAND: Once they see it, then they can believe it. And if they believe it, then they can begin to organize their life to be successful at whatever that is. That's really what we're talking about. You can learn that business, learn what you have to do to be involved in that business, to be successful at it; then you can start to build wealth.

T.I.: Visionaries have the ideas; they have the vision. Entrepreneurship comes from the belief in yourself that you can do something. Even when nobody else is saying, "Oh yeah, that's a good idea. Yeah, you should do that." If you're waiting on that, nine times out of ten, you're gonna be stuck doing nothing. You gotta believe in your motherf*cking self.

*   *   *

Perseverance and resilience are two things people of color have in excess; it is what has allowed us to stay above water. We are starting to see these traits take hold for a select few in business. Now those practices should become widespread and commonplace among a larger swath of the community. Poverty has hampered generations of Black people. The issues that accompany poverty, including underfunded and underperforming schools, poor health habits, and lack of self-esteem, often keep people from meeting their full potential.

In some corners, growing up in poverty is a rite of passage; if you didn't eat mayonnaise sandwich and sugar water for dinner, then you aren't "Black enough." Let's be clear: being poor should not be a prerequisite for being labeled authentically Black; your Black card is not reliant on your family being financially needy at one time. More and more opportunities are available. Finance should no longer be apprehensive ground for Black America to walk on. We must learn how to create wealth and grow income. There must also be greater expectations, demands from others to share the wealth, and a greater obligation for our community to learn the money game.

We are seeing those lessons play themselves out. Not satisfied with simply a career in entertainment, comedian Byron Allen has become a media mogul whose portfolio includes the Weather Channel, the Grio, and eleven television stations across the country. Another entertainment mogul, Tyler Perry, said "running from poverty" was the impetus that helped build his wealth (much of it on the back of his Madea character). In 2019, he became the only African American to be the sole owner of a movie studio. Janice Bryant Howroyd has realized ownership to the tune of almost $3 billion, the amount her staffing solutions firm is poised to hit. These are three examples of people who understood the importance of ownership, the change it made in their lives, and the power it gives them to influence and impact the lives of other people of color.

We must decide to chart a better course to ensuring a more fiscally sound lifestyle. Economic solutions to poverty, debt reduction, business development, and personal saving and investment can advance our continued march to equal rights. Building relationships, future planning, and economic cooperation with other people of color are all ways to grow money soundly. Black America must become less reliant on others to provide the financial backing for our advocacy and our future. No longer should financial stability be seen as an impossibility for the majority of Black families. There is money to be made; there is too much wealth in this country not to partake in it. It's time for African Americans to take a larger slice of the money pie.

STARTING YOUR OWN CONVERSATION

- What unique challenges do Black-owned businesses face in this day and age? Are things better now than in the past for African American entrepreneurs? Why or why not?

- Have your local or state policy makers helped Black-owned businesses thrive? If so, how?

- How can you invest more in Black-owned businesses in your community?

- Who are your Black financial role models? What do you admire about their approach to finances?

- How can you better invest in your own future and the economic legacy you'll leave behind for your descendants?

THE MADEA DILEMMA

BLACK REPRESENTATION IN ENTERTAINMENT AND THE MEDIA

TODD BOYD	Academic & Author
BRITTNEY COOPER	Academic & Author
TIFFANY CROSS	Managing Editor of *The Beat DC*
MICHAEL ERIC DYSON	Academic & Author
JEFF FRIDAY	Founder of the American Black Film Festival
SARAH GLOVER	President of the National Association of Black Journalists
BUTCH GRAVES	President & CEO of Earl Graves Publishing
JEMELE HILL	Journalist & Broadcaster
DERRICK JOHNSON	President & CEO of NAACP
KILLER MIKE	Rapper & Activist
VAN LATHAN	Television Producer
MALCOLM D. LEE	Film Director & Screenwriter
BRITTANY PACKNETT	Vice President of Teach for America
APRIL REIGN	Founder of #OscarsSoWhite
AL SHARPTON	President of the National Action Network
SUSAN TAYLOR	Former Publisher of *Essence* & Founder of the National Cares Mentoring Movement
T.I.	Rapper & Activist

Even with the success of *Black Panther*, actors like Tiffany Haddish and Dwayne "The Rock" Johnson making marks in Hollywood, and the prominence of super producers Will Packer and Shonda Rhimes, the question of whether Hollywood is still "so White" remains.

Hollywood sets expectations and shapes what we think and believe. They've made us believe that blondes have more fun and that the cowboy with the white hat and white horse is the good guy. Images are shaped in Tinseltown, and the world follows. Movies and television shows have driven the tastes, fads, and stereotypes that become real for the world. For people of color, those images haven't often been glamorous or positive. Since the infancy of the movie industry in the early 1900s until very recently, people of color have been depicted stereotypically or not at all. From Mammy to Madea, movies often reinforced dubious images of African Americans. D. W. Griffith's *Birth of a Nation*, a Civil War–era film released in 1915, even portrayed the Ku Klux Klan as a good force and depicted Black men as unintelligent and sexually hungry.

For decades other minorities were practically ignored by Hollywood. That might have been a blessing based on the prevalence of ugly characterizations. Blacks on the big screen were slaves, maids, or criminals—from the housekeepers in *Gone with the Wind* to the first Black movie star, Stepin Fetchit—and this reinforced how many Whites felt about Blacks. Fetchit, whose real name was Lincoln Perry, became a wealthy man but at the cost of being shunned by much of Black America, who saw his characters as perpetuating negative stereotypes about Blacks.

Slowly, over decades, these kinds of stereotypes became less exaggerated and less prevalent but were still present. Television provided more opportunities while still presenting myopic and one-dimensional characters of color. Nevertheless, Blacks forged their way into Hollywood and TV studios and showcased their supreme talents in front of and behind the camera. Sidney Poitier, Cicely Tyson, Denzel Washington, and Regina King are just a few of the finest actors of their generations. Melvin Van Peebles, the late John Singleton, and F. Gary Gray are among those who sat in director's chairs and guided movies to completion, a feat even rarer than starring on the big screen. We are starting to see real change and more balance in what is being produced about and by people of color. Even with this advancement, many of the same questions are being raised: Are the images negative? Are we complicit in fostering those stereotypes by producing and supporting the images we long railed against?

These questions are consequential because images still set the tone for how the world sees others and how we see ourselves. Hollywood might be the biggest opinion shaper in the world.

HOW DOES ENTERTAINMENT INFLUENCE BLACK IDENTITY?

JEFF FRIDAY: You can't overstate the importance of entertainment to how we view ourselves. I'd like to think that our self-identity was shaped and formed from other sources like church and Mom and Dad and neighborhood and Miss Jones next door. Even a book by James Baldwin. But how we see ourselves and how we behave, the values that we teach, and the standards that we set are too influenced by the media we don't control.

The economics of Hollywood forces us to pander to the taste of White people, and we very rarely get a chance to tell true stories, to give accurate depictions of our lives because what we often hear is "that won't sell." A Black heroic piece won't sell, but a Black piece that has "nigga, nigga, nigga" throughout will absolutely sell. Part of my mission as a film and television producer and a film festival financier is to shake things up and to help Black people work together.

Television and film producer Jeff Friday founded the American Black Film Festival. He created the annual gathering after realizing the huge void for independent Black films. Started in 1997, the film festival has become one of the nation's most prominent and influential.

DERRICK JOHNSON: How people see us on the big screen or on television is how they treat us in the streets and in public policy. For the NAACP Image Awards, it is a part of our mission to make sure we garner positive images that come from our community. Celebrating the fiftieth anniversary of the Image Awards this year was, for me, personally gratifying. You have not only a *Black Panther* on one side but *The BlacKkKlansman* on the other side. Both projected positive images of who we are and our potential. It is becoming clearer that not only can we present positive images, we can do so with the business model to generate revenue, which would then open up the door for more portrayals of who we are as a people. We are a rich and diverse people with many stories to tell. The more we produce stories that generate revenue, the more stories we can tell about who we are and the collective.

MICHAEL ERIC DYSON: It's still a pittance; we still, for instance, have the White savior movies being made. Take Mahershala Ali, an extraordinary actor. I was glad he was awarded for his extraordinary acting in *Green Book*, but [it's] another White savior story. These films undermine the capacity of Black people to narrate our own stories or, when we do, to have them celebrated or economically supported with the same vigor that White folk who are interested in telling our stories do. That is a problem.

We are taking back who we are, and we are finding pride in the ownership of who we are. I think we are doing the right thing in making sure that our social handprint is on everything that is to be gained from our culture and from all the things we create in our community.

BRITTANY PACKNETT: We have to take our rightful place as culture creators and trendsetters. I can't remember whose quote it is, but I've heard someone say, "Ghetto is just creativity that hasn't been stolen yet." We are taking back who we are, and we are finding pride in the ownership of who we are. I think we are doing the right thing in making sure that our social handprint is on everything that is to be gained from our culture and from all the things we create in our community.

ED GORDON: In 2015, April Reign's casual tweet about no acknowledgments of Black actors or actresses in the major acting categories for the second year in a row ignited a firestorm that burned through the industry. Her spontaneous tweet #OscarsSoWhite started a viral sensation and a closer, more serious look at diversity in the film industry.

JEFF FRIDAY: #OscarsSoWhite is probably the most transformative thing to happen in Hollywood in my professional lifetime. Everything we're seeing now is a result of that embarrassment. Every studio has a new diversity program; there are mandates for television. You can't do a show like *Friends* (a virtually all-White show); that probably doesn't exist today. Jerry Seinfeld is a creative genius, but that show doesn't play in 2020. If you go to networks and look at the casting boards, it's the rainbow now, and it's largely because of Hollywood being embarrassed. We should thank that movement for what we are experiencing now.

APRIL REIGN: #OscarsSoWhite shone a light on the disparities that existed and also highlighted the fact that a good story told well will be profitable not only financially but within the entertainment community and will stand the test of time. More opportunities should be given to traditionally underrepresented folks, and look at what they can do once that happens. Look at *Moonlight*. That is a movie that would be timeless, whether it was made in 1997 or 2017.

*   *   *

Tyler Perry's speech at the 2019 BET Awards was stirring. After being awarded the network's Ultimate Icon Award, he brought the crowd to its feet as he inspired listeners to take matters into their own hands and own their creations. He talked about how his success allowed him to build a sprawling film studio on the grounds of a Confederate army base. He noted, "The land once holding 3.9 million enslaved Negroes is now owned by one Negro." Perry's phenomenal success is awe-inspiring, and his do-for-self business model is certainly a template for others.

Perry's iconic character, Madea—a tough-talking, foulmouthed grandmother—has helped skyrocket his career and led him to become one of the most successful African Americans in Hollywood history. However, though he is lauded by many, some people felt that the character was belittling and a troubling example of how Black people are negatively portrayed on screen. That criticism reached its zenith in 2009 after Spike Lee and I did an interview in which Lee suggested that Perry's television shows and movies where demeaning and that "the imagery is troubling." Perry's success is undeniable. Yet for many who love Perry personally, it's often his art that remains a dilemma.

HOW DO YOU FEEL ABOUT MADEA AS A REPRESENTATION?

TODD BOYD: I never liked what Tyler Perry was doing. I think it's a throwback to the days of Stepin Fetchit, Rochester, Willie Best, Hattie McDaniel—a long list of Black performers from another era who perpetrated these negative stereotypes. Tyler Perry was doing a modern version of it.

KILLER MIKE: When I first saw Madea, I thought I hated it. This is when Tyler Perry was doing the plays. My grandmother used to have me go to stores and buy the VHS tapes. I saw the joy and the laughter that it brought to her. It was the same as when she watched *The Jeffersons* or *Sanford and Son* or when I watched *Martin* or *The Cosby Show* later. I understood that entertainment is just entertainment. Now, if you want to control the narrative better, you need more Black people in the writers' room. You need more Black people in the production company, and you need Black media!

JEFF FRIDAY: We should spend our time looking at the things that are commendable. He's an entrepreneur. We should evaluate whether he is hiring Black people or not. That's what matters, because you can do the most poignant work and only deal with White people.

＊　＊　＊

When Tyler Perry opened his studio in October 2019, the star-studded event was an outpouring of love and pride for Perry, who has shown that if you're not invited to the table, you build your own. He understood better than most that Hollywood often neglects Black audiences and overlooks Black talent, so rather than feel hurt or stymied, he built his own. Perry's creation of an entertainment empire has won over many, including Spike Lee. Over the years, Lee and Perry have differed in artistic approach and had disagreements that made media headlines. But those days seemed past; Perry named a sound stage after Lee. During the studio opening, Lee said it was "an honor" while calling the opening of the studio "historic."

The irony is that Perry's Madea character, whom some saw as demeaning to Blacks, is perhaps the biggest reason that he has become arguably the most powerful African American in the movie industry. This has given him the power to offer opportunities and employment to people of color.

The debate around "positive" images of Blacks didn't start with Tyler Perry. Our community has been divided about that for decades. Television shows such as *Beulah* and *Good Times* met with criticism for stereotypes. Movies like *Soul Plane* were chastised for playing to low comedic sensibilities. Hip-hop images and videos have often been lambasted almost from the beginning.

ARE CONCERNS ABOUT BLACK IMAGES ABOUT PROTECTING OUR DIGNITY OR ABOUT RESPONDING TO WHAT OTHERS THINK?

APRIL REIGN: We have to be careful about caring too much about what folks think outside of our community. Everyone has a Madea in their family. Everyone. And you could say the same thing about *Belly* or *Straight Out of Compton* or *Poetic Justice* or so many others that show the everyday life of the majority of us. We're not all middle class or upper class. Why would we want to police joy and restrain Black folks from having it, when, once we leave that darkened theater, we are all faced with a very similar struggle?

MICHAEL ERIC DYSON: It's not just an image. It's an image that is reflective of our complexity. Black people talk about positive versus negative. We need to talk about productive versus destructive. A lot of Black people don't want to see certain values and certain visions of Black people prevail, and I get it. We look at TV and say, "Oh my god, there's Junebug again with a scarf around his head being interviewed on the local news."

T.I.: Everybody's story is important, at least to that individual. So you don't have the power or authority—none of us do—to say, "Your story is not important enough to be portrayed" or "Your story's not important enough to tell." It's shades of Black. Just because this shade ain't your shade don't mean that it's not important.

BUTCH GRAVES: We have a decision to make: At what point do reputation and image matter? If the only thing that matters is putting a dollar in your pocket, then you'll sell your soul to the devil. What I am saying is, if the only images that we put out or are allowed to put out reflect buffoonery, then don't be confused when people don't treat you with the love or respect that you believe you should be accorded. We have to have balance. Everything can't be rappers with diamonds in their mouth, gold teeth, pants falling off their ass. How many *Friday* and *Friday after Next* and *The Friday after the Friday after Next* can you show?

MALCOLM D. LEE: I feel like there is a schizophrenia. There are so many things that we like that entertain us, that we relate to, but that we don't want shown to a larger society. I remember when *Flavor of Love* first hit the airwaves. I was like, "Oh God, this is just the worst parts of us, and people are consuming it." Not just Black people. There are things that are going to offend us and things that we're going to find really entertaining.

MICHAEL ERIC DYSON: Have we portrayed ourselves in fashions that don't always reflect the complexity, the complications, the nuance, the beauty of our culture? Of course. But there's also a dearth of opportunities. People like Spike Lee, Barry Jenkins, Ryan Coogler, and Ava DuVernay are seizing the reins of representational authority and making the media serve us and not vice versa. It's a mixed bag, but it's definitely a beautiful thing to see the proliferation of images across the board reflect deeper and more consistent values of Blackness. Still a long way to go. But there has been tremendous progress at the same time.

According to Comscore, a media and measurement and analytics company, since 2005, Tyler Perry's twenty-one movies have generated over $1 billion in ticket sales. In 2019, Perry opened Tyler Perry Studio, a 330-acre former military installation built by slaves. Tyler Perry became the first African American to own a major movie studio.

* * *

Black artists and creatives carry the extra burden of being harshly judged because there are so few positive and complex images of people of color. We tend to be overly critical of the work that other Blacks create. Jamie Foxx told me about the burden of the Black comic having to think about doing a joke about loving watermelon and chicken when a Jewish comic can joke about eating bagels and lox without reprisal. Our images have been so maligned and falsified over the years that our sensitivity is heightened, especially regarding what others think of us. For years Black America has been divided on how much our artists should play in the world of stereotypes. Much of Perry's success came at a time when the scope of Black work on television and movies was limited. His work became so popular and ubiquitous that his over-the-top characters became even more so, and what might be deemed stereotypical became more glaring.

The expectation that all Perry's movies should be deep, multilayered cinematic masterpieces is impractical. Moreover, that has not been Perry's lane up to this point in his career. I've told him that Madea is this generation's Geraldine, the female alter ego made famous by comedian Flip Wilson in the '70s. That character had detractors, too, but was mostly beloved. Those times were more forgiving, and Black people were just happy to see someone who looked like them on TV.

The great poet Maya Angelou and I also discussed the question of our images in the media. I asked if she was at all disappointed because so many of our depictions were oversexualized or buffoonish. "Of course, they could be better," she said and quickly followed in her melodious voice, "but, Mr. Gordon"—as she always graciously called me—"I remember a time when I never saw anyone who looked like me on any screen. This is better than being invisible."

Over the last few years, we have seen a wider range of images coming out of Hollywood. That has lifted the impossible onus of Perry's work to be representative for all Black people and allowed for a better appreciation of it. We shouldn't miss the bigger picture of what Tyler Perry has done with the success from the multibillion-dollar Madea franchise. He has provided other people of color with countless opportunities; actors, crew members, and many others have been given chances that were often closed before Perry's success brought him the power he wields now. Over the course of his career, Perry has amassed wealth that he has often used to help people of color, including lending his personal plane to fly aid to the Bahamas after Hurricane Dorian. As long as there is fair representation of our images, I believe Perry's many charitable efforts and his power as a producer and mogul are worth the occasional cringeworthy moments a couple of his characters may bring to some.

WHAT DOES THE FUTURE OF BLACK ENTERTAINMENT LOOK LIKE?

JEFF FRIDAY: I am happy to hear people are changing their temperature on Tyler, and the reason is that we're experiencing Barry Jenkins's work and George Tillman's and so on and so forth. Now we don't feel so limited. You've got Kenya Barris doing great, smart comedy. Now you can watch Kenya one night and Tyler one night and Ava [DuVernay] one night and Ryan Coogler and feel cool about it.

MALCOLM D. LEE: I've tried to do things that I feel we need in our entertainment. When I made *Best Man Holiday*, I thought, *There's not been a movie where Black people can just go to the movie and actually emote.* We don't have a *Terms of Endearment.* We don't have a movie where we can see men really displaying their emotions and women too, of course, but in a way that touches the heart and touches the soul. I wanna do that.

Malcolm D. Lee has a stellar track record in Hollywood. Movie talent runs in his family. Spike Lee is his cousin. His list of box office hits are impressive; The Best Man *franchise,* Night School, *and* Girls Trip *are some of his biggest titles.*

JEMELE HILL: We want balance. We often struggle with what's the proper way to support that balance. There is a hunger for our stories to be told and not just in some frivolous way. A lot of times, we patronized certain options because they were the only options, and now that there are more options, I like to think our palate is opening up.

We feel as if all of the entertainment that we have to consume must be PBS-level quality. It doesn't have to be. We should strive for balance; if you're going to have a *Love & Hip Hop* franchise, let's find a way to also support a nightly news program on BET. I'm not saying take away one to get the other; I'm saying we need a little bit more balance.

BRITTANY PACKNETT: We are freeing ourselves of the idea that we should really care what White people actually think of our culture. The way we wear our hair or the way we speak or how we dress or how we entertain. What our music sounds like or how long our nails are. I just recognized, and what I find ironic are [the] same trends that mainstream culture denigrated are the same ones they're copying now. We went from cornrows being unprofessional to them being featured in fashion magazines and being called boxer braids when they were worn by White celebrities.

* 　 * 　 *

Led by *Black Panther*, which became the highest-grossing movie of 2018, taking in an astonishing $1 billion, movies with Black casts made bank at theaters. Other Black films that were movie gold included *Us*, *Girls Trip*, *A Madea Family Funeral*, and *Get Out*. A growing number of broadcast outlets have given more space for content starring people of color. *The Good Fight*, *Empire*, and *Black-ish* are hit shows with majority Black casts. Issa Rae, Viola Davis, and Taraji P. Henson have become fixtures on TV. The desire for a wider representation of Black content and characters is slowly coming to fruition. We can't deny there have been tremendous strides.

WHAT IS BEING DONE TO CONTINUE THE ADVANCEMENT IN FILM AND TELEVISION?

MALCOLM D. LEE: We'd never done a movie prior to *Girls Trip* where we balance heart with raunch. I feel a responsibility to not only depict us in certain ways but also to try to push the depictions of Blackness further. Somebody like Jordan Peele's really doing it in a very dynamic way. In some ways it's subtle; in some ways it's very overt, like *Us*. Just the depiction of a very brown-skinned family at the center of the movie, and nobody mentions Blackness. It makes $70 million on the opening weekend and not just because Black folks went to see it. That's 'cause a lot of people went to see it and did not care that it was all Black.

JEFF FRIDAY: I agree, and what's great is our younger generations have choices; they have balance. The kids did go see *Us*, a horror movie with dark-skinned Black people. *Black Panther's* phenomenal success—you can't deny that kind of box office, over a billion dollars. It breaks the myth that content led by people of color won't perform internationally. Content, whether it's people of color or not, performs based on content and marketing budget and numbers of screens and number of territories. If you approach Black content like you approach every other content, we could have avoided the last twenty-five years of hearing Black doesn't sell. Follow that with *Get Out*, *Us*, *Hidden Figures*, *Moonlight* winning the Oscar. It's been this wave of Blackness. I believe things are changing. The influence of Hollywood is not going to be lessened; we've got to make sure Hollywood is accountable to our money and to our interest.

*   *   *

Perhaps even more important than the images dreamed up in Hollywood for the big and small screens are those images of African Americans shown by news outlets. The news media wants us to believe that the depictions of people of color in the news are representations of real life—unvarnished, balanced, objective reports of the way we live, reflective of who we are. But unbiased reporting is a myth.

Unbiased reporting used to be the goal. My generation of journalists was the last to work from the old news standard of multiple sourcing and trying to be neutral. You worked as best you could to stay in the middle lane—not too far right, not too far left. Accounting for the human element meant stories were reported from the understanding and lens of the person tasked with delivering the news. Hence, stories could be clouded by benign ignorance or malicious prejudice. Either does harm. Even with earnest attempts at being impartial, the news coverage of Black Americans has been slanted and stereotypical. My mother used to truly believe that news teams went out of their way to find the most inarticulate Black person to put on the news. We're all familiar with it: a reporter is on location talking to witnesses; the White couple calmly lets us know the details of what happened; the perky young blonde then tells us more, articulating what she saw; then the brother, eager to give you his account, loudly proclaims, "I seent it. I seent it!"

My mother's conspiracy theory was bolstered years later by the video of the news story featuring how Antoine Dodson defended his sister when a rapist entered her apartment. Dodson's "Hide yo kids, hide yo wife" interview became an internet sensation, going viral and becoming comedic fodder for some and a source of embarrassment for others.

After decades in the news business, I had to give more credence to my mother's notion that news media purposely showed Black folks in less than the best light. Countless times I sat in meetings, sometimes the only person of color in the room, and listened to White producers drone on about what they thought was happening in Black America or watched what they selected to represent the Black perspective. Though it was painful at times, I was often glad to have been in the room, knowing what may have been the final result without my input. One glaring example was coverage of the 1996 Democratic convention by MSNBC. A producer wanted to do a story about how Blacks in Chicago were going to vote. I was assigned the story, and she said, "Go over to the Cabrini-Green projects and get some reaction from Black voters."

"Is this to show how voters in that neighborhood are leaning politically?" I asked.

She said, "No, it's just to show Black voters, in general."

"I will do the story, but Blacks live all over Chicago, not just in the projects," I told her. "I will bring you a look at Black Chicago voters that is more reflective."

Her directive to go to "the projects" was not out of malice for Black folks but from an uninformed, stereotypical view of Blacks. That view is shared by many Whites in newsrooms and has little chance of changing based on analysis of US Census Bureau data and Pew Research Center findings that newsroom employees are less diverse than the country's overall workforce.

WHAT CAN WE DO ABOUT THE DECLINING NUMBERS OF BLACK OWNERSHIP?

SARAH GLOVER: We are living in a time where media ownership is challenging. We celebrate that *Essence* is owned by Richelieu, but we also know that without more Black-owned media, our stories do hang in the balance for the next hundred years in terms of the documentation of one of the most important fabrics of America, Black life.

Sarah Glover was the president of the National Association of Black Journalists from 2015 to 2019. The organization was founded in 1974 in Washington, DC, by a group of journalists. Among the association's primary goals is to advocate on behalf of Black journalists.

ED GORDON: Why was it important for you to buy *Essence* and return it to Black ownership?

Richelieu Dennis: You probably know the African proverb that says, "Until the lion learns how to write, every story will glorify the hunter." There's a narrative that has been put out about us as a people and about our culture that underlies a lot of how we get perceived when we're walking around, how we get treated when we go into a store. And we haven't controlled that narrative. There can be no more important thing than investing in platforms that allow us to share an accurate experience, to highlight and broadly distribute our true characters and our diversity and our strengths and our beauty.

Malcolm D. Lee: I remember when Obama was first elected. Here was this image of a model Black family. My wife and I were with two other couples, walking in the Village after dinner, and these White girls whisper, "Oh my God, look at them; they're so beautiful." It's like it was the first time they'd seen upwardly mobile Black people as normal. That does have value.

Butch Graves: He or she who controls the narrative controls the message. It's why we have chosen, at Black Enterprise, not to do negative stories on Black people. I refuse to. I don't need to, because the White press does that for me. So why do I have to go out and then reinforce the negative that they're already putting out about Black people?

If we lose the ability to reach directly to one another and control our images or control the narrative or what's said about us, what have you? There will be no independent thought about what's happening in the lives or in the world of African Americans. There was a time when there were a lot of Black newspapers and a lot of Black publications. That is no longer the case.

Most studies—including a 2019 media review by the Pew Research Center—show that Black Americans tend to be underrepresented in US newsrooms. And while there are more than one hundred Black newspapers in the United States, most have seen a steady decline for years, in keeping with trends throughout the whole industry. Only one of the newspapers audited, the *St. Louis American*, reported a circulation of more than fifty thousand.

*　　*　　*

Black ownership of media outlets is in decline. In a 2018 article, the Minority Media and Telecommunications Council suggested that the Federal Communications Commission may be engaging in minority ownership "suppression." Television, radio, newspaper, and magazine minority ownership is woefully low, and on a national level, their ownership is almost nonexistent. In that article the author cites the latest data from 2015, showing that "minority television ownership stands at 2.6% and is dropping fast," while minority radio ownership is "stagnant at about 5%."

Dennis and Graves are the anomaly. No longer a growing landscape, Black media ownership is fading. Once-vibrant publications—Black newspapers and magazines—now see declining readerships and ad revenues, making them vulnerable prey for larger White-owned companies. Johnson Publication, the legendary publisher of *Jet* and *Ebony*, eventually had to take on majority partners. Once-thriving local Black newspapers were unable to weather the economic storm and could no longer compete with larger, better-financed White rivals that had finally taken an interest in Black life, mostly for financial gain. They took a bigger share of the ad revenue than was being paid to Black-owned media. BET was sold to Viacom.

The sale of these outlets proved financially sound for those minority owners who cashed in, but it gave away a certain amount of influence that was held by a person of color. Black audience support for these outlets gets soft once mainstream media giants start to turn their attention to covering and producing stories on the Black condition. The question is, how reliably "Black" is it if the control is not in Black hands? That question remains even if a Black face is telling the story; rarely does that person have the final say in what is reported. For instance, according to the Radio Television Digital News Association, the percentage of local television Black news directors hovers around 5 percent, and Black general managers account for only 2.3 percent.

WHAT WILL HAPPEN IF WE CONTINUE TO LOSE OUR VOICE IN THE NEWS?

SARAH GLOVER: Diversity has eroded; if you look at the progress made in the '80s and '90s, it has eroded through layoffs and downsizing. What has happened with the strides in technology is the modes of doing journalism—the need for a printing press, a staff to do this story, and a staff to do that story—[and] so our industry has diminished. But that evolution has created a compression of jobs. My concern is that some companies use that change as an opportunity to cut, and it seems like when those cuts happen, diversity is the first thing that suffers.

BUTCH GRAVES: In an increasingly digital world, where everybody is a publisher, the messages can get jumbled, and so what we're finding is that more and more general-market folks are in fact buying our images, are buying our entities. And when that happens, you will have potentially a White person controlling the narrative and image around people of color. It's absolutely essential for African Americans to figure out how they can control the voice and narrative and how they deliver that narrative and the images of who we are, because in the absence of that, we're back to the 1950s.

SUSAN TAYLOR: What is disheartening is [the] loss of voice. We're online; we chat a lot. We have something to say about everybody, but we don't have the drum. We don't have those radio shows or what you had, Ed— television shows. We don't have our own space where we can really see ourselves, show ourselves. We don't have that anymore, and that loss is devastating.

MICHAEL ERIC DYSON: Think about what the media has done to Black people and brown people. Underrepresentation. Choosing who will cover the upcoming 2020 election, for instance. Some networks have rightly been excoriated for not having a single Black person involved in the producing or executive levels of the coverage. Most of the major media outlets, when it comes to thinking about, talking about, reflecting on the values, the interests, the visions of Black America, are radically underplayed and underrepresented in mainstream media. The media has had a long, inglorious history of misrepresenting Black folk.

KILLER MIKE: I don't know if we have Black media. Where are the Black newspapers? Are we supporting them? Are we supporting *Rolling Out*? Are we supporting Revolt TV? And if the answer is no, then we don't have media. We're subject to someone else's media. If you cannot put out on Black media a story that is written for Blacks, written by Blacks, that is owned by Blacks, and the viewership is primarily or starts off with a cornerstone that is Black, then I would argue that we don't have Black media. It's all just blackface.

VAN LATHAN: We need platforms that we trust around our own voices. That's not a conversation for Fox News. It might not even be a conversation for CNN. The conversation that we would have should take place on all platforms with people who we trust, that we know aren't trying to cook us. The key is doing it with each other on platforms that we trust. We can't talk family business outside the family.

TIFFANY CROSS: Ed, you and I worked together at BET. And we did some amazing things with your program and news specials that we did that spoke to our community. And yeah, people watched. But I also felt like there were people who would look at it differently had it aired on CNN or MSNBC. Here we were, presenting something to people on a silver platter, saying, "We found a home for you; we're making a home for you. Come join and be with us." People still wanted it to be validated by a White network.

AL SHARPTON: We need to ask ourselves, why did you let Black talk radio die? Why did you let Black TV die? It was in our interest to have that. When people watched Ed on BET, those were voters. "Well, they didn't make the numbers that a video got." But the video guy's crowd ain't voting! We have to have it. All you have to do is look how the conservatives did.

What did they do? They went and got their own TV network, Fox. They went and got their own talk shows, Rush Limbaugh, all the way across the board. How do you think we got beat down? It's not rocket science.

RICHELIEU DENNIS: Until we're the ones that are portraying our images, creating our narratives, and sharing our love for each other, it'll be up to somebody else to determine that, and that's a dangerous place to be.

* * *

Fellow journalist Roland Martin and I have discussed the difference in how we are perceived when we work for a Black media company versus a White one. There is no question that too many Blacks give more credence to majority companies than they do minority-owned outlets. We laugh when people have said to us, "Glad to see you back on real TV," when we appeared on "White" networks. I have worked in both spaces, both environments. The differences had nothing to do with intellect or skill. Both have a fair share of brilliant, creative people as well as those who never should have been hired. The biggest difference is money. Budget differences between mainstream media and minority-owned media are staggering.

The news media holds immense power in swaying the way of the world, especially in the corners of politics and commerce—two areas that control and influence much of the direction of the world. That kind of power is one of the reasons that ownership of broadcast entities is so coveted.

We are in a perplexing time socially and politically in this country. On any given day, we find the nation teetering on the verge of chaos. The news media's role in shaping public opinion and impacting the direction of America is as crucial as it has ever been. The current flimsy calm in an increasingly complicated world has made the dissemination of accurate information critical. Black America's narrative is too important to risk being managed by well-meaning thirtysomething White millennial producers who believe they understand Black America because they listen to Beyoncé and eat at restaurants in Harlem on the weekend. We need to report our own stories. Our perspectives should not be filtered.

We have sublimated Black programing, at our own peril, and given Black coverage in White media a greater degree of importance than it deserves. We must take back our narrative. We must encourage and reestablish the independent Black voice in the media. We must fund and own establishments that will shape, retain, and trumpet our stories. We must tell our stories and truths in a more complex and competitive way, because no one else will convey the Black narrative in a more heartfelt and authentic way.

STARTING YOUR OWN CONVERSATION

- How effectively do you think Black culture is being portrayed by the media today? What's missing?

- How do you support Black media in your daily life?

- Which Black entrepreneurs are currently dominating the entertainment industry? Which up-and-coming Black entrepreneurs do you think will play a large role in shaping the industry's future?

- Should there be community standards for how we represent Black people in the media, on TV shows, and in movies? Why or why not? And if so, who would be charged with establishing those standards?

- Let's ask a theoretical question: In your opinion, would it be better to pay to see a blockbuster film that is produced by a White man and that features a large, predominantly African American cast, or to pay to see a small indie film that is produced by a Black man and that features a much smaller African American cast? What factors would influence your decision making?

AM I BLACK ENOUGH FOR YA? 12

DEFINING BLACKNESS

TODD BOYD	Academic & Author
CHARLAMAGNE THA GOD	Radio Personality & Author
MICHAEL ERIC DYSON	Academic & Author
ALICIA GARZA	Cofounder of Black Lives Matter
JEMELE HILL	Journalist & Broadcaster
VAN JONES	Commentator & Author
VAN LATHAN	Television Producer
MALCOLM D. LEE	Director & Screenwriter
BRITTANY PACKNETT	Vice President of Teach for America
ANGELA RYE	Attorney & Political Analyst
BAKARI SELLERS	Attorney & Political Commentator
AL SHARPTON	President of the National Action Network
SHERMICHAEL SINGLETON	Republican Strategist
MICHAEL STEELE	Former Chair of the Republican National Committee

"**B**lack people all look alike" was one of those indignities that was meant to degrade us. The idea that all Black people look the same means we are, in essence, indistinguishable from one another. That is ridiculous. Black people are arguably the most diverse people in the world, from high yellow to jet black. Our diversity is the beauty of the race, though we don't always appreciate it. Because sameness was cast upon us, Black folks often push hard against the notion that we are all alike. We are constantly saying, "We're not monolithic."

While that is true, "majority thought" runs deep in our community, and if you land outside such thinking, be ready for the side-eye. Prefer pumpkin to sweet potato pie, and you might have a problem at Thanksgiving. Watching *Friends* instead of *Living Single* is blasphemous. Heaven forbid we find out you voted for Trump! No, Black America is not a monolith, but majority thinking is a reality.

We don't like when others see us as all the same, yet we don't like if one of us is too different. We shouldn't be expected to look, dress, and act the same, but it's difficult because much of the rest of the world treats us poorly and wants little to do with us. So we circle the wagons and vigorously protect those inside that circle. When we see people who seem to stray from the norm, we don't often react with acceptance: "Oh, they're just an individual." We unreasonably view him or her as someone who should be "canceled."

CAN A "BLACK CARD" BE REVOKED? IS THERE A LINE THAT CAN'T BE CROSSED?

ANGELA RYE: There's absolutely a line for me. If you're putting your own personal gain over what's in the best interest of the community, that's a line for me. Clarence Thomas is never invited to the picnic. Tim Scott is, sometimes—Mondays, Wednesdays, and Fridays. [laughs] He's done some things that are constructive and positive, but he also opposed a Black woman judge from South Carolina [whom] Congressman Jim Clyburn supported during the Obama years, who would have been a great pick. And now look at what we're getting. He's challenged Trump on some things. I don't think that we're monolithic, nor should we be, but we also need to be aware of the things that we are doing that could be really destructive to us, like Diamond and Silk, the Trump girls. Like, who are you actually? What are you doing? How is that helpful?

So even if we're not monolithic, I still think we have an obligation to sign a spiritual pledge of DO NO HARM. You can be in spaces that are different from rooms that I would want to sit in and still not do harm.

AL SHARPTON: Some cannot be invited back to the picnic only because when they're invited back, they won't behave. We must always give people a second chance. We did try to invite Clarence Thomas back. He told us he wasn't coming. He didn't want to come in the first place.

*   *   *

Ever since his nomination to the Supreme Court, Clarence Thomas has become the poster boy of Black sellout. Thomas, a Republican, became the second African American appointed to the high court. His nomination was controversial because of accusations from a former coworker, Anita Hill, that Thomas sexually harassed her when he was her supervisor at both the Department of Education and the Equal Employment Opportunity Commission. Her testimony during his confirmation hearings was groundbreaking for bringing light to the often-overlooked issue of sexual harassment in the workplace.

The other accusation that continues to plague Thomas to this day is that he harbors self-hatred. Many Blacks see Thomas as an Uncle Tom. This feeling was widely proclaimed in 1993 when *Emerge* magazine depicted Thomas on its cover wearing a headscarf tied like a mammy. Three years later Thomas would grace the cover again, this time dressed like a lawn jockey. Almost three decades since the first infamous cover, Thomas is still seen as an outcast by most of Black America.

Thomas, who rarely utters a word while presiding from the bench, has consistently voted against issues that the majority of Black Americans find important. From affirmative action to discrimination in jury selection, Thomas always falls on the side that makes life more difficult for people of color. When Thomas was appointed, many Black journalists and pundits were crestfallen. I tried to be optimistic, suggesting that over the years some justices had found the freedom of a lifetime appointment and made decisions less on partisan or ideological grounds and more on legal, moral, and ethical bases. Thomas has yet to become one of those justices. His ultraconservative views have made him a pariah in the Black community.

DO WE WALK AWAY FROM CLARENCE THOMAS AND PEOPLE LIKE HIM?

TODD BOYD: If you think about his age, you think about where he's from, a lot of people with similar circumstances think the same way; they're just not on the Supreme Court. He is not someone who is a descendant of the Black Panther Party; he didn't grow up in an urban area in the North or the Midwest or the West Coast. He's problematic in numerous ways, but there's an animosity to Clarence Thomas that is especially Black. People talk about haters. Clarence Thomas is a hater; he's not a Black guy who's trying to act White. He reminded me of a lot of Black people I've encountered over the course of my life. I suspect if you were to talk to a lot of people of his age from Savannah, Georgia, where he's from, I'm sure they wouldn't be that different than him. He's just a hater.

SHERMICHAEL SINGLETON: Justice Thomas told me [that] when he was in college he was a big, big Black Panther supporter. I don't know if a lot of people know that. Let me share what he shared with me about his interpretation of affirmative action: He knows there are some racial disparities, but he believes we're good enough to compete with Whites, so we don't need these things. People may disagree, but that's his thought process.

MICHAEL ERIC DYSON: Black people understand the trauma of Clarence Thomas. We don't often talk about this, and I'll just put that out there:

One of the reasons Clarence Thomas hates Black people so much is because he's a dark-skinned Black man in America. As a dark-skinned Black man in America of a certain generation—my daddy was blue-black, so I saw the way in which Black people treated him. I was a light-skinned Negro with curly hair and glasses, so I was treated differently. We talk about White privilege, but we won't speak about light privilege. Clarence Thomas was undoubtedly subject to some hurtful, traumatizing practices among Black people. Paper bag tests and privileges within Black America doled out on the basis of that. Look, I'm a yellow Negro, and I've had my share of people who've made assumptions about me.

MICHAEL STEELE: We don't have the debates that Booker T. and Du Bois would have over the state of Black America and how we as Black people need to own the state we're in. We're having debates over straight hair or kinky hair, over light skin or dark skin, [and] that's just utter bullsh*t. That tells me that's where we've allowed ourselves to settle at times. I think it becomes important for us to appreciate how we also limit ourselves and our ability to play at an accelerated level.

CHARLAMAGNE THA GOD: Clarence Thomas and people like him seem extreme and like they really are sellouts. White supremacists in Black skin in a lot of cases. If you are using your platform to do the work of your oppressor, to keep a foot on Black people's necks, that's treasonous to me. I don't respect you at all. Yeah, they need to stay over there!

I look at people like Van Jones. There were times that I had issues with things that Van was doing, but I had to say to myself, "Van is actually getting things done." Just because I'm not willing to engage with that administration on that level, I'm not going to make the same mistakes as my forefathers and call him an Uncle Tom and a coon and a sellout because he's really getting things done. You can go back and read *The Autobiography of Malcolm X.* You think Malcolm liked Martin? Malcolm used to say the same things about Martin Luther King Jr. Think about that.

VAN JONES: People who are sitting on a white-hot stove tend to be a little jumpy. The bane of our people is vented at whatever target is moving. I've been frustrated [that] TheRoot.com treats me now the same way that Fox News treated me when I was with the Obama administration. No matter what I did—if I demonstrated patriotism or love of country—they would never report that. I could do a thousand things that they would find admirable; they just ignored it. I did one thing that they didn't like, and it became a lead story on Fox News for a year after I left the Obama administration. Now I see the left doing the same thing. We literally got Demetrius Anderson, who was going to go back to prison for nothing; we got him saved, and he's not going to go back. We've done that kind of thing multiple times, and we sent it to *The Root*—"Hey, look, here's what we just did"—they won't cover it. But I say something positive about Kim Kardashian, Jared Kushner, or Donald Trump, in the context of them helping our people, [and] it's "Van Jones Is a Sellout." It's a big headline. Push it out, and it becomes clickbait for them. We have to put our people first, not our people's image first. Not what Black Twitter says first, but what actual Black people say.

> *We have to put our people first, not our people's image first. Not what Black Twitter says first, but what actual Black people say.*

Jones has taken heat for his relationship with the Trump administration. He was panned for what many called a fluff interview with Jared Kushner, Donald Trump's senior adviser and son-in-law. Jones has also worked closely with the administration to free wrongly incarcerated prisoners.

ED GORDON: So what does it mean to be Black in America today?

MALCOLM D. LEE: There's a narrow view of what it means to be Black. We've been brainwashed through media, over generations, about how we should behave. And then there's the cultural backlash about how we should behave. "I'm gonna be Black? What does that mean? I'm gonna be 'hood?

I'm gonna be ghetto?" No. "If I'm articulating, does that mean I'm trying to be White?" I've been fighting this kind of thing my entire life.

MICHAEL ERIC DYSON: That's why "Blacker Than Thou" can never work. Because Clarence Thomas is Black, Candace Owens is Black, Kanye West—even for those who find him problematic—is Black. It ain't their Blackness that we have to contend with. David Clarke? Black, too! The question is, to what degree does your humanity prevail? We're not only arguing about your Blackness. We are arguing about your humanity. You can still be Black; you just ain't part of what we understand to be the [confluence] of forces that will help rescue us. Redeem us. Restore us. Extend our virtues and values, and if you don't want to be part of that, then cool. We don't have to read you out of the ranks. You've already excommunicated yourself.

We're not only arguing about your Blackness. We are arguing about your humanity.

The Candace Owenses of the world are people who are willing to leverage their Blackness in defense of some vicious beliefs that are anti-Black. Black people can be anti-Black too. Black people can harbor racist viewpoints too. It used to be said we couldn't be racist, in terms of exercising authority, because we didn't have power in this country. That's true. But we can be bigots. We can self-hate; we can hate Blackness. In fact, we are sometimes smuggling in White supremacist views. White supremacy is operating within Black minds in the ventriloquist effect. Black mouths moving, White supremacist ideals flowing.

CHARLAMAGNE THA GOD: Candace Owens says she wants to liberate Black people. My only question for somebody like her is, "You're telling everybody to go be Republicans. What is the Republican Party promising us? What are the Republicans doing for us?" But her message is the liberation of Black people—same thing with Van Jones. He wants to liberate Black people from the prison system. We've got these engagers, and we have these resisters. The engagers are willing to engage with anybody and any administration to get something done on our behalf. The resisters are, "Nah, eff that. We are going to focus on our communities and our people. We're going to empower each other." Both are cool. As long as both of them have got the same end goal, what does it matter?

AL SHARPTON: Omarosa came to our National Action Network convention in '17 and spoke for Trump. She got booed. When she got booted out of the White House, I told her, "The only reason I'm going to put you on my show is I want you to expose Trump." That's the only reason I had her on. And the only reason I had her back is because she'd worked for both Trump and the guy from *National Enquirer* [David Pecker]. I thought we could teach other people that you're going to end up back here anyway, so don't go for the okey-doke. Maybe it's the minister in me.

CHARLAMAGNE THA GOD: Omarosa seems to have woken up. But did she wake up because she got fired or because she finally came to her senses?

MICHAEL ERIC DYSON: She came to an awareness—to many of us—too damn late. So all Black folks who go against the grain ain't in the same boat. Some wake up and smell the coffee and understand that it was Black before it had cream in it.

ANGELA RYE: I remember when Michael Steele was the chairman of the RNC, and I disagreed with him on a lot. But it's so funny because now, given where we are, that wasn't that bad. There are voting initiatives that Michael wants to be engaged in that are helpful to us, that the Republican Party would not be supportive of. He believes in the idea of a real democracy, probably because he's got ancestors who weren't allowed to participate. There's a thought. [laughs]

BAKARI SELLERS: I think it's more pronounced now than it ever has been. Kanye and Omarosa have crossed that line politically. Bill Cosby and R. Kelly have crossed that line by abusing our women. For a long period, people believed that Black folks would never stop putting up with [them], but that's no longer the case.

* * *

In 2005, during a live national telethon for the victims of Hurricane Katrina, a natural disaster that disproportionately impacted people of color in New Orleans, rapper Kanye West claimed that President George Bush "doesn't care about Black people." There had been questions about the government's slow response to assist those in need, most of whom were minority and poor. West's off-script moment spoke loudly for those who believed race was the reason for what some saw as the federal government's lack of urgency to assist the needy of New Orleans. Critics felt the mercurial rapper's comment was out of line, while many Black people saw a celebrity who didn't worry about his image and used a huge platform to speak truth to power.

According to studies analyzed by the Pew Research Center, interracial births have tripled since the 1980s. In a 2015 survey of interracial births, 12 percent were Black–American Indian, and 11 percent were Black-White. Most researchers believe that the multiracial population in America will continue to grow.

Juxtapose that Kanye with the one who supported Donald Trump and fawned over him during a White House visit, complete with West wearing a MAGA hat that he said made him feel like Superman. Was the dislike for Trump in the Black community strong enough to topple a megastar like West? Perhaps not, but West's appearance on TMZ, where he implied that slavery was "a choice" for Blacks, was enough to make a good number of African Americans feel that Kanye had burned his bridge back home.

HOW HAVE KANYE WEST'S MORE CONTROVERSIAL STATEMENTS AND ACTIONS CHANGED HIS RELATIONSHIP WITH THE BLACK COMMUNITY?

BRITTANY PACKNETT: I recognize everything he's done for the culture in years past, maybe even years in the future. Even the moments where I'm saying, "How is he holding his head up, and who's got you?" There are so many Black folks who are friends with Kanye, who are in association with Kanye, who've worked with Kanye, who could have given a phone call, who could have given him a text or reached out or said, "Brother, are you okay?" I'm not blaming them for his behavior. I am saying that he has to recognize that there's public accountability, and there also has to be some community accountability.

Todd Boyd: I spent some time with Kanye a while ago, and what was interesting to me was how different he was off-screen, away from the camera. I didn't get any of that attitude; what I got was insecurity, somebody who really is just not comfortable in his own skin. The way he went out of his way to embrace Trump. He's trying to be different, and by doing that, he dug a hole for himself, and he had to keep on digging. The next thing you know, he's sitting up in the White House, engaging in a coon show, talking about how good the MAGA hat made him feel. That's not some Black guy trying to be White; it's a Black guy trying to get attention and trying to do everything possible to be different.

I have issues with things both West and [Clarence] Thomas have said, things they've done, but I don't think [Kanye is] somebody who's not trying to be Black. Some might see them as trying to seek White approval or perform for White audiences. But, to me, those things are "Black," not something Black that I want to identify with, or something that I wanna do. But it's not the first time I've seen it, and I imagine it won't be the last.

Van Lathan: When Kanye went on television and said that George Bush didn't care about Black people because of the hurricane that wiped out my community, I'm watching someone speaking for me and who seems to be in lockstep with the things that are trying to take me out, the things that are trying to hurt young Black America, the things that are trying to hurt the disenfranchised and marginalized people. Then he's standing in the TMZ newsroom—a room full of White people, my coworkers—and he's saying all of these vile, crazy things about my ancestors who, beyond any other group of untouchables, they are the most untouchable. Their grandchildren got beat up and had dogs and hoses turned on them. So I don't care who you are. If you stand up in a room full of White people and say those people chose that life, me and you are going to have words in front of the whole world, okay? You have to be able to hold people accountable, but you hold them accountable the way you would somebody in your family. "I appreciate your genius, my brother, but this is how I feel like you are missing the point." You never want to take somebody's platform away from them or poke holes in it, but if something is being done that is actually starting to hurt the community, then you have to speak up. What I love about being Black is my people have carte blanche to get me to tighten up when I need it. I don't mind accountability from Black people; I don't mind accountability from people in my community. That's what I expect from them. And they should expect it from me as well. We just have to do it in a way that doesn't destroy one another. There's no one anywhere who loves Kanye West as much as I do. And I say *loves* in the present tense.

MICHAEL ERIC DYSON: I'm gonna tell you something about Black people, Doc. At the end of the day, if these people evince any understanding that what they have done is wrong, Black people will take them back. Michael Jackson, whom we loved and understood—I remember Jesse Jackson went in the court with Michael and was there with him. After he got off for charges of child molestation, I called Jesse and asked, "What did he say?" Jesse said, "I ain't heard from him." And I love Michael Jackson.

So there's no question that Black people are the most forgiving people on earth, and why shouldn't we be? If we can forgive a White boy who goes into a Black church and murders nine people, and before their bodies are cold, they offer forgiveness to him, whether or not you think that's good or productive, it is a simple definition of our Black humanity. And this is a redemptive character of Black people for the world, not just for our community.

TAMIKA MALLORY: Black folks are forgiving—we'll begin to open doors for Black folks to enter the space again. We don't just cancel people; that's just not who we are. But you can hurt yourself in a way that even when you're in the room again, it doesn't mean that you're significant. Some Black folks have definitely crossed that line, particularly in this Trump era.

BRITTANY PACKNETT: Sometimes we bring folks back to the cookout, but there's a line that has to be drawn when someone does persistent damage, someone like R. Kelly. It took a long time for our cookout invitation to finally be rescinded. Everyone was busy whispering about it and not paying attention to the Black women who were trying to shout about it. Finally, his reckoning has begun. I am not God, so I can't judge anyone's damnation. But I do know that he is someone who persistently did harm to our community, and we all knew it. That should be a line that we hold firm on.

ALICIA GARZA: R. Kelly has been abusing, sexually assaulting, and sexually violating Black girls and Black young women for close to two decades now. And he has been doing so in plain sight. On the contrary, many of us were content for Clarence Thomas to be in that position of power because we wanted representation at the Supreme Court level, and in order to get that representation [we needed Thomas].

JEMELE HILL: I look at a lot of the people we have put on a similar pedestal, from Bill Cosby to R. Kelly. These are people we have embraced and seen as family members, as we tend to do with Black people who attain a certain level of success. And for them to commit traitorous acts against our own people was unforgivable. A lot of people don't understand that love is correction. If we didn't love the prospect of us doing better and thinking better, then accountability wouldn't be a part of this equation. We have to do this, because it is born out of love.

Defining color and "Blackness" has always been tricky in America, even among Blacks. The "one-drop rule" is an example of a social construct and legal principle in certain states that stated that any person with one drop of Black (sub-Saharan) blood is to be considered Black. Another example, the brown bag test, was practiced within the Black community, in which members would discriminate against anyone darker than the bag's color.

*   *   *

We need to expand the definition of *Black*. The problem is, who defines what is authentically Black? Who determines what is Black enough and what isn't? Is it color? We are still caught up in the question of light folks not being "Black enough" and dark folks being "too Black." If that's the gauge, then you're saying that Clarence Thomas is "Blacker" than Louis Farrakhan. Want to stay with that one? Is it the way you dress and carry yourself? Perhaps it's your level of education? Did you have to be born into hard times?

It's a quandary that African Americans have long struggled with. There has never been a singular voice, never a monolithic definition of what is authentically Black. Deviance is often viewed as off-putting.

From the days of capturing slaves from Africa, there has always been a leeriness of those who don't pass the "cultural test." The test should actually be whether you are engaged for the greater good. Our methods don't need to be the same, but our desire to benefit all in the community should be the overall aim.

We are better with a diverse group of opinions and voices. We are better with different approaches and plans. We are better with different schools of thought. We are better with a shared understanding that there is no one way to be Black.

STARTING YOUR OWN CONVERSATION

- What does *being Black* mean to you? How do you define your own Blackness?

- How have your family members, friends, and colleagues contributed to your idea of what it means to be Black? How does that compare to what the national media says about Blackness?

- Is there a "Black card"? And should others be able to rescind it or take it away?

- There is much disagreement about whether the Republican Party is aligned with Black interests, which is why many Black Republicans—such as Clarence Thomas and Omarosa Manigault Newman—are considered pariahs in the Black community. Do you agree with this? Why or why not?

- Van Lathan stresses that loving people means you're willing to call them out when you see them falter, and in that way, "No one loves Kanye West as much as I do." How does the respect and "love" you have for others in the Black community shape your critique of them?

CONCLUSION: THE NEW NARRATIVE

The discussions shared throughout these pages have allowed me to look deep into the state of Black America today and what must still be done to make sure that our journey continues to move forward all people of color in our nation. These conversations emphasize the need for a new direction and new narratives to guide us through the twenty-first century and beyond. I am encouraged by the things we all have in common, including what I believe is the consensus in the Black community that we need to find new roads. That's not to say that we must throw out everything that has helped us get to this point, but we should not be so stuck in tradition that we are unable to rationally evaluate what is still working for us and what should be abandoned.

During our conversation, Michael Eric Dyson noted, "It's always been a small group of Black people, of conscientious Black people, who have spurred revolution or change or evolution. It's only a few. We romanticize it as if all of us were involved. Also, we look at the sexy spectacular, [like] the March on Washington, as opposed to the unsexy normal—twenty people in the room trying to figure out what to do, thirty people in a church trying to figure out how to move forward. People trying to come up with programs, and so on and so forth. That's the unsexy normal that we have to acknowledge."

While I want the entire Black community to engage in this change, I'm hopeful that a few can start to bring forward the change that we so desperately need. Police brutality, education, employment, voting rights—wherever consensus can be found on an issue, a group of like-minded people can spur a revolution.

These discussions have also revealed that we can keep the momentum going by combining the strengths and clout of established organizations and longtime leaders with the energy, expertise, and new ideas from millennials. This is not to be Pollyanna. This marriage would not be simple, nor would it be without snags. There will certainly be some amount of fallout, but if commitment to our fight is bigger than our desire for the spotlight or organizational self-aggrandizement, the results could be stellar.

The candor of the participants in these conversations has demonstrated that, above all else, we need to be more honest with ourselves and with each other. We need better cooperation between generations. A number of the old guard believe their relationships with those following in their footsteps is more collaborative than it actually is. Those next in line sometimes feel as if their elders are more interested in being paternal than being partners. Moving forward together will require leaders to subjugate their egos. They'll need to find at least one common interest that allows both generations to bring their strengths to the table. These talks also gave me a better understanding of where that middle ground may be, as participants found common ground in the most productive ways to forge ahead and take on those who want to hold us back.

The generational changing of the guard that has begun is refreshing. Activism has always been a survival mechanism for African Americans. The brave push back—sometimes risking life and limb—against prejudicial institutions and systems; that has kept Blacks from being totally shut out by racism.

Activism is often sparked by actions that trigger emotions. Black America has been triggered, and there has been a corresponding resurgence in activism. A new generation has been moved by the election of Barack Obama, sickened by the murder of Trayvon Martin, motivated by the kneeling of Colin Kaepernick, and disgusted by the election of Donald Trump and the overall injustice of a country that has yet to find a way to meet its promise of "liberty and justice for all."

While I was talking with CNN analyst Laura Coates, she remarked, "Polite activists never make change. I don't mean they have to be uncivil, but if politeness means that you give people a pass just because they think it's enough that you're in the room, then you've missed the point of the invitation. You've missed the point if you say, 'Oh, good, look. I have been deemed worthy enough for an invitation by this person' or 'I have been deemed worthy enough to have a seat at X, Y, or Z table,' as opposed to saying, 'I built the table and made the meal. I set the menu, and I am the topic of dinner conversation. Why would I not be at this table?'"

And she's right. We need more than just an invite to the party. We should be allowed to dance and pick some of the music too. I know that many in the next generation have adopted this mind-set, and that change in attitude is crucial to our advancement. A new spirit is in the air.

A crucial part of this advancement requires taking new approaches to wealth building. The new narrative for money starts with changing the legacy left behind by the previous generations of Blacks who entered the workforce. During our conversation, *Black Enterprise* publisher Butch Graves suggested to me that we need to have a fearless approach to becoming more financially independent. "Young people don't look at the thought of them going to work somewhere for thirty-five years and getting a watch—that doesn't even enter their mind-set. They want to get out there and try to do their thing, and they have a sense that something—they don't know what it's going to be—but something will come true, and that's not necessarily a dangerous mind-set. It's actually healthy. They think, 'Something's going to work out. I'm going to be able to get this business going.' So that's a good thing; that entrepreneurial spirit is a good thing."

Professional athletes and entertainers have already taken the lead in this regard. Many are using their primary income to participate in other economic ventures. This multiple-income route turned Magic Johnson into a power player in the business world and Jay-Z into a billionaire. CNN commentator Van Jones said, "I look with great admiration to people like Robert Smith, who built his company and, now that he's a billionaire, contributes to certain causes. I look with a great deal of admiration to people like Jay-Z or Diddy and Oprah Winfrey. They have leveraged their notoriety and built real enterprises. The next generation can do like Robert Smith and skip the notoriety and just build. There might just need to be a quieter approach to some of this asset building." As these ideas and practices trickle down and become more common in Black America, we will be able to start building great wealth for ourselves and move our community beyond the grip of poverty.

Education is a huge part of that too. Today's young Blacks are arguably the most educated generation of African Americans in history. If the highly learned elite, as well as the educated middle class, reach back to those currently being failed by the American public school system, it could help lift them up and get them the resources they need to succeed. Educator and activist Jitu Brown echoed that need to help young kids move up in the world. "I started off working with youth—training kids through enrichment programs in schools. My life experience tells me that if you're consistent, if you have high expectations, then any child can learn. Today, we have an education system that is clearly biased to fail our young people. Clearly, we adopted the [idea that] no schools are bad; it's [just] because the kids don't want to listen."

As many of these interviewees noted, we have to stop convincing ourselves that many of the public school systems our kids attend aren't that bad. They are. We have to stop pretending that these children are being prepared for the modern world. They aren't. Education has become a big business for public and private industry. Charter, public, and some private schools are all vying for children, and for some of these institutions, children are simply profit opportunities. Failing schools should be a reclamation project for the entire Black community. We can hold up the great educational achievements of this new generation of Black women to prove that Black students can achieve, as our sisters—in record numbers—are proving.

Representation—in all facets of life—is also crucial to the development of our community, and fortunately, we are starting to see more diverse representation of people of color in the entertainment industry. The diversity of images and stories today is undeniably and vastly more positive than it was just a few years ago. From movies to television, we're demanding real depictions of people who look like us—and we're finally starting to be heard. Some of these changes were accelerated by the #OscarsSoWhite movement, which shone a light on how often Black performances are overlooked by the Academy and how often Black actors are portrayed as secondary or stereotypical characters.

As Blacks, we need to be able to tell our own stories—and we're finally getting the chance to do so. The idea that what were once only considered "Black stories" have universal appeal is starting to take hold. Still, there's a long way to go, as Jeff Friday, founder of the American Black Film Festival, reminded us: "Individuals have made progress. There are people who are very influential, so influential that they own their content and lease that content to studios to distribute. But, for the most part, people of color have very little financial influence in Hollywood. The number of people of color who have any kind of financial leverage now in the town is about ten."

However, we must remember that, in the end, the consumer will always win out. As has often been said, Hollywood's real color isn't white or black or brown—it's green. If people watch the content, it will flourish; if not, it will not survive. Voting with our dollars and being more intentional in terms of the content we support are the best ways to define what films and TV shows about Black folks get made.

Still, there exists an intracultural dividing line of taste when it comes to our entertainment. We must respect that a Tyler Perry movie is just as important as a television show by Shonda Rhimes—Madea is every bit as representative of Black America as Olivia Pope. Director Malcolm D. Lee opined that all we really want to see on the screen is ourselves. "Like all this artistry—whether it's visual art, painting, drawing, dance, music, film, writing, literature—it's got to inspire. Not just entertain. You [need to] really make people think, make people feel good. We always want to see images of ourselves and be empowered and validated. That's why *Black Panther* worked. That's why *Girls Trip* worked. That's why *Get Out* worked. That's why *Us* worked. We are seeing ourselves in ways that we have wanted to. We see ourselves on a big screen and say, 'That's me, that's my friend, that's my mother, that's my father, that's my sister, that's my cousin.' We also know, 'That's my mind, that's my imagination on the screen.'"

The state of Black America remains intriguing. Some African Americans are living the promise of the American dream—educated, thriving in their jobs, giving back to their communities—and a few have acquired real wealth. Others are trapped in an endless cycle of poverty and despair, with little hope of escaping the shackles of racism. Collectively, we're complicated, fluid, changing. And we need a strong foundation for all Black Americans to stand on.

Ultimately, these conversations confirm that, as a group, we need an agenda—a shared template that the majority of us can agree on in theory and act on in practice. As we go into the crucial 2020 election, we should move toward speaking in a unified voice. As former attorney general Eric Holder said, "We are not yet at the place where we need to be. Some things are better, but they're not yet where they should be if you look at our incarceration, if you look [at] all the economic statistics, if you look at the possibilities that are still foreclosed to people because of the color of their skin. We're still not yet at a place where the African American community—where Black America—needs to be. However, I would say that we're better than we were fifty years ago, [or even] twenty years ago, and [we're] still striving to get to the place where we need to be."

It's true that we are in a far better place than we were years ago. The real question is this: Will we be able to say the same thing a decade or two from now? I left all of these conversations feeling optimistic that Black America has a real chance to make positive advancements in the lives of the bulk of our families. But that will take everyone making a dedicated commitment to finding new, more productive ways to overcome the prejudices and barriers we still run up against.

We are in a critical period. We are in a time when racism is being weaponized in ways we have not seen for years to slow, stop, and eradicate the tremendous gains we've already made. The conversations in this book remind us that we have a duty not to allow our community to slide backward. We owe a debt to those brave souls who fought for equality, and we must continue to pay it.

At the end of the day, we hold the power of change in our own hands. I hope this book has inspired you to start your own conversations and to look for ways that you can help create new narratives of change. Black power and independence are in the air, and finally grasping them may only be a conversation away. It's time to start talking!

ACKNOWLEDGMENTS

My sincere thanks and deepest gratitude to all the extraordinary people who gave of their time to participate in these conversations. Most of all, thank you for your dedication to our community and your continued efforts to make life better for all people of color. Thanks to my friend and booker extraordinaire, Carol Johnson Green, for always helping me reach my dreams. Thanks to my literary agent, Regina Brooks of Serendipity Literary Agency, for reppin' me. Adrienne Ingrum, your help made it a book! You're a pleasure to work with; you're the best. Appreciation to Krishan Trotman for taking a leap of faith on the book's concept and to her team at Hachette Publishing—Mary Ann Naples, Michelle Aielli, Michael Barrs, Odette Fleming, Michael Giarratano, and Carrie Napolitano—for all they do. To my wife, Leslie, your love and encouragement kept me going and writing, especially on the days I didn't want to. To the rest of my family and friends, thanks for leaving me alone so I could finish!

ABOUT THE AUTHOR

*H*ard-hitting, inspiring, intelligent, honest, and *direct*—these are some of
the words used to describe the style and approach of Emmy Award–
winning broadcaster Ed Gordon. Known for his stellar interactions with
newsmakers from the worlds of politics, entertainment, and sports, Gordon
is the president of Ed Gordon Media, a multiservice production company.

Gordon hosted and executive produced *Ed Gordon*, an hour-long quar-
terly newsmagazine on Bounce TV. This program featured many inspirational
and moving interviews, such as an emotional interview with the Mothers
of the Movement, a group of women whose children have been killed by
senseless violence, and a look at the controversy surrounding the movie *The
Birth of a Nation* (2016) and its star and director, Nate Parker. Other high-
lights included a profile of powerhouse congresswoman Maxine Waters and
exclusive interviews with comedian Steve Harvey, R&B singer Maxwell, and
the cast of the mega-successful movie *Girls Trip*.

Additionally, Gordon hosted and executive-produced the nationally syndicated one-on-one program *Conversations with Ed Gordon*. The signature
program allowed Gordon to bring newsmakers and celebrities up close and
personal with viewers. Over the years, guests have included Oprah Winfrey,
Denzel Washington, Kevin Hart, and Janet Jackson, among many others.
Previously, he has also been a contributing correspondent for the CBS news
show *60 Minutes II*, a contributor for NBC's *Today Show* and *Dateline*, the
host of NPR's *News and Notes with Ed Gordon*, and the MSNBC anchor and
host of the nationally syndicated television programs *Our World* and *Weekly
with Ed Gordon*. He further distinguished himself during two stints at BET.

He's had many roles at the network, including host of *BET Tonight*, anchor of *BET News*, and creator of his signature one-on-one series *Conversations with Ed Gordon*. Gordon also anchored BET's coverage of the 2012 presidential election, Obama's second inauguration, Nelson Mandela's funeral from South Africa, and the fiftieth anniversary of the historic March on Washington.

But Gordon's reach doesn't stop there. He is also featured on *The Steve Harvey Morning Show*, where he gives his perspective on current national headlines, and he records *Right Now with Ed Gordon*, which provides daily commentaries for radio stations across the country. He also hosts the nationally syndicated radio program *Weekend with Ed Gordon*, a two-hour program featuring a mix of talk, information, entertainment, and music. It's been called "a fun, smart radio show for grown folks."

Aside from his own media ventures, Gordon continues to be at the forefront of news. He conducted one-on-one interviews with President Barack Obama during his historic presidency. He has covered many of the world's most defining events throughout his career, from the historic 2008 US presidential election to the freeing of South Africa's Nelson Mandela to the beating of Rodney King to the upheavals in Haiti and Cuba. He's also provided comprehensive coverage and up-to-the-minute reports on many other domestic and international events, including the tragic 9/11 attacks on America.

Gordon's impressive interview portfolio also includes conversations with the following newsmakers: President Bill Clinton, Grammy Award–winning performer Beyoncé, Academy Award winners Jamie Foxx and Halle Berry, Nation of Islam leader Minister Louis Farrakhan, actor Idris Elba, and the late musician Michael Jackson.

Some of Gordon's other notable works that have garnered the admiration and respect of viewers and colleagues include the infamous O. J. Simpson interview; an exclusive interview with pop superstar Janet Jackson about her secret marriage and painful divorce; no-holds-barred interviews with controversial senator Trent Lott and embattled singer R. Kelly; the critically acclaimed one-on-one interview with Tupac Shakur (often noted as the rapper's definitive interview); and a fiery interview with White House staffer Omarosa Manigault Newman in 2017, which made national headlines.

In addition to receiving an Emmy for his work, Gordon is the recipient of many other awards recognizing his talent and professionalism, including the NAACP Image Award and the prestigious Journalist of the Year Award from the National Association of Black Journalists.

ABOUT THE CONTRIBUTORS

Stacey Abrams: Democratic politician, attorney, and author. She was the party's nominee in the 2018 Georgia gubernatorial election. Abrams was a member of the Georgia House of Representatives from 2011 to 2017. She is seen as a possible future US senator or presidential candidate.

William Barber: Minister and political activist. Bishop Barber is pastor of Greenleaf Christian Church in Goldsboro, North Carolina. He leads the antipoverty movement Poor People's Campaign, which was named in honor of a campaign of the same name founded by Martin Luther King Jr. in 1968. Barber is also a national board member of the NAACP.

Harry Belafonte: Legendary entertainer and activist. In the 1950s, he broke color barriers in entertainment and is credited with becoming the first solo artist whose album sold a million copies. He was an active supporter of the civil rights movement in the 1950s and 1960s and remains a champion of justice issues.

Marilyn Booker: Corporate executive. Booker is the head of Morgan Stanley's Urban Market Group. She is a twenty-five-year veteran of the wealth-building field. Booker is dedicated to increasing the financial literacy of people of color, especially young African Americans.

Todd Boyd: Professor and author. Boyd is a professor at the University of Southern California. Boyd, an "opinion shaper," often appears on broadcast and media outlets. His writing credits include the book *Am I Black Enough for You?* and the movie *The Wood*.

Jitu Brown: Chicago activist and national director of the Journey for Justice Alliance, an alliance of grassroots community, youth, and parent-led organizations in over thirty cities across the country, demanding community-driven alternatives to the privatization and dismantling of public school systems.

Tarana Burke: Civil rights activist. Burke is the founder of the #MeToo movement. She started her activism while attending college in the 1990s. She is also a champion of gender equity and a crusader against sexual harassment and abuse.

Charlamagne tha God: Radio personality, author, and influencer. Charlamagne (Lenard McKelvey) is a cohost of *The Breakfast Club*, a nationally syndicated morning radio program. He is also a best-selling author and a strong mental health advocate for people of color.

Laura Coates: Attorney, analyst, and professor. Coates is a legal analyst for CNN and the host of *The Laura Coates Show* on SiriusXM. She is also an adjunct professor of law at George Washington University. She was a trial attorney at the Department of Justice during the George W. Bush and Obama administrations.

Brittney Cooper: Associate professor in the Department of Women's and Gender Studies at Rutgers University. She is also an author and speaker whose areas of research include Black women's organizations, Black women intellectuals, and hip-hop feminism.

James Craig: Chief of police for the city of Detroit. Craig has held that position since 2013. He started his career as an officer in 1977, and over the years, he has worked on police forces in Los Angeles; Cincinnati; and Portland, Maine.

Tiffany Cross: Editor and commentator. Cross is the cofounder and managing editor of *The Beat DC*, a daily newsletter focusing on politics and policy for people of color. She is also a frequent guest on cable news outlets. She has worked on numerous political campaigns and in organized labor.

Ben Crump: Attorney and activist. Crump is one of today's most successful civil rights attorneys and one of the faces of the current fight for racial justice. Crump has represented the families of Trayvon Martin, Michael Brown, and many others. In his fight for equality, he has taken on multiple police forces and Harvard University.

Richelieu Dennis: Entrepreneur and philanthropist. Dennis is the founder, CEO, and executive chair of Sundial Brands and the founder and chair of Essence Ventures. He also oversees the $100 million New Voices Fund, which invests in businesses owned by women of color.

Michael Eric Dyson: Academic, preacher, activist, and author. Dyson is a professor at Georgetown University. He is one of today's foremost intellectuals and has authored numerous books. He is often seen as one of the leading voices on Black culture.

Jeff Friday: Entrepreneur and movie producer. Friday is the founder of the American Black Film Festival, which is considered one of the most influential film festivals in the country. Friday is a force in Hollywood and is also president of his own production company.

Sybrina Fulton: Mother of slain teen Trayvon Martin and activist. Martin's death became a flashpoint for the Black Lives Matter movement, and Fulton has become a symbol of strength and a leading voice in the fight for racial justice in America.

Alicia Garza: Civil rights activist and writer. Garza is a cofounder of the Black Lives Matter movement. She also spotlights issues surrounding a myriad of social concerns and is a partner in Black Futures Lab, an initiative working to build political and social power for minority communities.

Sarah Glover: Journalist. Glover is the president of the National Association of Black Journalists. A veteran in the industry, she is also the manager of social media strategy for NBC-owned television stations.

Earl "Butch" Graves: Graves is the CEO of Earl G. Graves Publishing Company and the publisher of *Black Enterprise* magazine. Graves serves on a number of corporate boards and is a staunch proponent of and advocate for greater diversity in corporate America.

Jemele Hill: Journalist. She is a writer for *The Atlantic* and a cofounder of Lodge Freeway Media, a broadcasting and media company. Hill was a host on ESPN from 2006 to 2018. She is an outspoken political voice on social media and a vocal Trump critic.

Eric Holder: Former US attorney general in the Obama administration. He was the first African American to hold that position. Holder previously served as a judge of the Superior Court of the District of Columbia and was later appointed by President Bill Clinton as the US attorney for the District of Columbia and deputy attorney general.

Ericka Huggins: Activist and educator. Huggins is a professor of sociology at Laney College in Oakland, California, and at Berkeley (California) City College. She was a member of the Black Panther Party and the director of the Black Panther Party's Oakland Community School from 1973 to 1981.

D. L. Hughley: Entertainer and social commentator. Hughley is one of today's most successful comedians and the host of the nationally syndicated radio program *The D. L. Hughley Show*. He is also one of today's most astute observers of society and one of the keenest satirists on the comedy scene.

Hakeem Jeffries: Jeffries is a US representative from the state of New York. He serves as the head of the House Democratic Caucus and is considered a rising star in the Democratic Party. Before being elected to Congress, he served in the New York State Assembly and was a corporate lawyer.

Derrick Johnson: Civil rights leader and activist. Johnson is the president and CEO of the NAACP. Johnson was named to that position in 2017 and is a longtime member of the organization. His goal is to reinvigorate the NAACP. Prior to this, Johnson founded One Voice, Inc., to improve the quality of life for African Americans through civic engagement training and initiatives.

Van Jones: Commentator, author, and influencer. Jones is a regular on CNN and a best-selling author. He is also a cofounder of several nonprofit organizations. In 2009, he served as President Barack Obama's special adviser for green jobs.

Killer Mike: Rapper, activist, and entrepreneur. Killer Mike (Mike Render) is a Grammy Award–winning rapper and actor. He has also become a national voice in the social and political arenas. He advocates for and encourages political participation and entrepreneurship among African Americans.

Van Lathan: Television producer and influencer. Lathan was a producer at TMZ, best known for his infamous challenge of Kanye West's comments about slavery being a choice. Lathan is also a social media influencer and the host of a popular podcast, *The Red Pill.*

Malcolm D. Lee: Film director and screenwriter. Lee is one of today's most successful movie directors in Hollywood. His credits include *The Best Man* (a franchise), *Girls Trip*, and *Night School.* His movies have grossed almost $500 million.

Tamika Mallory: Political activist. Mallory is the copresident of the 2019 Women's March. She is also a leading activist in the Black Lives Matter and gun control movements. She has been involved in activism since the age of eleven.

Julianne Malveaux: Economist, author, social and political commentator, and businesswoman. She serves on numerous economic policy boards and was the president of Bennett College from 2007 to 2012.

DeRay Mckesson: Civil rights activist. He came to prominence during the Black Lives Matter protests in Ferguson, Missouri, and Baltimore, Maryland. Mckesson was a candidate for mayor of Baltimore in 2016. He cofounded Campaign Zero, a policy platform to end police violence.

Marc Morial: Civil rights leader and president of the National Urban League. Before being named as head of the Urban League in 2003, he was elected mayor of New Orleans and served two terms from 1994 to 2002; he also served in the Louisiana Senate from 1992 to 1994.

Brittany Packnett: Packnett is the vice president of the national community alliance Teach for America, a nonprofit organization that works to strengthen educational equity. After being involved in the Ferguson, Missouri, protests, she cofounded Campaign Zero, a policy platform designed to end police violence.

Steve Perry: Educator, motivational speaker, and author. The founder of Capital Preparatory Schools, Perry is on the front lines of the charter school movement and has been embroiled in controversial debates over the future of education for children of color.

April Reign: Activist and lawyer. Her #OscarsSoWhite hashtag sparked a movement to challenge Hollywood's lack of diversity and to encourage the movie industry to become more racially inclusive. She is also an advocate for women's right to choose.

Angela Rye: Attorney, political analyst, and strategist. She is the CEO of IMPACT Strategies, a political advocacy firm. Rye is also a political commentator on CNN and was the executive director and general counsel to the Congressional Black Caucus.

Bakari Sellers: Attorney and political commentator. Sellers is a political commentator for CNN. He was also a representative in South Carolina's statehouse from 2006 to 2014. He ran for lieutenant governor of the state in 2015.

Al Sharpton: Civil rights leader and media host. Sharpton is the president of the National Action Network and a longtime civil rights activist. He is one of today's most powerful influencers, with his voice reaching millions through his platforms on cable television and syndicated radio.

Shermichael Singleton: Political analyst. Singleton is a political commentator who appears regularly on MSNBC. He is also a writer and political consultant. He has worked on three presidential campaigns—for Newt Gingrich, Mitt Romney, and Ben Carson. He was the youngest-ever Department of Housing and Urban Development deputy chief of staff and was fired after writing an op-ed that criticized President Donald Trump's characterization of Black voters.

Tommie Smith: Olympic track gold medalist and lecturer. Smith and his teammate, John Carlos, created one of the most important moments in America's fight for equality. Their raised one-gloved-fist protest at the 1968 Olympics has become an enduring image in the fight for civil rights.

Michael Steele: MSNBC analyst and former chair of the Republican National Committee. He was also lieutenant governor of Maryland from 2003 to 2007 and the first African American elected to statewide office in Maryland.

Susan Taylor: Editor and author. Taylor is the founder of the National Cares Mentoring Movement, an organization dedicated to helping children by galvanizing communities and breaking the cycle of generational poverty. Taylor was also the editor in chief of *Essence* magazine from 1981 to 2000.

T.I.: Rapper, actor, entrepreneur, and activist. T.I. (Clifford Harris) is a multiplatinum-selling music artist who has become a leading activist in the civil rights movement. T.I. uses his celebrity platform to advance African American causes. He has called for a number of boycotts, including boycotts of high-fashion brands over blackface controversies.

Iyanla Vanzant: Inspirational speaker and life coach. She is also a best-selling author and television personality who has made a career out of helping others deal with issues and trauma in their lives. She is one of today's most sought-after motivational speakers.

Maxine Waters: Democratic US representative from California. She is one of the most powerful people in Congress today and is the chair of the House Financial Services Committee. The fifteen-term congresswoman is a staunch critic of President Donald Trump.